HOLDEN CAULFIELD

Major Literary Characters

THE ANCIENT WORLD THROUGH THE SEVENTEENTH CENTURY

ACHILLES
Homer, *Iliad*

CALIBAN
William Shakespeare, *The Tempest*
Robert Browning, *Caliban upon Setebos*

CLEOPATRA
William Shakespeare, *Antony and Cleopatra*
John Dryden, *All for Love*
George Bernard Shaw, *Caesar and Cleopatra*

DON QUIXOTE
Miguel de Cervantes, *Don Quixote*
Franz Kafka, *Parables*

FALSTAFF
William Shakespeare, *Henry IV, Part I, Henry IV, Part II, The Merry Wives of Windsor*

FAUST
Christopher Marlowe, *Doctor Faustus*
Johann Wolfgang von Goethe, *Faust*
Thomas Mann, *Doctor Faustus*

HAMLET
William Shakespeare, *Hamlet*

IAGO
William Shakespeare, *Othello*

JULIUS CAESAR
William Shakespeare, *Julius Caesar*
George Bernard Shaw, *Caesar and Cleopatra*

KING LEAR
William Shakespeare, *King Lear*

MACBETH
William Shakespeare, *Macbeth*

ODYSSEUS/ULYSSES
Homer, *Odyssey*
James Joyce, *Ulysses*

OEDIPUS
Sophocles, *Oedipus Rex, Oedipus at Colonus*

OTHELLO
William Shakespeare, *Othello*

ROSALIND
William Shakespeare, *As You Like It*

SANCHO PANZA
Miguel de Cervantes, *Don Quixote*
Franz Kafka, *Parables*

SATAN
The Book of Job
John Milton, *Paradise Lost*

SHYLOCK
William Shakespeare, *The Merchant of Venice*

THE WIFE OF BATH
Geoffrey Chaucer, *The Canterbury Tales*

THE EIGHTEENTH AND NINETEENTH CENTURIES

AHAB
Herman Melville, *Moby-Dick*

ISABEL ARCHER
Henry James, *Portrait of a Lady*

EMMA BOVARY
Gustave Flaubert, *Madame Bovary*

DOROTHEA BROOKE
George Eliot, *Middlemarch*

CHELSEA HOUSE PUBLISHERS

Major Literary Characters

DAVID COPPERFIELD
Charles Dickens, *David Copperfield*

ROBINSON CRUSOE
Daniel Defoe, *Robinson Crusoe*

DON JUAN
Molière, *Don Juan*
Lord Byron, *Don Juan*

HUCK FINN
Mark Twain, *The Adventures of Tom Sawyer, Adventures of Huckleberry Finn*

CLARISSA HARLOWE
Samuel Richardson, *Clarissa*

HEATHCLIFF
Emily Brontë, *Wuthering Heights*

ANNA KARENINA
Leo Tolstoy, *Anna Karenina*

MR. PICKWICK
Charles Dickens, *The Pickwick Papers*

HESTER PRYNNE
Nathaniel Hawthorne, *The Scarlet Letter*

BECKY SHARP
William Makepeace Thackeray, *Vanity Fair*

LAMBERT STRETHER
Henry James, *The Ambassadors*

EUSTACIA VYE
Thomas Hardy, *The Return of the Native*

TWENTIETH CENTURY

ÁNTONIA
Willa Cather, *My Ántonia*

BRETT ASHLEY
Ernest Hemingway, *The Sun Also Rises*

HANS CASTORP
Thomas Mann, *The Magic Mountain*

HOLDEN CAULFIELD
J. D. Salinger, *The Catcher in the Rye*

CADDY COMPSON
William Faulkner, *The Sound and the Fury*

JANIE CRAWFORD
Zora Neale Hurston, *Their Eyes Were Watching God*

CLARISSA DALLOWAY
Virginia Woolf, *Mrs. Dalloway*

DILSEY
William Faulkner, *The Sound and the Fury*

GATSBY
F. Scott Fitzgerald, *The Great Gatsby*

HERZOG
Saul Bellow, *Herzog*

JOAN OF ARC
William Shakespeare, *Henry VI*
George Bernard Shaw, *Saint Joan*

LOLITA
Vladimir Nabokov, *Lolita*

WILLY LOMAN
Arthur Miller, *Death of a Salesman*

MARLOW
Joseph Conrad, *Lord Jim, Heart of Darkness, Youth, Chance*

PORTNOY
Philip Roth, *Portnoy's Complaint*

BIGGER THOMAS
Richard Wright, *Native Son*

CHELSEA HOUSE PUBLISHERS

Major Literary Characters

HOLDEN CAULFIELD

Edited and with an introduction by
HAROLD BLOOM

CHELSEA HOUSE PUBLISHERS
New York ◇ Philadelphia

Jacket illustration: Painting of Holden Caulfield by James Avati (1953) (photograph by Stanley Meltzoff). *Inset:* Title page of the first edition of *The Catcher in the Rye* (Boston: Little, Brown, 1951).

Chelsea House Publishers

Editor-in-Chief Remmel T. Nunn
Managing Editor Karyn Gullen Browne
Picture Editor Adrian G. Allen
Art Director Maria Epes
Manufacturing Manager Gerald Levine

Major Literary Characters

Managing Editor S. T. Joshi
Copy Chief Richard Fumosa
Designer Maria Epes

Staff for HOLDEN CAULFIELD

Researcher Jerome J. Aliotta
Picture Researchers Joan Beard, Vicky Haluska
Assistant Art Director Loraine Machlin
Production Manager Joseph Romano
Production Coordinator Marie Claire Cebrian

Printed and bound in the United States of America

3 5 7 9 8 6 4 2

Library of Congress Cataloging-in-Publication Data

Holden Caulfield / edited and with an introduction by Harold Bloom.
p.   cm.—(Major literary characters)
Includes bibliographical references (p.   ).
ISBN 0-7910-0953-X.—ISBN 0-7910-1008-2 (pbk.)
1. Salinger, J. D. (Jerome David), 1919–   Catcher in the rye.
2. Salinger, J. D. (Jerome David), 1919–   —Characters—Holden Caulfield.
3. Caulfield, Holden (Fictitious character)   I. Bloom, Harold.
II. Series.
PS3537.A426C328 1990
813'.54-dc20
90-1678
CIP

CONTENTS

THE ANALYSIS OF CHARACTER

Harold Bloom

"Character," according to our dictionaries, still has as a primary meaning a graphic symbol, such as a letter of the alphabet. This meaning reflects the word's apparent origin in the ancient Greek *charactēr*, a sharp stylus. *Charactēr* also meant the mark of the stylus' incisions. Recent fashions in literary criticism have reduced "character" in literature to a matter of marks upon a page. But our word "character" also has a very different meaning, matching that of the ancient Greek *ēthos*, "habitual way of life." Shall we say then that literary character is an imitation of human character, or is it just a grouping of marks? The issue is between a critic like Dr. Samuel Johnson, for whom words were as much like people as like things, and a critic like the late Roland Barthes, who told us that "the fact can only exist linguistically, as a term of discourse." Who is closer to our experience of reading literature, Johnson or Barthes? What difference does it make, if we side with one critic rather than the other?

Barthes is famous, like Foucault and other recent French theorists, for having added to Nietzsche's proclamation of the death of God a subsidiary demise, that of the literary author. If there are no authors, then there are no fictional personages, presumably because literature does not refer to a world outside language. Words indeed necessarily refer to other words in the first place, but the impact of words ultimately is drawn from a universe of fact. Stories, poems, and plays are recognizable as such because they are human utterances within traditions of utterances, and traditions, by achieving authority, become a kind of fact, or at least the sense of a fact. Our sense that literary characters, within the context of a fictive cosmos, indeed are fictional personages is also a kind of fact. The meaning and value of every character in a successful work of literary representation depend upon our ideas of persons in the factual reality of our lives.

Literary character is always an invention, and inventions generally are indebted to prior inventions. Shakespeare is the inventor of literary character as we know it; he reformed the universal human expectations for the verbal imitation of personality, and the reformation appears now to be permanent and uncannily inevitable. Remarkable as the Bible and Homer are at representing personages, their characters are relatively unchanging. They age within their stories, but their habitual modes of being do not develop. Jacob and Achilles unfold before us, but without metamorphoses. Lear and Macbeth, Hamlet and Othello severely modify themselves not only by their actions, but by their utterances, and most of all through *overhearing themselves,* whether they speak to themselves or to others. Pondering what they themselves have said, they will to change, and actually do change, sometimes extravagantly yet always persuasively. Or else they suffer change, without willing it, but in reaction not so much to their language as to their relation to that language.

I do not think it useful to say that Shakespeare successfully imitated elements in our characters. Rather, it could be argued that he compelled aspects of character to appear that previously were concealed, or not available to representation. This is not to say that Shakespeare is God, but to remind us that language is not God either. The mimesis of character in Shakespeare's dramas now seems to us normative, and indeed became the accepted mode almost immediately, as Ben Jonson shrewdly and somewhat grudgingly implied. And yet, Shakespearean representation has surprisingly little in common with the imitation of reality in Jonson or in Christopher Marlowe. The origins of Shakespeare's originality in the portrayal of men and women are to be found in the *Canterbury Tales* of Geoffrey Chaucer, insofar as they can be located anywhere before Shakespeare himself. Chaucer's savage and superb Pardoner overhears his own tale-telling, as well as his mocking rehearsal of his own spiel, and through this overhearing he is emboldened to forget himself, and enthusiastically urges all his fellow-pilgrims to come forward to be fleeced by him. His self-awareness, and apocalyptically rancid sense of spiritual fall, are preludes to the even grander abysses of the perverted will in Iago and in Edmund. What might be called the character trait of a negative charisma may be Chaucer's invention, but came to its perfection in Shakespearean mimesis.

The analysis of character is as much Shakespeare's invention as the representation of character is, since Iago and Edmund are adepts at analyzing both themselves and their victims. Hamlet, whose overwhelming charisma has many negative components, is certainly the most comprehensive of all literary characters, and so necessarily prophesies the labyrinthine complexities of the will in Iago and Edmund. Charisma, according to Max Weber, its first codifier, is primarily a natural endowment, and implies a primordial and idiosyncratic power over nature, and so finally over death. Hamlet's uncanniness is at its most suggestive in the scene of his long dying, where the audience, through the mediation of Horatio, itself is compelled to meditate upon suicide, if only because outliving the prince of Denmark scarcely seems an option.

Shakespearean representation has usurped not only our sense of literary character, but our sense of ourselves as characters, with Hamlet playing the part of the largest of these usurpations. Insofar as we have an idea of human disinterestedness, we tend to derive it from the Hamlet of Act V, whose quietism has about it a ghostly authority. Oscar Wilde, in his profound and profoundly witty dialogue, "The Decay of Lying," expressed a permanent insight when he insisted that art shaped every era, far more than any age formed art. Life imitates art, we imitate Shakespeare, because without Shakespeare we would perish for lack of images. Wilde's grandest audacity demystifies Shakespearean mimesis with a Shakespearean vivaciousness: "This unfortunate aphorism about art holding the mirror up to Nature is deliberately said by Hamlet in order to convince the bystanders of his absolute insanity in all art-matters." Of *Hamlet*'s influence upon the ages Wilde remarked that: "The world has grown sad because a puppet was once melancholy." "Puppet" is Wilde's own deconstruction, a brilliant reminder that Shakespeare's artistry of illusion has so mastered reality as to have changed reality, evidently forever.

The analysis of character, as a critical pursuit, seems to me as much a Shakespearean invention as literary character was, since much of what we know about how to analyze character necessarily follows Shakespearean procedures. His hero-villains, from Richard III through Iago, Edmund, and Macbeth, are shrewd and endless questers into their own self-motivations. If we could bear to see Hamlet, in his unwearied negations, as another hero-villain, then we would judge him the supreme analyst of the darker recalcitrances in the selfhood. Freud followed the pre-Socratic Empedocles, in arguing that character is fate, a frightening doctrine that maintains the fear that there are no accidents, that overdetermination rules us all of our lives. Hamlet assumes the same, yet adds to this argument the terrible passivity he manifests in Act V. Throughout Shakespeare's tragedies, the most interesting personages seem doom-eager, reminding us again that a Shakespearean reading of Freud would be more illuminating than a Freudian exegesis of Shakespeare. We learn more when we discover Hamlet in the Freudian Death Drive, than when we read *Beyond the Pleasure Principle* into *Hamlet*.

In Shakespearean comedy, character achieves its true literary apotheosis, which is the representation of the inner freedom that can be created by great wit alone. Rosalind and Falstaff, perhaps alone among Shakespeare's personages, match Hamlet in wit, though hardly in the metaphysics of consciousness. Whether in the comic or the modern mode, Shakespeare has set the standard of measurement in the balance between character and passion.

In Shakespeare the self is more dramatized than theatricalized, which is why a Shakespearean reading of Freud works out so well. Character-formation after the passing of the Oedipal stage takes the place of fetishistic fragmentings of the self. Critics who now call literary character into question, and who proclaim also the death of the author, invariably also regard all notions, literary and human, of a stable character as being mere reductions of deeper pre-Oedipal desires. It becomes clear that the fortunes of literary character rise and fall with the prestige of normative conceptions of the ego. Shakespeare's Iago, who wars against being, may be the first deconstructionist of the self, with his proclamation of "I am not what I am." This constitutes the necessary prologue to any view that would regard a fixed ego as a virtual abnormality. But deconstructions of the self are no more modern than Modernism is. Like literary modernism, the decentered ego came out of the Hellenistic culture of ancient Alexandria. The Gnostic heretics believed that the psyche, like the body, was a fallen entity, mechanically fashioned by the Demiurge or false creator. They held however that each of us possessed also a spark or pneuma, which was a fragment of the original Abyss or true, alien God. The soul or psyche within every one of us was thus at war with the self or pneuma, and only that sparklike self could be saved.

Shakespeare, following after Chaucer in this respect, was the first and remains still the greatest master of representing character both as a stable soul and a wavering self. There is a substance that endures in Shakespeare's figures, and there is also a quicksilver rendition of the unsettling sparks. Racine and Tolstoy, Balzac and Dickens, follow in Shakespeare's wake by giving us some sense of pre-Oedipal sparks or drives, and considerably more sense of post-Oedipal character and personality, stabilizations or sublimations of the fetish-seeking drives. Critics like Leo Bersani and René Girard argue eloquently against our taking this mimesis as the only proper work of literature. I would suggest that strong fictions of the self, from the Bible through Samuel Beckett, necessarily participate in both modes, the sublimation of desire, and the persistence of a primordial desire. The mystery of Hamlet or of Lear is intimately invested in the tangled mixture of the two modes of representation.

Psychic mobility is proposed by Bersani as the ideal to which deconstructions of the literary self may yet guide us. The ideal has its pathos, but the realities of literary representation seem to me very different, perhaps destructively so. When a novelist like D. H. Lawrence sought to reduce his characters to Eros and the Death Drive, he still had to persuade us of his authority at mimesis by lavishing upon the figures of *The Rainbow* and *Women in Love* all of the vivid stigmata of normative personality. Birkin and Ursula may represent antithetical and uncanny drives, but they develop and change as characters pondering their own pronouncements and reactions to self and others. The cost of a non-Shakespearean representation is enormous. Pynchon, in *The Crying of Lot 49* and *Gravity's Rainbow*, evades the burden of the normative by resorting to something like Christopher Marlowe's art of caricature in *The Jew of Malta*. Marlowe's Barabas is a marvelous rhetorician, yet he is a cartoon alongside the troublingly equivocal Shylock. Pynchon's personages are deliberate cartoons also, as flat as comic strips. Marlowe's achievement, and Pynchon's, are beyond dispute, yet they are like the prelude and the postlude to Shakespearean reality. They do not wish to engage with our hunger for the empirical world and so they enter the problematic cosmos of literary fantasy.

No writer, not even Shakespeare or Proust, alters the available stock that we agree to call reality, but Shakespeare, more than any other, does show us how much of reality we could encounter if only we retained adequate desire. The strong literary representation of character is already an analysis of character, and is part of the healing work of a literary culture, which implicitly seeks to cure violence through a normative mimesis of ego, *as if it were stable*, whether in actuality it is or is not. I do not believe that this is a social quest taken on by literary culture, but rather that we confront here the aesthetic essence of what makes a culture *literary*, rather than metaphysical or ethical or religious. A culture becomes literary when its conceptual modes have failed it, which means when religion, philosophy, and science have begun to lose their authority. If they cannot heal violence, then literature attempts to do so, which may be only a turning inside out of the critical arguments of Girard and Bersani.

I conclude by offering a particular instance or special case as a paradigm for the healing enterprise that is at once the representation and the analysis of literary character. Let us call it the aesthetics of being outraged, or rather of successfully representing the state of being outraged. W. C. Fields was one modern master of such representation, and Nathanael West was another, as was Faulkner before him. Here also the greatest master remains Shakespeare, whose Macbeth, himself a bloody outrage, yet retains our imaginative sympathy precisely because he grows increasingly outraged as he experiences the equivocation of the fiend that lies like truth. The double-natured promises and the prophecies of the weird sisters finally induce in Macbeth an apocalyptic version of the stage actor's anxiety at missing cues, the horror of a phantasmagoric stage fright of missing one's time, of always reacting too late. Macbeth, a veritable monster of solipsistic inwardness but no intellectual, counters his dilemma by fresh murders, that prolong him in time yet provoke him only to a perpetually freshened sense of being outraged, as all his expectations become still worse confounded. We are moved by Macbeth, however estrangedly, because his terrible inwardness is a paradigm for our own solipsism, but also because none of us can resist a strong and successful representation of the human in a state of being outraged.

The ultimate outrage is the necessity of dying, an outrage concealed in a multitude of masks, including the tyrannical ambitions of Macbeth. I suspect that our outrage at being outraged is the most difficult of all our affects for us to represent to ourselves, which is why we are so inclined to imaginative sympathy for a character who strongly conveys that affect to us. The Shrike of West's *Miss Lonelyhearts* or Faulkner's Joe Christmas of *Light in August* are crucial modern instances, but such figures can be located in many other works, since the ability to represent this extreme emotion is one of the tests that strong writers are driven to set for themselves.

However a reader seeks to reduce literary character to a question of marks on a page, she will come at last to the impasse constituted by the thought of death, her death, and before that to all the stations of being outraged that memorialize her own drive towards death. In reading, she quests for evidences that are strong representations, whether of her desire or her despair. Such questings constitute the necessary basis for the analysis of literary character, an enterprise that always will survive every vagary of critical fashion.

EDITOR'S NOTE

This volume gathers together a representative selection of the best criticism that has been devoted to Holden Caulfield, considered as a major literary character. I am grateful to Jerry Aliotta for his assistance in editing this book.

My introduction centers upon the religious element in Holden's troubled nature. A selection of extracts from the criticism of Holden follows, tracing the entire history of Holden's reception, from 1951 through 1980. Included are suggestive remarks by William Faulkner, and a number of attempts to set Holden both in the contexts of literary tradition and of American society in the first three decades after the publication of *The Catcher in the Rye.*

Fuller critical essays begin with Donald P. Costello's account of Holden's language, and with a contrast between Twain's Huck Finn and Holden by Arvin R. Wells. Jonathan Baumbach's analysis of Holden's saintly quality is now classical, as is Clinton W. Trowbridge's description of symbolic elements in the hero's portrayal. A Russian perspective, surprising in its emphases, is provided by Vera Panova, after which David J. Burrows meditates on Holden's relations with Allie, his dead brother, and with Phoebe, his little sister and salvation.

William Glasser offers an exegesis of how the people of Holden's vision have fallen into the quotidian of "phoniness," while Duane Edwards emphasizes what he judges to be Holden's latent homosexuality. A more accurate view of Holden as an image of potential healing is presented by James Lundquist.

A sensitive essay by Edwin Haviland Miller centers upon Holden's deep grief over his brother Allie's death, after which we are given an informed attempt by R. J. Huber to bring Holden's difficulties into the area dealt with by the Individual Psychology of Alfred Adler, with its emphasis upon the darker consequences of social alienation.

This volume concludes with Alan Nadel's study of what he categorizes as Holden's "speech of contradictions," which he relates to the unhappy era of the Cold War, and the specter of Senator Joseph McCarthy.

INTRODUCTION

As a literary character, Holden Caulfield has now demonstrated his durability and likely permanence. Forty years of readership have not dimmed his poignance, his ability to represent the idealism and the refusal to be deceived that have marked the American tradition of representing adolescence. He holds his place in the sequence that goes from Huck Finn through Huck's descendants in Hemingway, Scott Fitzgerald, and Faulkner, on to the outraged protagonists of Philip Roth's moral fictions. What Toqueville called our "habits of the heart," the American balances between individualism and social concern, continue to find a crucial representative in Holden, whose appeal has survived the enormous changes in American sensibility over these last forty years.

Holden's literary strength has little to do with his author's overt religious concerns, whether Buddhist or Christian. Haunted always by a brother's death, Holden evades the adolescent obsession with the sexual drive only to yield himself to the shadows of the Death Drive. His pathos is that of the survivor who can find no guidance in the art of survival. Teachers, parents, sages are unavailable to him, primarily because of his borderline sense that maturity and deathliness are the same state, an illusion of identity that in itself is deathly. The innocent and the beautiful, Yeats wrote, have no enemy except time, but poor Holden is too belated to make so confident a High Romantic assertion.

Holden essentially is a narrative voice, stemming directly from Fitzgerald's Nick Carraway, with Huck Finn hovering farther back. The largest difference is that Holden is desperate; even his humor balances on the verge of madness. Still, his desperation is vivacious; he is on the verge, but always with verve. All readers receive him into their affection, which may be the largest clue to his book's enduring charm. As a representation of a sixteen-year-old youth, the portrait of Holden achieves a timeless quality that is at variance with the novel's true status as a period piece, a vision of America in the aftermath of World War II. The timelessness of Salinger's hero has less to do with his refusal to mature than with his religious refusal of time. The American Religion, almost from its origins, has been closer to Gnos-

I

ticism than to Christianity. Time in Christianity is an agent of redemption; the
Incarnation breaks into time, and after that time becomes another form of God's
mercy. But time, in Gnosticism, is the enemy, because time results from the
Creation-Fall in which we were thrown out from our original fullness into this world
of separations and angers. Holden is haunted by the characteristic Gnostic sense
that what is best and oldest in him is no part of the Creation. Doubtless, Holden's
religiosity is the result not so much of Salinger's interest in oriental esotericisms, but
of Salinger's debt to Fitzgerald and Hemingway, whose protagonists tend to be
pure embodiments of the American Religion. Freedom for Gatsby or for Jake
Barnes, as for Huck Finn, comes only in solitude, and cannot be realized in the
sexual life, which is shackled by time. Love is possible for Holden, but only for his
dead brother, or for his ten-year-old sister, Phoebe. Holden, watching Phoebe in
the rain, is in communion with Nick Carraway at Gatsby's funeral, and with Frederic
Henry walking away after Catherine's death. In all these scenes, the rain constitutes
an American Gnostic baptism, a rendering free through knowledge.

The innocence of Holden Caulfield, unlike that of Huck Finn, takes its informing context from the American Religion, that curious amalgam of Emersonian
idealism and national messianism. Holden possesses neither a saving doctrine nor
spiritual authorities to whom he can turn, yet his sensibility is wholly religious.
Because of his inner isolation, and his lack of teachers, Holden courts the doom of
the New Testament's Legion, the insane tomb-haunter infested by demons. Hence
Holden's grim declaration, which is at once the darkest and the most significant
sentence in his book: "If you want to know the truth, the guy I like best in the Bible,
next to Jesus, was that lunatic and all, that lived in the tombs." *The Catcher in the
Rye* essentially is a quest or romance in which Holden narrowly evades the madness of Legion, in order to survive as a wistful version of an alienated American
Adam, dreaming of a Jesus-like role as a savior of children: "What I have to do, I
have to catch everybody if they start to go over the cliff—" By catching himself, just
in time, Holden at least has made a fresh beginning.

As a literary character, Holden hardly will sustain comparisons with figures in
Shakespeare and Dickens, though such incongruous juxtapositions have been attempted. Holden's legitimate forebears are located where we might expect them
to be found, in Hemingway and in Fitzgerald, writers who may be said to have set
the limits for Salinger's intense but narrow art. We can see Holden as a latter-day,
potential version of Nick Carraway or Jake Barnes, or as a substitution for Hemingway's projections of himself in his final writings. Holden's capacity for sympathy
with others is immense, and so is his aversion to everything that is inauthentic. This
double capacity informs the eloquent pathos of his closing remarks:

> . . . D.B. asked me what I thought about all this stuff I just finished telling you
> about. I didn't know what the hell to say. If you want to know the truth, I don't
> *know* what I think about it. I'm sorry I told so many people about it. About all
> I know is, I sort of *miss* everybody I told about. Even old Stradlater and Ackley,

for instance. I think I even miss that goddam Maurice. It's funny. Don't ever tell anybody anything. If you do, you start missing everybody.

This affection of a narrator for his characters prophesies Holden's almost full return from alienation. Perhaps he will become his creator, Salinger; perhaps, like Huck Finn, he will light out for another territory. Either way, he will have the prospect of progressing from survival to freedom. His ability to move so many readers has something to do with how vulnerable and likeable he is, but perhaps more to do with the intimations he incarnates, which are religious, and which return us to that curious spirituality I have called the American Religion. What shadows Holden always is his brother Allie's early death; what saves Holden is his love for his sister Phoebe. It is the mark of the American Religion that death is not accept- able to it. One thinks of the post-Christian faiths that originated in the United States, and that have survived: Mormonism, Christian Science, Seventh-Day Adventism, Jehovah's Witnesses. In common, they deny literal death, as though we could progress to godhood without the necessity of dying. At the root of these imaginings is an impulse that Holden profoundly shares: a passion for survival, at every cost. What is most American about Holden is the complex alliance between a despera- tion for survival, and a self-destructiveness that seems in love with death. Holden may not be a universal figure, but he is one of the most representative of Ameri- cans. In him we read some of our national paradoxes, central to our literature and to our still-emerging American spirituality.

Fables of our innocence are a recurrent element in American literature, and are a crucial component of the American Religion. If I were asked to nominate the most distinguished parables of that innocence in modern American fiction, I would choose Faulkner's *As I Lay Dying,* Nathanael West's *Miss Lonelyhearts,* and Pyn- chon's *The Crying of Lot 49.* Darl Bundren, Miss Lonelyhearts, and Oedipa Maas are all maddened by intimations of a primal goodness lost yet still beckoning in America, and their quests for that original intensity of being remain purposive, however catastrophic. But these are all parables of the dark side, and need to be complemented by the more nostalgic fables of *The Sun Also Rises, The Great Gatsby,* and their younger and weaker brother, *The Catcher in the Rye.* Jake Barnes and Nick Carraway are necessarily wiser and graver than Holden Caulfield, but he participates in their nostalgia, in their affection for everyone whose stories they narrate. If Holden participates also in their purposelessness, that is because the lack of quest is as much the cost of confirmation in the American Religion as is the darker intensity of drive in the protagonists of Faulkner, West, and Pynchon.

—H. B.

CRITICAL EXTRACTS

T. MORRIS LONGSTRETH

Mr. Salinger is a war veteran in his early thirties who has written short stories for the *New Yorker* and other magazines. This, his first novel, is the mid-summer selection of the Book-of-the-Month Club. A sixteen-year-old schoolboy, Holden Caulfield, tells the story—with the paradoxical result that it is not fit for children to read.

Mr. Salinger says, "All of my best friends are children. It's almost unbearable to me to realize that my book will be kept on a shelf out of their reach." Many adults as well will not wish to condition themselves to Holden's language. Indeed, one finds it hard to believe that a true lover of children could father this tale.

Twice there is a reminder of Shakespeare. It comes near Macbeth's despairing definition of life, "a tale told by an idiot . . . signifying nothing." And Salinger has taken a more sensitive than normal child, just as Shakespeare took a more than normally sensitive man in Hamlet. It could be debated long just how irrational is Holden Caulfield, as likewise, Hamlet.

Holden, who is the clown, villain, and even, moderately, the hero of this tale, is asked not to return to his school after Christmas. This is his third expulsion and he cannot endure to face his parents, so he hides out in New York, where his conduct is a nightmarish medley of loneliness, bravado, and supineness. Jerome David Salinger is an extremely skillful writer, and Holden's dead-pan narrative is quick-moving, absurd, and wholly repellent in its mingled vulgarity, naiveté, and sly perversion.

The Catcher in the Rye purports to be the *Seventeen* of our times, though it is as remote in conception from the Tarkington masterpiece, still much alive, as the television age from Indiana in 1916.

Holden Caulfield is so supersensitive to others' faults that he has no friends, among boys at least. He is as unbalanced as a rooster on a tightrope. He asks a girl to elope with him and then calls her names. He suffers from loneliness because he has about shut himself away from the normal activities of boyhood, games, the outdoors, friendship.

He is capable of love for a dead brother, for a lively younger sister, for all young things, as his explanation of the book's title makes clear—an oddly psychopathic one, it must be noted. (For Holden has mistaken the words of "Coming Through the Rye," as "If a body *catch* a body," and fancies himself the heroic rescuer of children in danger of plunging over a cliff in the field.)

But he is also capable of wholesome revulsion from contact with the human dregs, and impulsively seeks a kind of absolution by offering help to others. He hates what is wrong with the movies and in the end he forgets himself and his hoped-for escape into freedom to help his sister. He is alive, human, preposterous, profane and pathetic beyond belief.

Fortunately, there cannot be many of him yet. But one fears that a book like this given wide circulation may multiply his kind—as too easily happens when immorality and perversion are recounted by writers of talent whose work is countenanced in the name of art or good intention.

—T. MORRIS LONGSTRETH, "New Novels in the News," *Christian Science Monitor*, July 19, 1951, p. 11

HARVEY BREIT

Somewhere about halfway in Salinger's novel, the bright, terrible, and possibly normal sixteen-year-old protagonist follows a little boy who is singing quietly to himself "If a body catch a body coming through the rye." Later when the youthful hero's younger sister challenges him, demanding to know if there is anything in the world that he likes or wants to be, he can only think he wants to be "the catcher in the rye." It is significant because the novel, for all its surface guilelessness, is a critique of the contemporary, grown-up world.

It isn't important whether Salinger had it in mind or not, but reading *The Catcher in the Rye* made me think of *Adventures of Huckleberry Finn*. Holden Caulfield struck me as an urban, a transplanted Huck Finn. He has a colloquialism as marked as Huck's: "You remember I said before that Ackley was a slob in his personal habits? Well, so was Stradlater, but in a different way. Stradlater was more of a secret slob. He always looked all right, Stradlater, but for instance, you should've seen the razor he shaved himself with. It was always rusty as hell and full of lather and hairs and crap." Like Huck, Holden is neither comical nor misanthropic. He is an observer. Unlike Huck, he makes judgments by the dozen, but these are not to be taken seriously; they are conceits. There is a drollery, too, that is common to both, and a quality of seeing that creates farce.

What is crucial is where Huck and Holden part company. T. S. Eliot once pointed out that we see the world through Huck's eyes. Well, we do not see it through Holden's. We see Holden as a smiling adult sees a boy, and we smile at his spectral, incredible world. I think that is the decisive failure: whatever is serious and implicit in the novel is overwhelmed by the more powerful comic element. What remains is a brilliant *tour de force,* one that has sufficient power and cleverness to make the reader chuckle and—rare indeed—even laugh aloud.

—HARVEY BREIT, "Reader's Choice," *Atlantic Monthly* 188, No. 2
(August 1951): 82

ERNEST JONES

Holden Caulfield is friendly, "democratic," well-bred, and snobbish in ways peculiar to adolescence. He has the beginnings of taste; "corny" is a term frequent in his speech. A virgin, he never knows exactly what any girl may be expecting of him and is afraid to make love to the prostitute supplied by an obliging bellhop. He mistakes whatever is spontaneous in his behavior for madness: "But I'm crazy. I swear to God I am"; if he acts on impulse he feels guilty, though also boastful: "I'm the most terrific liar you ever saw in your life." Bravado and buffoonery imperfectly disguise his conviction of madness and guilt.

His sense of alienation is almost complete—from parents, from friends, from society in general as represented by the prep school from which he has been expelled and the night-club and hotel world of New York in which he endures a week-end exile while hiding out from his family. With his alienation go assorted hatreds—of the movies, of night clubs, of social and intellectual pretension, and so on. And physical disgust: pimples, sex, an old man picking his nose are all equally cause for nausea. It is of little importance that the alienation, the hatreds, and the disgust are those of a sixteen-year-old. Any reader, sharing or remembering some-thing like them, will agree with the conclusion to be drawn from this unhappy odyssey: to borrow a line from Auden, "We must love one another or die." After every other human being has failed him, Caulfield still has his loving ten-year-old sister to love; she embodies the innocence we all hope we have preserved and the wisdom we all hope we have acquired.

The skill with which all this has been worked into 277 pages is most ingenious. But as it proceeds on its insights, which are not really insights since they are so general, *The Catcher in the Rye* becomes more and more a case history of all of us. Radically this writing depends on the reader's recollection of merely similar difficulties; the unique crisis and the unique anguish are not re-created. These emotional ups and downs become increasingly factitious—so much must be in-cluded to elicit memories of so many callow heartbreaks—and though always lively in its parts, the book as a whole is predictable and boring.

—ERNEST JONES, "Case History of All of Us," *Nation,*
September 1, 1951, p. 176

✗ RILEY HUGHES

Holden Caulfield, an artist at getting himself thrown out of prep schools and all, is the ribald narrator of this account of academic and social shortcomings. Like Charles Lamb, he is a victim of some very imperfect sympathies; he hates phonies, teachers ("You don't have to think too hard when you talk to a teacher"), and, well, phonies. He wants to protect people, especially "little kids"; most of the time he finds himself acting "like a madman."

The Catcher in the Rye tells of the madman's week end he has in New York, after walking out on prep school. It's a mad mélange of ice-skating at Radio City, interviewing a prostitute in his hotel room, escaping from a homosexual, and so on. Not only do some of the events stretch probability, but Holden's character as iconoclast, a kind of latter-day Tom Sawyer or Huck Finn, is made monotonous and phony by the formidably excessive use of amateur swearing and coarse language.

—RILEY HUGHES, "New Novels," *Catholic World* No. 1040
(November 1951): 154

⚜ JOHN W. ALDRIDGE

Mr. Salinger's *The Catcher in the Rye,* like *Adventures of Huckleberry Finn,* is a study in the spiritual picaresque, the journey that for the young is all one way, from holy innocence to such knowledge as the world offers, from the reality which illusion demands and thinks it sees to the illusion which reality insists, at the point of madness, we settle for. But the great difference between the two novels is the measure not merely of the change in time and history of a cultural situation, but of the changed moral circumstances in which innocence typically finds itself in crisis and lends itself to drama. The innocence of *Huckleberry Finn* is a compound of frontier ignorance, juvenile delinquency, and penny-dreadful heroism. It begs for the challenge of thugs, thieves, swindlers, and feuds, and that is what it gets and delights in, takes such delight in, in fact, that even when the dangers become real and the escapes increasingly narrow, we know it is all in fun, that this is innocence living out its concocted daydream of glory in which no one really gets hurt, and even the corpses climb to their feet and dust themselves off at dinnertime. Still, in the suspension of our disbelief, in the planned illusion of the novel itself, the innocence and the world of violence appear to be seriously and effectively opposed. The innocence is the raft to which Huck and Jim, in flight from the dangers of the shore, make their narrow escapes. It is the river itself, time, faith, continuity, moving endlessly and dependably beside and between the temporary and futile altercations of men. And it is the raft and the river together which give the innocence of *Huckleberry Finn* its focus and breadth of implication, so that it exists at once on the level of naïveté at which it responds to adventure and on the level of maturity at which it lends itself to allegory.

The innocence of Mr. Salinger's Holden Caulfield, on the other hand, is a compound of urban intelligence, juvenile contempt, and *New Yorker* sentimentalism, and the only challenge it begs for, the only challenge it has left to beg for, is the challenge of the genuine, the truly human, in a world which has lost both the means of adventure and the means of love. But it is in the nature of Holden's dilemma, his spiritual confinement in this world, that he lacks a concrete basis, can find no concrete embodiment, for the ideal against which he judges, and finds wanting, the life around him. He has objects for his contempt but no objects other than his sister for his love—no raft, no river, no Jim, and no Tom. He is forced, consequently, simply to register his contempt, his developing disillusionment; and it is inevitable that he should seem after a time to be registering it in a vacuum, for just as he can find no concrete equivalent in life for the ideal which he wishes life to embody, so the persons on whom he registers his contempt seem inadequate to it and unjustly accused by it. The boorish prep school roommate, the hypocritical teacher, the stupid women in the Lavender Room, the resentful prostitute, the conventional girl friend, the bewildered cab driver, the affected young man at the theater, the old friend who reveals that his interest in Holden is homosexual—these people are all truly objectionable and deserve the places Holden assigns them in his secret hierarchy of class with its categories of phonies, bores, deceivers, and perverts. But they are nonetheless human, albeit dehumanized, and constitute a fair average of what the culture affords. They are part of the truth which Holden does not see and, as it turns out, is never able to see—that this is what one part of humanity *is;* the lies, the phoniness, the hypocrisy are the compromises which innocence is forced by the world to make. This is the reality on which Holden's illusion is finally broken, but no recognition follows, and no conversion. He remains at the end what he was at the beginning—cynical, defiant, and blind. And as for ourselves, there is identification but no insight, a sense of pathos but not of tragedy. It may be that Mr. Salinger made the most of his subject, but his subject was not adequate to his intention, just as Holden's world is not adequate to his contempt, and that is probably because it does not possess sufficient humanity to make the search for humanity dramatically feasible.

—JOHN W. ALDRIDGE, "The Society of Three Novels," *In Search of Heresy: American Literature in an Age of Conformity* (New York: McGraw-Hill, 1956), pp. 129–31

CHARLES H. KEGEL

Like Stephen Dedalus of *A Portrait of the Artist as a Young Man,* Caulfield is in search of the Word. His problem is one of communication: as a teen-ager, he simply cannot get through to the adult world which surrounds him; as a *sensitive* teen-ager, he cannot even get through to others of his own age. The same impulse which caused Dedalus to contemplate subtle and slight differences in the meaning of words—"Canker is a disease of plants,/Cancer one of animals"—activates a comparable sensitivity in Caulfield, especially with word formulas. After his interview, for example, with Mr. Spencer, his history teacher at Pencey, Caulfield says, "He yelled something at me, but I couldn't exactly hear him. I'm pretty sure he yelled 'Good luck!' at me. I hope not. I hope to hell not. I'd never yell 'Good luck!' at anybody. It sounds terrible, when you think about it."

Caulfield places most of his attention, however, on the sympathetic rapport which must exist between communicators. He asks but one thing of those he talks with, sincerity; he asks only that they *mean* what they say. If they tell him, as does Maurice, the elevator operator, that the price of goods is "Five bucks a throw," Caulfield expects to pay only five dollars. If they ask, as did Mrs. Antolini, about the health of his mother, Caulfield expects sincere concern about his mother's health; he expects that the questioner *actually* wants an answer to her question and will not interrupt him half way through it. Throughout the novel, he is troubled with people who are not listening to what he says, who are talking only to be polite, not because they want to communicate ideas. Like Hamlet, a "sad, screwed-up type guy" like himself, Caulfield is bothered by words and word formulas which only "seem," which are "phony." The honesty and sincerity which he cannot find in others, he attempts to maintain in himself. His repeated assertions that something he has said is *"really"* so demonstrate his attempt to keep faith with the Word. He is particularly distressed by the occasional realization that he too must be phony to exist in the adult world. With regard to the insincere "Glad to've met you" formula, he laments that "If you want to stay alive, you have to say that stuff, though."

As I have indicated, the main reason for Caulfield's communicative difficulty lies in his absolute hatred of phoniness. And he finds that phoniness, that hypocrisy, not only in the world of his personal contacts, but in the world of art as well. He detests phony books, phony music, phony movies and plays. He sees Hamlet as a "sad, screwed-up type guy" and wants him played that way instead of "like a goddam general." Likewise he is bothered by the way people "clap for the wrong things" and hence corrupt the promising artist. Very poignantly he understands the plight of Ernie, the piano player, or of brother D.B., once a sincere writer, but now "out in Hollywood . . . being a prostitute." He wants more Thomas Hardys—"old Thomas Hardy" Caulfield calls him endearingly—because he knows that the creator of "old Eustacia Vye" refused to prostitute himself, refused to be phony.

Holden Caulfield's inability to communicate satisfactorily with others represents itself symbolically in the uncompleted telephone calls and undelivered messages which permeate the novel. Seeing a phone booth is almost more than he can stand, for he almost constantly feels like "giving somebody a buzz." On fifteen separate occasions he gets the urge to communicate by phone, yet only four calls are completed, and those with unfortunate results. Usually the urge dies without his having even attempted to place the call; he seems fearful of what the results will be and rationalizes, "I wasn't in the mood." Likewise, none of the several verbal messages he asks others to deliver for him gets through to the intended receiver; he simply cannot succeed in making contact.

Growing logically out of this prolonged incommunicability is Caulfield's intention to become a deaf-mute. So repulsed is he by the phoniness around him that he despairs of communicating with anybody, and in a passage fraught with import, he contemplates a retreat within himself.

> I figured I could get a job at a filling station somewhere, putting gas and oil in people's cars. I didn't care what kind of a job it was, though. Just so people didn't know me and I didn't know anybody. I thought what I'd do was, I'd pretend I was one of those deaf-mutes. That way I wouldn't have to have any goddam stupid useless conversations with anybody. If anybody wanted to tell me something, they'd have to write it on a piece of paper and shove it over to me. They'd get bored as hell doing that after a while, and then I'd be through with having conversations for the rest of my life. Everybody'd think I was just a poor deaf-mute bastard and they'd leave me alone. . . . I'd cook all my own food, and later on, if I wanted to get married or something, I'd meet this beautiful girl that was also a deaf-mute and we'd get married. She'd come to live in my cabin with me, and if she wanted to say anything to me, she'd have to write it on a goddam piece of paper, like everybody else.

Significantly, the fact that a message does get through to Phoebe—the only successful communication in the entire novel—leads toward the abandonment of the deaf-mute retreat. The Rousseauistic-Wordsworthian theme of childhood innocence and sincerity which Salinger had played upon so effectively in "For Esmé—with Love and Squalor" works its magic again. It is Phoebe who furnishes the clue to the solution of his problem, and when he refuses to ride the carrousel with her and thus gives up his idealistic attempts "to grab for the gold ring," he has initiated his transition from adolescence to adulthood. He does not, of course, capitulate to the phoniness of life, but he attains an attitude of tolerance, understanding, and love which will make it endurable. There can be no doubt but that when he returns to New York—for he, unlike Dedalus, will return home—he will be in the mood to give "old Jane a buzz."

—CHARLES H. KEGEL, "Incommunicability in Salinger's
The Catcher in the Rye," Western Humanities Review
11, No. 1 (Winter 1957): 188–90

FREDERIC I. CARPENTER

Like *Huck Finn, The Catcher in the Rye* is narrated in the first person, and in the vernacular, by a boy who is badly "mixed up." But both Huck and Holden are intellectually honest, and both succeed in communicating their confusion and in suggesting some of the reasons for it. Both are ambivalent, and even flaunt their confusion—Huck by praising Tom Sawyer's plans as "mixed up and splendid," and Holden by defiantly wearing his red hunting cap backwards through New York City. In the end Huck plans to "light out for the territory," and Holden thinks of fleeing West, but is dissuaded by his attachment to his family, and is sent to a psychiatrist instead.

Of course the two novels differ as much as they resemble each other, and I do not mean to suggest that *The Catcher . . .* is a rival of *Huck Finn.* Where Huck was the typical American democrat, Holden is a snob who criticizes his friends for the shabby suitcases they carry. Where Huck lived in the rich heartland of America, Holden is the product of an exclusive New York City. Salinger himself seems almost the typical New Yorker, and his short stories emphasize the emotional starvation and brittleness of the city life, which his novel only suggests. Yet his New York and its problems are perhaps as central to modern America as Mark Twain's Mississippi River was to the pioneer nineteenth century.

The quality which makes Huck Finn and Holden Caulfield brothers under the skin—and which runs through all the best of these novels—is a common hatred of hypocrisy and a search for integrity. And this emerges in spite of—or perhaps as a reaction against—the love of play-acting which is a natural and inevitable aspect of all adolescence. Just as Huck plays along with Tom's mixed up schemes, and observes the deceptions of the Duke and the Dauphin with reluctant admiration, so Holden ironically admires the amatory techniques of his roommate Stradlater who speaks in "this sincere voice," and himself makes up absurd phantasies for the mother of a classmate whom he meets on the train. Yet Holden's chief contempt is for "all those phonies," and his admiration goes out to the genuine sincerity of the two nuns he meets, and of his sister Phoebe.

Perhaps the central theme of these novels of adolescence is the individual's search for genuine values. At the end Phoebe typically corrects her brother's misquotation of the poem:

" 'If a body catch a body comin' through the rye' "
"It's 'If a body *meet* a body . . .' "

In the confused rye fields of life the worldly characters seek to "catch" people, and in revulsion Holden imagines "catching" all innocent children to protect them from destruction. "I know it's crazy," admits Holden, who suffers a nervous breakdown at the end. And similarly Huck Finn ended by exclaiming: "I can't stand it. I been there before." In their confusion, these heroes desperately seek truth.

But the ambivalence of adolescence, which runs after experience yet fears it, and admires the mixed up and splendid world while still idealizing innocence, merely reflects the similar ambivalence of American society. And here *The Catcher . . .* goes beyond *Huck Finn*—partly in that it describes an older boy who confronts the larger problems of sex which Huck Finn never faced, and partly in that it describes an America which also has reached "an end to innocence." Where Huck had been able to escape "civilization and its discontents" by "lighting out for the territory," now Holden must consult a psychiatrist and face those problems of growing up which our maturing society must also face.

—FREDERIC I. CARPENTER, "The Adolescent in American Fiction,"
English Journal 46, No. 6 (September 1957): 315–16

WILLIAM FAULKNER

(April 24, 1958)

Q. I've sometimes thought that the tragedy of Holden Caulfield was that he did not fall, in a way. That if he fell off into humanity he might have found it.

A. Well, he would have to have been tougher than he was. If he had been tougher than that there wouldn't have been any story in the first place. But his story was an intelligent, very sensitive young man who was—in this day and time was an anachronism, was almost an obsolescence, trying to cope with a struggle with the present-day world which he was not fitted for, when he didn't want money, he didn't want position, anything, he just wanted to find man and wanted something to love, and he couldn't. There was nothing there. The nearest he came to it was his sister who was a child and though she tried to love him she couldn't understand his problem. The only other human beings he ran into he had preconceptions to doubt—the teacher which could have helped him, and he suddenly began to suspect the teacher's motives.

> —WILLIAM FAULKNER, *Faulkner in the University: Class Conferences at the University of Virginia 1957–1958*, ed. Frederick L. Gwynn and Joseph L. Blotner (Charlottesville: University Press of Virginia, 1959), pp. 246–47

FREDERICK L. GWYNN & JOSEPH L. BLOTNER

This novel's exciting resemblances to *Adventures of Huckleberry Finn* have been justly noted by a number of critics—the comic irony, the colloquial language, the picaresque structure, and the theme of anti-phoniness—and it is not inconceivable that some day Holden Caulfield may be as well known an American boy as Huck Finn. For a reader goes through much the same pattern of relishing both boys: first it is the release provided by their rebellion against society, then the inspiration of their honesty against sham, and then the sympathetic awareness of their melancholy roles. After the reader recovers from the releasing joy of Holden's invective (e.g., "Her son was doubtless the biggest bastard that ever went to Pencey, in the whole crumby history of the school") and of his exposure of phoniness (e.g., a Radio City Christmas complete with what has been identified as the movie of James Hilton's *Random Harvest*), he goes on to appreciate the pathos of Holden's loneliness and frustration.

But nervous cynicism and neurosis are not enough for fiction in depth, and the next step for a reader should be to realize that Holden Caulfield is actually a saintly Christian person (there is no need to call him a Christ-figure). True, he has little notion of the love of God, and he thinks that "all the children in our family are atheists." But (1) he himself never does a wrong thing: instead of commandments, Holden breaks only garage windows (when his brother dies) and the no-smoking rule in the Pencey dormitory. (2) He sacrifices himself in a constant war against evil, even though he has a poignantly Manichean awareness of its ubiquity ("If you had a million years to do it in, you couldn't rub out even *half* the [ubiquitously scrawled dirty words] in the world.") And most important, (3) his reward is to understand that if one considers humanity, one must love it. The text for Holden's behavior is his insistence—oddly enough, to his Quaker friend Childs on absolute primitive Christianity: "Jesus never sent old Judas to Hell. . . . I think any one of the Disciples would've sent him to Hell and all—and fast, too—but I'll bet anything Jesus didn't do it."

For Jesus and Holden Caulfield truly love their neighbors, especially the poor in goods, appearance, and spirit. Holden not only gives ten dollars to the nuns in the station but also he is depressed by their meagre breakfast and the fact that they will never be "going anywhere swanky for lunch." He worries about where the ducks in Central Park can go when the water freezes, and how wretched his mother would feel if he died—"because she still isn't over my brother Allie yet." He is kind to the repulsive Ackley, with his "Sinus trouble, pimples, lousy teeth, halitosis, crumby fingernails," and he tries to obviate Slagle's envy of his Mark Cross luggage. Most significantly, for an adolescent undergoing the torturing growing pains of sex, he sympathizes with the girl's situation—with the ugly daughter of Pencey's head-master, with both the ugly girl and the beautiful girl in the nightclub undergoing male treatment from their escorts, with the prostitute Sunny, with the girl whom Luce has enjoyed and now derogates, and especially with Jane Gallagher, the girl whose fear Holden appreciates (she wouldn't move her checker kings out of the back row) and whose virtue he fears Stradlater has taken. And like his Jesus with his Judas, he still forgives Stradlater and the bellboy Maurice who have betrayed and beaten him. Indeed, this is the old-fashioned moral, stated haltingly at the very end by Holden Caulfield, who wishes to be the Catcher in the Rye suffering little children to come to him and be saved from falling over the cliff. He puts it this way: "About all I know is, I sort of *miss* everybody I told about. Even old Stradlater and Ackley, for instance. I think I even miss that goddam Maurice. It's funny. Don't ever tell anybody anything. If you do, you start missing everybody." In less concrete words: If you are aware of the human comedy, you must love individual human beings. The ending of *The Catcher in the Rye* is just as artistically weak—and as humanly satisfying—as that of *Huckleberry Finn*.

—FREDERICK L. GWYNN AND JOSEPH L. BLOTNER, *"The Catcher in the Rye* (1951)," *The Fiction of J. D. Salinger* (Pittsburgh: University of Pittsburgh Press, 1958), pp. 28–31

PAUL BRESLOW

Salinger ⟨. . .⟩ pleases his beat audience with an occasional sharp jab at the world in which they live because he is not telling them to stop what they're doing; his segment of the beat audience finds irony and satire a sword easily turned inward.

It is in this way that *The Catcher in the Rye* is read as a beat allegory of the middle-class American reconciling himself to a nonsensical existence. When Holden Caulfield rejects his school and a future business career, it is a gesture known to the beat reader as mental reservation about what, eventually, Holden will embrace. The only alternatives to school and participation in the foolish world so distasteful to Holden appear in his daydreams as being a rancher, or pretending to be a deaf-mute and supporting himself by working in a gas station. The absurdity of these and, throughout the novel, the absurdity of any other escapist existence, makes it clear to beat people that some sort of adjustment to respectability is the only possible outcome of the boy's discontent. This is beat realism, the softening of the agony of disillusionment through a conviction of personal emotional superiority; it is the use of love not as sex, not as a creative power, not as a social spirit, but as the possession of a socially passive (though enlightened) soul seeking mystical salvation.

—PAUL BRESLOW, "The Support of the Mysteries: A Look at the Literary
Prophets of the Beat Middle Class," *Studies on the Left* I, No. I
(Fall 1959): 26–27

CHRISTOPHER PARKER

So what was Caulfield's problem—if he had one. He'd met a dilemma—like all the rest of us; he didn't give in and he didn't ignore (like most of the rest of us). And he couldn't find any other solution except good old Phoebe on the carrousel. You could say he was trying to find himself, his identity, and all that; but that's a lot of categorical nonsense—who isn't? It's evident that he was also fed up with hypocrisy—but I think Caulfield's real problem is that he was trying desperately to be sincere in an insincere world, with FUCK YOU signs on the walls of children's corridors, wheezing bald caddy-driving alumni who want to find their initials carved in the door of the can, Antolinis who have the answers but don't use them, and Mr. Vinsons who yell "Digression!" at you every time you become excited enough in an idea you have to forget about the classroom exercise and start talking about the idea. Caulfield was outside of himself looking for others. He wasn't a critical smart-aleck—far, far from it. I'm not trying to say that Caulfield's way is right and society's is wrong—but I do think that Caulfield, the individual, is far more human and right than those of us on the outside asking him if he's going to apply himself or not.

The good thing about Caulfield is that he's trying to do it all by himself—no Beatnik—no Bohemian—no Ivy League—just Holden Caulfield. He knows the others are just as phony as the "American Dream," and he also knows that he's being a bit of a phony; he realizes he's in a bad way but he doesn't know what to do about it.

Why do I like *The Catcher?* Because it puts forth in a fairly good argument the problems which boys of my age face, and also perhaps the inadequacy with which some of us attempt to cope with them. I have great admiration for Caulfield because he didn't compromise. I think he was relatively free of self-worship—his cause was certainly justified, if not just. I think Salinger deals fairly with him—he gives enough grounds to argue either pro or con. Some people condemn Caulfield as "not liking anything," but he does—he likes the only things really worth liking, whereas most of us like all the things that aren't worth liking. Because he is sincere he won't settle for less.

I think most fellows who read *The Catcher* don't think about it enough— what's really behind it all. They think he's a cool guy, so they imitate his casual talk and nonchalant attitude. Salinger didn't invent the talk, nor Holden Caulfield for that matter, but it's certainly become much more popular since. I don't even think most fellows notice it's called the *"Catcher* in the Rye" when in the song it's really supposed to be "meet a body," not "catch a body."

I can feel every impulse and emotion that Caulfield experiences—and he's by no means consistent. Sometimes he does exactly what he calls phony in another. That's why I think the book is good—it shows the dilemma of needing people and yet not wanting them. For instance, as Caulfield says after he's asked Sally (whom he despises) to go for a trip and she refuses: "The terrible part, though, is that I *meant* it when I asked her. That's the terrible part. I swear to God I'm a madman." He cannot break completely away from what he knows is phony. Does he make an effort to get along? I certainly think he does, but when it comes to the point of getting along or going phony, he sacrifices the first and ends up with Stradlater's fist in his mouth. The idiot Stradlater stays in school and Caulfield gets the ax—and it's not because he's lazy—he does it deliberately—because he just can't do stupid things like describing a room. Rather he describes his brother Allie's baseball mitt with poetry written on it. If he were unintelligent, there would have been no problem. It is because he was really looking, sincerely, for a pure thing outside himself, that I admire him.

Hope I gave a crazy kid's view of a crazy kid.

—CHRISTOPHER PARKER, " 'Why the Hell *Not* Smash All the Windows?,' "
Salinger: A Critical and Personal Portrait, ed. Henry Anatole Grunwald
(New York: Harper & Brothers, 1962), pp. 257–58

ALVIN D. ALLEY

I can name several teachers who cringe at the mention of Salinger or *The Catcher in the Rye.* I have heard these same teachers call the book "trash," but they never are able to give valid reasons. Such teachers have arrogated to themselves the attributes of a Solomon, if not of God Himself. Every student of mine who has read *Catcher in the Rye* (which includes those of low, average, and high intelligence) has readily identified himself with its hero, Holden Caulfield. They see in him, not the ideal young man, but a young man in search of himself, in search of his place in the human scheme of things, and in conflict with the narrowness of the society in which he lives. Students come away from the book with a better understanding of themselves and with a deeper penetration into American life. I have asked students to write compositions on the episodes or elements in the novel which shocked them. In almost all the replies the students said quite frankly they were not shocked. And why should they be? Stand with a group of teenagers, and you will hear language such as that of *Catcher in the Rye,* and admittedly most teachers who call the book "trash" are referring primarily to the language Salinger uses. The same principle applies to novels dealing with the military. Having worked for six years as an education counselor for the armed forces, I can not imagine a novel dealing with them that would ring true if there were not a kind of vulgarity in the dialogue.

—ALVIN D. ALLEY, "Puritanism: Scourge of Education Today?,"
Clearing House 38, No. 7 (March 1964): 394–95

PATRICK COSTELLO

Two considerations justify the addition of yet another article to the vast bulk of existing commentary on the work of J. D. Salinger: so much of what has already been written is clearly and simply wrong; and *The Catcher in the Rye* continues to exert a more profound fascination and influence on the college freshman and sophomore than any other book, Golding's *Lord of the Flies* notwithstanding. The purpose of this essay is to correct a seemingly universal misreading of a centrally important scene in the book, and by so doing to enlarge the scope of an observation that has been frequently but too timidly or incompletely made.

In Shakespeare's *Othello* there are many matters which cause disagreement among the play's critics, but there is general accord on one facet of Iago's character. Shakespeare has made it perfectly clear that here is a man who can conceive of no other love relationship than that which is dictated by lust: for him the words love and lust are one and the same. The idea of purity like the idea of selflessness is preposterous to him. It is this failure to conceive of love in any other terms that brings about his destruction, when his own wife, Emilia, responds to a much nobler impulse than that which he allows. Hence the adjective "honest," which is applied to Iago by almost every character in the play, carries a multiple irony, for to the Elizabethans the word "honest" also meant chaste or pure.

To view much of the Salinger criticism, and indeed much of contemporary literary criticism in general, is to realize that the "honest Iago" mentality is dominating a considerable, if not a major, portion of our society. We, as basically sane, civilized human beings, are in much the same position as Othello. If we allow "honest Iago" to infect us with his insanity, we too shall be destroyed. And this is exactly what J. D. Salinger has been telling us in *The Catcher in the Rye.* It is a commonplace that the book condemns the "phony" society which Holden has to confront, but to see just how perverse and befuddled this society is, we have had to wait till that portion of it which devotes itself to literary criticism has made its collective pronouncement.

Numerous commentators writing on *The Catcher in the Rye* have indicated that the scene between Holden and Mr. Antolini in the latter's apartment is of crucial importance both to Holden and the novel. Unfortunately these writers have not been nearly as felicitous in their treatment of the scene as they have been in recognizing its significance. Most of them assume that Mr. Antolini is a homosexual and go on from there. A small minority say the matter is ambiguous and cautiously feel their way out of any commitment. This second group is only somewhat more perceptive; there is an ambiguity in Holden's mind: "Maybe he was only patting my head for the hell of it." But Salinger does give the reader, who is observing and not experiencing Holden's problems, evidence enough for a clear judgment.

In proceeding to such a clear, correct judgment we must briefly review the events of the scene. Holden, at the point of physical and emotional exhaustion intensified by the effect on his nervous system of a considerable overdose of alcohol imbibed earlier in the evening, goes to sleep on Antolini's living room couch, which he and Mr. Antolini have hastily made up into a bed. This is hardly the condition under which one is likely to drop into a deep, peaceful slumber. Holden awakes suddenly and feels a hand on his head. Mr. Antolini is sitting on the floor beside him and is patting him on the head. Holden construes this to be a homosexual action and reacts quite normally by becoming afraid. In his panic, he leaves the apartment despite the extreme lateness of the hour. Shortly thereafter he begins to doubt whether he has judged Mr. Antolini rightly.

Why did Holden make such an initial judgment? Two oft-noted characteristics of Holden's habit of mind are his being quite sensitive to and affected by that which occurs around him, and the highly associative quality of his thought processes. He has told us that immediately before going to sleep, "I laid awake for just a couple seconds thinking about all that stuff Mr. Antolini had told me."

This "stuff" is some remarkably sound advice stressing the necessity of basing his life on a vital humility. It might be noted that this is in consonance with the traditional Christian teaching that humility is the foundation of the moral life. The heart of Mr. Antolini's advice is in the classic, one-sentence refutation of the romantic agony: " 'The mark of the immature man is that he wants to die nobly for a cause, while the mark of a mature man is that he wants to live humbly for one.' " Mr. Antolini tells him that this sentence was written by a psychoanalyst named Wilhelm Stekel.

Now if we will reflect on Holden's patterns of association we will see that one object calls to mind another in the same category. When he thinks of Estelle Fletcher, the authentic Negro vocalist who sings "Little Shirley Beans," he immediately thinks of unauthentic white girl singers. The Lunts call to mind Laurence Olivier, and so on. Sometimes the association in Holden's mind is not immediate, but it seems that eventually opposites within a given category are paired off: in girl friends the phony Sally Hayes is balanced by the genuine Jane Gallagher, and Ackley as inauthentic Catholic is countered by the two nuns as authentic Catholics.

Where does this lead us? It leads to the opposite number of Wilhelm Stekel, the sound psychoanalyst. It seems natural that Holden would recall the other psychoanalyst who had figured in his conversation so recently, the father of Carl Luce. Luce had said, "He's helped me to *adjust* myself to a certain extent, but an extensive analysis hasn't been necessary." This is one of the most howling ironies in the entire book; Luce is one of the most sexually mixed up characters imaginable. While at the Whooton School, he would take younger boys like Holden into his room and give them sex talks, especially about perverts: "Old Luce knew who every flit and Lesbian in the United States was. . . . Sometimes it was hard to believe, the people he said were flits. . . . He said you could turn into one practically overnight, if you had the traits and all. He used to scare the hell out of us. I kept waiting to turn into a flit or something." Just as the movies have made a lasting impression on Holden, so Luce has poisoned his mind. Like Othello, Holden has been prepared to see evil where it doesn't exist.

What do we know of Mr. Antolini? First of all he is a teacher, a teacher who has compassion. Remember it was he who covered with his own coat the body of the boy driven to suicide, and carried the body to the infirmary. A real teacher, not an 8:00 to 3:00 clock puncher, he has maintained interest in his pupils after they have left him. Holden considers him to be the best teacher he has had. Mr. Antolini must of a necessity have a paternal feeling towards his pupils. Is it not an established tradition in Western education that the teacher acts *in loco parentis?* He has married a woman considerably older than himself; there is little likelihood of their being able to have children of their own. He knows that Holden is a boy of much promise who is having difficulties. The boy has turned to him as to a father. The advice he gives Holden is not a list of platitudes. Holden, even in the condition he is in, recognizes this: "It was nice of him to go to all that trouble. It really was." But in spite of his desire to teach Holden, Mr. Antolini plays the good parent when Holden yawns. He realizes the boy's state and breaks off his lecture immediately.

Consider the dedicated, childless teacher watching his pathetically adolescent ex-pupil fall into exhausted sleep. Mr. Antolini has been drinking; the emotions are nearer the surface. Finally he is an Italian, the only character with an Italian name in the book. Is there any one who has known Italians, who hasn't seen a father kiss his son, regardless of the son's age, on greeting and parting? The Italian does not place the same restrictions on his natural, legitimate inclinations as does the Anglo-Saxon.

He becomes flustered at Holden's reaction, but who would not? We have been told that Mr. Antolini is "sophisticated," a teacher at New York University. Certainly he knows the world's attitudes; he is not unaware of the "honest Iago" mentality. It is an easily demonstrable fallacy that the innocent always remain calm in the face of accusation.

The tragedy of this situation is that Holden rejects the one person who is willing and apparently able to help him, the one man who treats him as a person, a human being yearning for a grasp of real adulthood. It is this poisoning of Holden's judgment by adult society as he sees it about him that quite justly bears Salinger's greatest condemnation. How just and how far reaching the condemnation really is becomes apparent when we see that the segment of society responsible for critical reading has been polluted even more thoroughly than Holden. After considering the Carl Luce-like treatment that has been given Mr. Antolini in previous critical commentary, it is no wonder Salinger, in his latest publication, *Seymour, an Introduction,* refers to the universities as "neo-Freudian Arts and Letters clinics." The society which allows the Carl Luce mentality to become its leading voice commits that sin for which the verdict is—it were better for him to have a mill stone tied around his neck. . . .

—PATRICK COSTELLO, "Salinger and 'Honest Iago,' " *Renascence*
16, No. 4 (Summer 1964): 171–74

JAMES E. MILLER, JR.

Holden Caulfield, the fumbling adolescent nauseated by the grossness of the world's body, may be the characteristic hero of contemporary fiction and the modern world. There can be no doubt that for today's American youth, Holden is an embodiment of their secret terrors and their accumulated hostilities, their slender joys and their magnified agonies. In his persistent innocence and his blundering virtue, he may represent to the rest of the world an adolescent America uncertainly searching for the lost garden, suspicious of alien or intimate entanglements, reluctant to encounter the horrors of reality. ⟨. . .⟩

The Catcher in the Rye is a deceptively simple, enormously rich book whose sources of appeal run in deep and complexly varied veins. The very young are likely to identify with Holden and to see the adult world in which he sojourns as completely phony and worthless; the book thus becomes a handbook for rebels and a guide to identification of squares. The older generation is likely to identify with some part of the society that is satirized, and to see Holden as a bright but sick boy whose psyche needs adjustment before he can, as he will, find his niche and settle down. Holden as ideal rebel or Holden as neurotic misfit—the evidence for either interpretation lies loosely on the surface of the novel. Beneath the surface lies the evidence for a more complicated as well as more convincing Holden than some of his admirers are willing to recognize.

—JAMES E. MILLER, JR., *J. D. Salinger* (Minneapolis:
University of Minnesota Press, 1965), pp. 5, 8

ROBERT P. MOORE

The usual charge made against Salinger's *Catcher in the Rye,* which may well be one of the most controversial books of our time, is that it is a dirty book. It includes four letter words that, some suppose, the adolescent in America is being introduced to for the first time. It includes dirty scenes in hotel rooms, and it includes crude and violent scenes in dormitory rooms.

Another charge is that, like *Adventures of Huckleberry Finn,* it is a negative, subversive, and immoral book. Holden Caulfield rejects his school, and the school rejects him. Holden is without ambition, without creed, without purpose. He is a drifter, a wanderer, an adventurer who seeks not adventure but smut and the negative satisfactions of a negative rebellion.

And, of course, in a very inaccurate and superficial sense, to the unseeing, unperceptive, and puritanical eye, much of this is not without foundation. There is negation in the book, and there is dirt and crudeness and subversion and immorality. But it is the world around Holden Caulfield that is negative. It is the world around Holden Caulfield that writes the dirty words on the walls, that does the crude things that make the sensitive cringe, that is immoral and duplicitous and vengeful. The world around Holden but never Holden himself.

The point central to the novel is that Holden is the innocent youth in a world of cruel and hypocritical adults. He is the twentieth-century, unromantic version of Melville's Billy Budd. He is the knight-errant trying to make some sense, find some meaning, gain some understanding of a world that won't listen to him, a world that doesn't care, a world that segregates the sixteen-year-old, separate and never, never equal, a blind, callous, fumbling, bumbling world that often reduces him to tears.

—ROBERT P. MOORE, "The World of Holden," *English Journal*
54, No. 3 (March 1965): 159

DAVID D. GALLOWAY

Few heroes of contemporary literature have aroused so much devotion, imitation, or controversy as J. D. Salinger's Holden Caulfield, the disaffiliated adolescent whose lost weekend in New York is chronicled in *The Catcher in the Rye.* As an impressionable adolescent making his first tentative movements into an adult world, Holden becomes a sensitive register by which the values of that world can be judged. From the opening pages of this novel the world is seen to be fragmentary, distorted, and absurd—in Holden's own special vernacular, "phony." It is an environment in which real communication on a sensitive level is impossible, and when Holden unsuccessfully tries to explain his spiritual pain to Sally Hayes, there is certainly more than a coincidental suggestion of Eliot's "J. Alfred Prufrock" in the frustrated cry, " 'You don't see what I meant at all.' "

Holden does not refuse to grow up so much as he agonizes over the state of being grown up. The innocent world of childhood is amply represented in *The Catcher in the Rye,* but Holden, as a frustrated, disillusioned, anxious hero, stands for modern man rather than merely for the modern adolescent. He is self-conscious and often ridiculous, but he is also an anguished human being of special sensitivity.

Even though he is often childishly ingenuous, and his language is frequently comic, Holden must be seen as both a representative and a critic of the modern environment, as the highly subjective tone of the novel suggests.

As a misfit Holden has literary predecessors in such early Salinger stories as "The Hang of It," "The Varioni Brothers," "Soft-Boiled Sergeant," "This Sandwich Has No Mayonnaise," and "The Stranger." Holden is not unlike Rabbit Angstrom or Augie March in seeking the environment in which he can perform at his best, and the result is a painful contemporary odyssey. As the novel opens, Holden is in the process of rejecting yet another uncongenial environment, Pencey Prep. There he feels surrounded by phonies, just as he had felt surrounded by them at Elkton Hills, his previous school: "One of the biggest reasons I left Elkton Hills was because I was surrounded by phonies. That's all. They were coming in the goddam window." That "Goddam Elkton Hills" is far more than an example of the social snobbery of an Eastern prep school. It comes to stand for a world in which values and perspectives have become so distorted that there seems little if any room for the sensitive individual who attempts to order the flux of human existence or to bring it into the light of a consistent aesthetic perspective. To this significant degree, the milieu in which Salinger heroes function is "absurd." Like Camus's absurd man, the Salinger hero tries to live by ethical standards in an indifferent, often nihilistic universe. An important distinction, however, must be drawn between Camus's absurd man and the absurd man in Salinger's fiction. This distinction is primarily one of consciousness, for Camus's heroes consciously acknowledge the absurdity of their struggle against reality. While the reader is in a position to see the absurdity of Holden's quixotic gestures and of Zooey's ultimate, transcendent "love" stance, he is never entirely certain that the characters themselves see their own struggles as absurd, though Zooey at least approaches this essential awareness. These characters, however, do demonstrate "disproportions" on the level of values which make the myth of the absurd applicable to their struggles. The context of the absurd does not perhaps explain as much about Salinger as it did about Updike, Styron, or Bellow, but it does help us to see what Salinger has tried to accomplish in his writing and to understand his relationship to other contemporary novelists.

Few areas of modern life escape Holden Caulfield's indictment. Among those most severely challenged are the movies (to which his brother D.B., a writer, has prostituted himself) and religious enthusiasm. Holden explains that the children in his family are all "atheists" because his parents are of different religious persuasions (foreshadowing the Irish-Jewish Glass family). Thus Holden's biting but revealing point of view is not clouded by specific religious commitments, and he can love the nuns whom he meets in Grand Central Station even though he feels that Catholicism usually throws up insurmountable barriers to communication. Just as he loves the nuns for their simplicity and honesty, he sees through the selfish religious pose of "this guy Ossenburger," an undertaker who contributes a dormitory wing to Pencey.

The phoniness of Hollywood and of religion as it is often practiced in the contemporary world come together to form a dramatic whole in the Christmas pageant which Holden attends at Radio City. Following the Rockettes and a man who roller-skated under tables, "they had this Christmas thing they have at Radio City every year":

> All these angels start coming out of the boxes and everywhere, guys carrying crucifixes and stuff all over the place, and the whole bunch of them— *thousands* of them—singing "Come All Ye Faithful!" like mad. Big deal. It's supposed to be religious as hell, I know, and very pretty and all, but I can't see anything religious or pretty, for God's sake, about a bunch of actors carrying crucifixes all over the stage.

The blatant, graceless *kitsch* of the movie which follows the stage show (and which has been identified as James Hilton's *Random Harvest*) is an equally commercial deception, an artificial substitute for the love and generosity which Americans have forgotten how to express. After his experience with a Radio City Christmas, Holden feels yet more agonizingly frustrated and alone. "I'm sort of glad they've got the atomic bomb invented," he comments. "If there's ever another war, I'm going to sit right the hell on top of it. I'll volunteer for it, I swear to God I will."

Wherever Holden turns, his craving for truth seems to be frustrated by the phoniness of the world. From his hotel window he looks out upon scenes of perversion and distortion; in bars and night clubs he hears only the laconic accents of shallow supersophisticates or self-satisfied intellectuals. When he finds innocence or purity it is always jeopardized by evil or apathy, and he searches desperately for something to sustain him. An answer seems to come from Mr. Antolini, a former English teacher who explains to Holden that the fall he is riding for is " 'a special kind of fall, a horrible kind. The man falling isn't permitted to feel or hear himself hit bottom. He just keeps falling and falling. The whole arrangement's designed for men who, at some time or other in their lives, were looking for something their own environment couldn't supply them with. So they gave up looking.' " Mr. Antolini urges Holden to continue to search in humility for a cause worth living for. Such a search, he assures Holden, has been chronicled by educated and scholarly men, and he promises to guide the boy into an intellectual channel that will both stimulate and comfort him. Whatever consolation there may have been in this message is destroyed when Holden awakens to find Mr. Antolini petting him—and he flees from yet another example of the world's perversion.

What prompts Holden's quest is his desire for unity, a desire that is expressed in the comfort and safety which he always felt in the Museum of Natural History:

> The best thing, though, in that museum was that everything always stayed right where it was. Nobody'd move. You could go there a hundred thousand times, and that Eskimo would still be just finished catching those two fish, the birds would still be on their way south, the deers would still be drinking out of that water hole, with their pretty antlers and their pretty, skinny legs, and that

squaw with the naked bosom would still be weaving that same blanket. Nobody'd be different.

That such a reassuringly ordered universe is an improbable dream is emphasized by the fact that, when Holden visits the Museum near the conclusion of his New York odyssey, he sees the words " 'Fuck you' . . . written with a red crayon or something, right under the glass part of the wall, under the stones." Holden wishes to erase the interminable "Fuck you's" on all the alley walls and school corridors and sidewalks in the world, and this intention to cancel out vulgarity and phoniness is a poignant if naive example of the absurd.

The Catcher in the Rye is an important articulation of one of the possible responses which man may make to an essentially destructive life experience. Since, Holden reasons, there is no fulfillment in the adult world, since all it can offer man is frustration or corruption, the only worthwhile task to which he can devote himself is that of the protector who stops children before they enter the world of destruction and phoniness and keeps them in a state of arrested innocence:

> "Anyway, I keep picturing all these little kids playing some game in this big field of rye and all. Thousands of little kids, and nobody's around—nobody big, I mean, except me. And I'm standing on the edge of some crazy cliff. What I have to do, I have to catch everybody if they start to go over the cliff—I mean if they're running and they don't look where they're going I have to come out from somewhere and *catch* them. That's all I'd do all day. I'd just be the catcher in the rye and all. I know it's crazy, but that's the only thing I'd really like to be. I know it's crazy."

Holden's reiteration of the word "crazy" reminds us that his ambition is also "absurd," for his Christ-like intention (suffering the little children to come unto him) is opposed to the reality in which children like his own sister, Phoebe, are carted off to the Lister Foundation to see movies on euthanasia and move along grimy school corridors which flaunt the words "Fuck you!" at them. While Holden has a vision of his role in the world, he is unable either to live the absurdity he has outlined or to develop an absurd faith. The reasons for this failure on his part are simple and obvious. First, even though we are clearly intended to see him as a representative of modern man, Holden is an adolescent, and both his experience and his perspectives are too limited for him to offer any kind of finalized "answer" to the phoniness of the world. Second, and perhaps most important, his vision carries within itself a destructive contradiction. While Holden's intention is absurd in its opposition to reality, the goal of his intention is to help innocent children to *avoid* reality. His conclusion negates his premise insofar as it eliminates one of the two crucial terms of the absurd confrontation and offers no formula by which man can live in and with his world. Holden's intention is moving and vaguely saintly, but it involves a nostalgia which, according to Camus, the absurd man must reject.

(Indeed, Holden himself rejects it when he decides that he must not attempt to protect Phoebe during her final ride on the carrousel.)

What Salinger leaves us with in this novel is an often biting image of the absurd contemporary milieu. The idea of perpetuating the innocence of childhood is a philosophically untenable position, and the only other unrejected proposals in the novel are so vague that their full importance can be seen only in Salinger's later work. The first of these proposals for a stance at once self-protective and human-istically fulfilling is made by Carl Luce, who suggests a vague mystical discipline derived from Eastern philosophy as a solution to Holden's spiritual agony, but Luce's approach to this discipline seems supersophisticated and "phony." In the epilogue to the novel Holden suggests the possibility of re-entering society when he says, "I sort of *miss* everybody I told about. Even old Stradlater and Ackley, for instance. I think I even miss that goddam Maurice." Holden misses even the phonies of the world because his experience has taught him something about the necessity of loving, and here Salinger sounds what is to become his major and most complex theme.

—DAVID D. GALLOWAY, "The Love Ethic," *The Absurd Hero in American Fiction: Updike, Styron, Bellow, Salinger* (Austin: University of Texas Press, 1966), pp. 140–45

✳ MARIO L. D'AVANZO

Perhaps the most celebrated literary champion of *The Great Gatsby* in the past few years has been Holden Caulfield. In *The Catcher in the Rye* Holden remarks: "I was crazy about *The Great Gatsby*. Old Gatsby. Old sport. That killed me." In attempting to account for his strong attraction for "old Gatsby" ("old" being a term of affection in Holden's vocabulary), one finds some important clues in Fitzgerald's novel which help to illuminate the character of Holden. Several other meaningful literary references are to be found in *Catcher*—Burns, Hemingway, Shakespeare, Dickens, Lardner—but I think the reference to Gatsby is most significant.

The central, common characteristic of both Gatsby and Holden is the adherence to a powerful, abiding illusion, while around them swirls a corrupt, hostile, essentially phony world. Both have integrity and contemplate an ideal world. Gatsby's pursuit of a pure vision of happiness in marriage with Daisy, who becomes a religion or "grail" to him, is surely attractive to Holden, for he too loves with worshipful dedication. His brother Allie is a saint; and Phoebe is his dearest companion. Gatsby's life is dedicated to recapturing the past and maintaining a paradise of youth, love, and perpetual beauty. He is a watchdog, continually surveying Daisy's house. So too is Holden in his desire to keep children contained in the rye field and away from the cliff that drops off into the experiential world. He would be their catcher as Gatsby would be Daisy's custodian and solemn protector of their dream-world. Holden's self-appointed role as catcher is like Gatsby's "Platonic conception of himself." Indeed, Gatsby's character is a key to understanding Holden, especially the celebrated passage on Gatsby's youth: "So he invented just the sort of Jay Gatsby that a seventeen-year-old boy would be likely to invent, and to this conception he was faithful to the end."

Even though Gatsby and Holden entertain unreal visions—the world is perhaps too painfully mutable for each—there is something admirable in their fidelity to an ideal world each contemplates. Holden likes Gatsby precisely because "old Gatsby" is unswervingly constant in his aim and has an indestructible, almost childlike belief in his ability to recapture the past.

Gatsby's absurd posing would appear to be acceptable to Holden, who also play-acts and fibs with a similar innocence. Gatsby's only intent is to win Daisy by whatever means he thinks will impress her or her friends. For all his social posing and dubious business dealings, he really acts guilelessly. No wonder Holden admires Gatsby. He too is an isolated being who loves deeply, acts kindly, charitably, and trustingly, despite what he thinks about the adult world. They are two noble kinsmen dreaming their dreams and pursuing their ideals in a cruel, visionless world.

If Gatsby finds it difficult to distinguish between illusion and reality (he never sees Daisy in proper focus, as Nick does), Holden has the same problem. He must navigate between the real and ideal worlds without sinking fully into Gatsby's romantic illusory world. With the help of a psychiatrist, Holden's idealism will perhaps be tempered as he adjusts to the real world. If not, he will feel the betrayal that Gatsby knew. Perhaps he will be saved from Gatsby's fate, if he comes to understand that one cannot exist fully in Gatsby's invented world. In this regard Holden is a disturbed Gatsby who is learning to see rightly but not necessarily denying the validity of a tempered idealism. As the model character of innocence and illusion in American literature, Gatsby has a successor in Holden Caulfield. Salinger acknowledges that debt in the text of the novel.

—MARIO L. D'AVANZO, "Gatsby and Holden Caulfield,"
Fitzgerald Newsletter No. 38 (Summer 1967): 4–6

CLINTON W. TROWBRIDGE

To some, I fear, what I am about to argue will seem the most blatant form of mistruth, horrendous, even, in its lack of taste, a kind of literary sacrilege, in fact. Surely we have reached the end, they will say, when one can consider comparing the immortal Hamlet, Prince of Denmark, with the adolescent protagonist of Salinger's *The Catcher in the Rye*. And I can sympathize with their feelings of outrage. Salinger's "hero" has been compared to many literary figures, from Huck Finn to David Copperfield. So many different attitudes have been taken toward him. Let's stop talking about him and write about something else. Isn't the subject getting boring? Perhaps so, but Holden, at least for me, will not go away. He continues to pester the mind, and recently, while reading A. C. Bradley's analysis of Hamlet's character, I couldn't resist the idea that much of what Bradley was saying about Hamlet applied to Holden as well. So, let the critics carp. I, at least, have felt illumined. And perhaps the comparison is not as absurd as it first appears.

Of course, there is no similarity between the events of the play and those of the novel. What struck me while reading Bradley was how perfectly his analysis of Hamlet's character applied to Holden's, how deeply, in fact, he was going into Holden's character as well, revealing, among other things, its potentially tragic nature.

For a moment the temptation to play anagrams, to ponder the significance of Shakespeare, Salinger, H*A*M*L*E*T, H*O*L*D*E*N, became almost too much for me, but fortunately the visionary eyes clouded over and I returned to what was, relatively speaking, earth.

After demolishing the theories of other critics, Bradley concludes that the essence of Hamlet's character is contained in a three-fold analysis of it. First, that rather than being melancholy by temperament, in the usual sense of "profoundly sad," he is a person of unusual nervous instability, one liable to extreme and profound alterations of mood, a potential manic-depressive type. Romantic, we might say. Second, this Hamlet is also a person of "exquisite moral sensibility," hypersensitive to goodness, a moral idealist who, when he cannot wholly love the world chooses wholly to despise it rather than live in it with its imperfections. He is also a person who tends to see only good as real but who, when evil is forced upon him as a reality, loses his awareness of good almost altogether. Third, there is Hamlet's particular type of intellectual genius: an unusual quickness of mind, a great agility in shifting mental attitudes, a remarkable ability to penetrate appearances once they are seen as such, a passion for generalizing about life, and a curiosity about life, ideas, and people that is so strong that one doubts the possibility of his ever satisfying it.

Bradley goes on to say that the tragedy of Hamlet is that these very characteristics, which formerly were the reasons for his superiority, because of an incident in his life—his mother's hasty marriage to his father's brother and what he later learns about his mother's adultery and his father's murder—are now the very qualities that bring about his destruction. Bradley sees his inability to act as being the result of an intense moral disillusionment, one that produces a depression so great as to constitute utter world-weariness and a frustration as well as perversion of intellectual genius. The Hamlet of the play, then, as Bradley sees him, *is* melancholy in the sense that he is almost continually depressed and thus incapable of positive action, is moving toward death, spiritual as well as physical, and yet is a figure whose story is tragic because we are constantly made aware of the greatness that he once had. As Bradley says, the tragic feeling is the profound awareness of waste.

Before discussing the manner in which these remarks apply to Holden, let me hasten to say that Holden is redeemed from the tragic catastrophe. He is, at least minimally, brought back to life; in fact, as I have tried to show elsewhere ("The Symbolic Structure of *The Catcher in the Rye," Sewanee Review*, Summer 1966), he might be said to have been saved from tragedy. That is one supreme and vital difference between them. Another, of course, is that I would hardly argue that Salinger's depiction of the Hamlet character is as profound or as deeply moving as Shakespeare's. But let us now look at the evidence.

The evidence is so omnipresent that one's initial reaction is to regard it as self-evident, but we had better at least sketch it out. In the first place, everyone seems to agree, detractors and worshipers alike, that Holden is some crazy kid. To say that he is moody is to understate indeed. Surely his nervous instability, his tendency toward a manic-depressive form of Romanticism, needs no corroboration.

His "extreme moral sensibility" is also pretty obviously there. Virtually everything in his world is regarded as "phony"; nor does he exempt himself from "calumny." And there are other more exact parallels. His idealization of Allie, the only perfect person he has ever known, he says, is similar to Hamlet's attitude toward his father. As Hamlet's "almost blunted purpose" is sharpened by the reappearance of his father's ghost, so Holden's suidical tendencies are held in check by the memory of Allie, who keeps Holden from destruction as he crosses the city streets. Holden's disillusionment with people is on the same vast scale as Hamlet's and encompasses an even greater variety of people: his brother, D.B., who has prostituted his talents by writing for Hollywood; his history teacher, Mr. Spencer, who laughs at the headmaster's jokes; his former English teacher, Mr. Antolini, who is seen, momentarily at least, as a pervert; most of all the "rogue and peasant slave" that is himself.

The process whereby each universalizes the significance of a particular disillusioning experience is also strikingly similar. Just as Hamlet's disillusionment with his mother's character extends itself to Ophelia and finally to women in general, so does Holden's conviction that to grow up is to grow phony force itself upon him.

Both characters are left virtually alone at the end, having either been betrayed by or alienated themselves from those who could have helped them. Holden's friends, Stradlater, Ackley, Carl Luce, Sally Hayes—the Rosencrantzes and Guildensterns of The Catcher—betray him and are rejected. They all had the opportunity of helping Holden, and while they are all in a sense as much enemies as friends, one of the results of their failure to aid and their inability to understand Holden is that he is left more and more alone. There are also, however, what might be called Horatio characters in The Catcher, figures who are relied on mainly for their steadfastness but who also have a quality of innocence and what might be called rationality about them: the nuns, the drummer at Radio City Music Hall, Jane Gallagher, who keeps her kings in the back row. Phoebe is certainly the most important of these characters, though she finally goes beyond her prototype and prevents the "noble heart" from "cracking."

Most important, surely, in considering the similarity between Hamlet and Holden as disillusioned, moral idealists, is the sense so deeply embedded in each of them that death is preferable to life in a world in which evil seems to predominate. Yet neither is capable of suicide.

If differences in age and in depth of mind are remembered, the thought that Holden is of the same type of intellectual genius as Hamlet should not be too offensive a suggestion, and, once again, the similarities are striking. Holden's remarkable quickness of mind shows itself most clearly in the spur-of-the-moment fantasies he weaves for Mrs. Morrow, for the nuns, and for Sunny. His agility in shifting mental attitudes is perhaps best seen in connection with Mr. Antolini who falls from savior to seducer "overnight." Holden's ability to see beneath appearances is one of the reasons why *The Catcher* can be read purely on the level of social satire. Combined with his passion for generalizing about life, it is this ability in him that helps produce his disillusioned ruminations on the phoniness of the world. As with Hamlet, this capacity to see the real behind what appears becomes a cynical habit of mind and so, ironically, finally places each in a nightmare world whose abominations as effectively hide reality as did the former fantasies of the world of appearance. Holden is perceptive when he sees the difference between the appearance and reality of Stradlater, "the secret slob," when he sees through the false charity of Sally Hayes's mother, when he senses the egotism behind Ernie's false humility; and taken all together, his vision constitutes a valid indictment of the phoniness of man and society. But Holden's perceptiveness, like Hamlet's, leads him too far. He condemns too rapidly and too harshly. The fact that he suspects that he does so proves that he can be equally perceptive about himself, that he cannot stop from doing so, that his perceptiveness is degenerating into cynicism. He forgets the nuns, Mr. and Mrs. Spencer, Mrs. Morrow, Horwitz, the divinely mad taxi driver, the drummer at Radio City Music Hall, and he concludes that to grow up is to become hopelessly corrupt. Not to grow up, then, must be to remain good; and there is the consequent false idealization of childhood, the past, ultimately the changeless world of the dead. Just as Claudius is no satyr, and just as Hamlet's father was probably no Hyperion, so the adult world cannot be seriously imagined as wholly evil and the world of the child as entirely good. While there is obviously truth in both heroes' conclusions, it is certainly equally obvious that what begins as perceptiveness degenerates into unperceptive melancholia.

Yet, in spite of the utter dejection, the only momentarily alleviated world-weariness of both characters, both keep to the end what is essentially an insatiable curiosity about life, ideas, people; and at the end, Holden, having been saved from catastrophe by Phoebe, can start again with all the questions that he has been so successful in answering, having been given one answer that will enable him to ask them all over again in a different light. He has been told, and he has come to realize, that the world can be, in fact must be, loved in spite of its imperfections.

If there is, then, a striking similarity between Hamlet as Bradley sees him and Holden Caulfield, what is so significant about this fact? After all, there are also many differences, the most important of which have to do with the relative "size" of the two. It is hard to conceive of a Holden whose very qualities here mentioned made him a truly superior creature at some time before the action of the novel. We are certainly not witnessing the fall of some Renaissance type, as Bradley argues that we are with Hamlet. Not only is the tragic stature missing but, as I have mentioned, the tragic conclusion is averted. Moving as he does toward catastrophe, Holden is kept from it; and while the novel can hardly be said to end happily, there is this salvation from death as well as the hope of recovery that Holden's newfound acceptance of life promises. In spite of their similarities, then, one might still feel that the two are created on such different scales that mention of them in the same breath constitutes something of a sacrilege.

Nevertheless, there is a great importance in recognizing the basic similarity between the characters of Hamlet and Holden; and it lies chiefly in the following "truths." Such recognition helps clarify Salinger's attitude toward his "hero" by giving additional support to those of us who, for other reasons, already view Holden as symbolizing the plight of the idealist in the modern world. Most importantly, however, it suggests why Holden Caulfield won't go away, why we can't stop thinking about him, why after almost as many words have already been spilled over him as over Hamlet himself, he continues to fascinate us, why he continues to remain so potent an influence on the now aging younger generation that he first spoke to, and why he continues to brand himself anew on the young. In fact, in this age of atrophy, in this thought-tormented, thought-tormenting time in which we live, perhaps it is not going too far to say that, for many of us, at least, our Hamlet is Holden.

—CLINTON W. TROWBRIDGE, "Hamlet and Holden," *English Journal* 57, No. 1 (January 1968): 26–29

BERNARD C. KINNICK

As an adolescent, Holden Caulfield's search for idealism, sincerity, and decency (in a sense a small-scale and private Utopia) strikes an accepting note with many. However, his actions and thoughts meet with naked rejection by many who would cry with one voice, "Holden, why don't you just grow up?" To me, Holden Caulfield represents the uniqueness in man in a world which has lost its spirit for the idealism so often expressed in man's past search for Utopia.

In J. D. Salinger's *The Catcher in the Rye,* we find more than merely a theme of man vs. society or the individual vs. conformity. Not so much a description of social life, but rather an intensified search and exploration of inner life—not so much a critique of a period in adolescent life or a series of particular situations, but of human condition—life itself. Holden is trying to find, in an urgent and excited way, idealism in the world—to wit, a private version of Utopia. He seeks, through a personal search, the often mentioned ideals of truth, beauty, and goodness. (This same search is more taken up with personal introspection than with an allegiance to any far removed dream.)

The adolescent Holden Caulfield is usually described as a rebel, either against the materialism and ugliness of our society or against the realities of the adult world. But actually he does not make a very satisfactory rebel because he is not for much of anything—that is, he lacks any real positive program for eradicating the evils he finds all around him. (Still, many may ask, why must a rebel be for anything? Is it not enough to *expose* the evils within a society?) Holden's only real friend, his sister Phoebe, complains that he (Holden) doesn't like anything that's happening. It would seem that the well-adjusted, successful, "adult rebel" would have a positive program; otherwise, after all, is he not merely an anarchist? Holden is not so much a rebel against society, but rather a searcher for idealism—a striving to find the good and the perfection in man which Rousseau so aptly espoused.

No doubt it would not be difficult to understand the phonies, the bores, and the deceivers whom Holden so dislikes. They actually "constitute a fair average" of what the culture affords. They are part of the truth which Holden does not see, is never able to see, or in fact refuses to see. The phonies, the bores, and the deceivers are one part of humanity—the lies, the phoniness, the hypocrisy are the compromises which innocence is forced by the world to make. Is this perhaps the reality on which Holden's search for idealism is finally broken?

Many adults feel that the adolescent (characterized here by Holden Caulfield) should "grow up," accept the world for what it is, and live in it. In essence, throw off any ideas of ever reaching for or becoming a part of an ideal world. At first notice, this is a sound but conservative recommendation. However, taken seriously and logically, the advice would put an end to any search for idealism, sincerity, and decency. True, it is the kind of advice that most are forced to give sooner or later—and to take. But, is it not possible that there are some adolescents (and adults) who are simply not like the majority, who cannot accept the human condition for what it is, who cannot resign themselves to the existence of injustice, ugliness, and pain? This refusal to accept the status quo in the world marks not only the adolescents—it also marks many adults who may be seen as an adolescent who has refused to "grow up," who is unable or unwilling to cover his inner life with the calluses necessary for the ordinary life. These individuals wage war with the-way-things-are. They are martyrs in the eternal search for idealism. Holden Caulfield, if he is a rebel at all, is a rebel against the human condition and as such he deserves his small share of nobility.

It is most important to protect and cherish the uniqueness of the adolescent who, rightly or wrongly, refuses to accept completely the existing reality of the adult world. Resistance to the world is not bad or evil in itself—rather, it may be that one thing that gives the adolescent his uniqueness as a human being. The continuous search of the adolescent for a semi-Utopian world where truth, beauty, and goodness would abound must be encouraged rather than stamped upon. Holden, like most adolescents, continues in an urgent pace to search for his true self and his place in the world. The adolescent's disillusionment and sense of failure arrive when his search for an ideal and decent world for his ideal and decent self to respond to, proves useless. Thus, the adolescent's rebellion is in part a protest against the ugly world transmitted to him and in part a sort of punishment for the world's lack of idealism.

A great part of the adolescent's idealism probably stems from his resistance to growing up. Still, it is rather difficult to criticize this resistance to entering a world lacking in the ideals found within the spirit of the young adolescent. Holden's distaste for his findings, in his collision with the outside world, seem to be warranted. If this be true, one should recognize the adolescent's need for viewing and experiencing himself from the inside—exploring his inner life where idealism and notions of Utopia are free to live and flourish. As reality closes in on the adolescent, he fights all the harder to escape it and preserve his vision of Utopia or self-made paradise. (Perhaps in cherishing the world of the adolescent, we cherish ourselves, or, rather, the memory of ourselves in youth. We admire what we once were, or think we were, or wanted to become.)

Adolescent idealism is found in Holden's quest for sincerity, for honesty between people. His repeated insistence, "I mean it, I really do," gives credence to this search. And when Holden does experience decency, as he does with his sister Phoebe, he reacts decently to it. Holden, as many adolescents, is extremely sensitive to the good and evil in society. He may often be criticized for being too sensitive about the realities of society to live in it. But might not the opposite be true? Perhaps the adolescent is too sensitive to ignore it, to look the other way, to withdraw, as the so-called well-adjusted and busy adults withdraw into their protective shells when faced with society's terrors and ugliness. Holden simply cannot accept the injustices, the ugliness, the lovelessness that surround him. He meets them head-on. It is to the adolescent's great credit that, in spite of numerous disillusionments, he stubbornly clings to his conviction that there *must* be a hidden core of sincerity somewhere among the world's hypocrisies. As long as the adolescent can hold on to the conviction that there are external counterparts to his ideal self, he can keep going. When this vision of his self-made Utopia is finally broken in his encounter with the world of reality, the adolescent must compromise or painfully withdraw in one of many ways from this same world of reality.

The idealistic rebellion of adolescence is a good thing when it is harnessed to idealistic and Utopian schemes, even though unworkable in the hard world of practicality. There *must* be some virtue in rebellion against a false, lying, and deceitful society. Most adolescents eventually come to terms with things as they are. They give up their Utopian and idealistic ideas of working any radical changes in the social structure or in the culture's value system. They try at least, painful as it may be, to find their own "realistic" place in society. Holden was unable to do this very thing. For this, he is both intensely praised and violently condemned.

Is Holden Caulfield an outsider in this world, or is he really an insider with the track all to himself?

—BERNARD C. KINNICK, "Holden Caulfield: Adolescents' Enduring Model," *High School Journal* 53, No. 8 (May 1970): 440–43

NANCY C. RALSTON

Almost twenty years ago a very sensitive, confused young man was introduced to the world of literature. While his problems were not terribly unique, his reactions and their documentation were unsettling in their intensity. J. D. Salinger caused a sensation in 1951 when he created Holden Caulfield, whose use and misuse of the English language was absurd with exaggeration, comical with colorful and some-times obscene adjectives, and pitiful with loneliness. The sensation has not entirely died down. It is not uncommon, though still somewhat surprising, to hear of some local controversy involving the banning of *The Catcher in the Rye* from a school library. This action is apparently taken under the unbelievably naive assumption that removing Holden from book shelves will thus prevent him from contaminating our pristine youth with his vivid language. This represents, of course, total ignorance of the current popularity of the book, now in its twenty-fourth printing in paperback form, and of its availability in the well-scanned, well-thumbed selections rotating on the racks of every corner drugstore. This type of psychological tunnel-vision also involves complete rejection of the advisability of providing an opportunity for the novel to be read and interpreted in an educational atmosphere such as an English class. Instead, under restricted circumstances involving outwardly enforced censor-ship, the book is assured digestion within a peer-oriented setting, which does not necessarily nor ordinarily foster a literary perspective or an intellectual point of view. Of greater significance, however, than *Catcher's* initial and vestigial impact is the impressive evidence that this book is still so *au courant.*

Ironically, were Holden a real rather than fictional character who had success-fully resolved most of his adolescent problems, he no doubt would be concerned today with such pressing matters as a receding hair line, middle-age spread, mutual funds, and the financing of his children's college education. As a member, in rea-sonably good standing, of the establishment, he conceivably would be alive, well, and running for the school board in western Michigan. In spite of this rather alarming and paradoxical projection, the twenty-year-old account of adolescent turmoil and emo-tional trauma remains a best-seller for young people who theoretically could be of the same age as the hypothetical progeny of Salinger's protagonist. However, the popularity of the novel on both the high school and college campus is dramatic evi-dence of its continued relevancy. More to the point, this is an indication that changes which have taken place in the world of the adolescent since 1951 have been in the realm of concrete situations and not in the underlying attitudes of young people.

Were Salinger tempted to up-date his novel (the mere suggestion of such tampering may be viewed by some as a sacrilege), he might find it appropriate to treat Holden's alienation and/or hypersensitivity in terms of his reactions to racial discrimination, poverty, war, environmental pollution, and other cancerous situa-tions. We might also be asked by the author to share Holden's experience with drugs rather than his out-dated adventures with liquor. It is difficult to predict exactly how he would respond to the accessibility and popularity of drugs and hallucinogens. He used drinking primarily as an attention-getting device rather than as a means of escape. He wasn't the kind of person who would wish to tune out what beauty he could discover in his life and it is highly doubtful, because of his level of intelligence, that he would fall for the "mind-expanding" propaganda. He would experiment with drugs, but not to a degrading extreme. While still highly critical of the phoniness exhibited by others, he probably would be more tolerant of the people responsible for such behavior, especially if those persons were his own peers. In this sense, he might not be so much of a loner now nor feel so alienated from his own group, since he would be more likely in this day and age to find soul-mates who would share his feelings. In fact, Holden could easily find companionship in one of many existing communes where he undoubtedly could wear his hunting cap unchallenged and do his own thing surrounded by kindred spirits until the inevitable disenchantment would set it.

Salinger would need to change some of the physical properties of his story— i.e., D.B. might conceivably become a copywriter for Dow-Chemical, the movies and plays would be of the topless and bottomless variety, the night clubs would become discotheques, Holden's hair and sideburns would be allowed to grow, thus exploiting the grey streak to its fullest advantage, and his clothing would be much more individualistic. The concrete examples of obsolescence would have to be discarded but there would be no need to tamper with the hero's psyche.

The boy's weaknesses—his unwillingness to apply himself academically, his frequent refusal to face the consequences of his behavior, his over-reaction to objects of his sentimentality, his harsh and intolerant criticism of others, the incessant stereotyping of all individuals with whom he finds fault, the inability to accept or adjust to a world he finds extremely frustrating—all are typical of today's youth. Even in the area of sex behavior, while his exposure might be on a more sophisticated level, his confusion would not be lessened. He might well still be saying, "Sex is something I just don't understand, I swear to God I don't."

That only the external and none of the internal factors of the story would need revision is a tribute to Salinger's insight into the hearts and minds of young people. He actually provided us with the forerunner of the disenchanted young person of today. In 1951, we were given an alarmingly accurate prediction of youthful alienation in a book which even described specific examples of its manifestations: complaints about ineffective teaching and irrelevant education, repugnance for social allegiances in the form of club or fraternity membership, and total lack of enthusiasm indigenous to rah-rah school spirit. Holden typically turned off anyone or anything which seemed superficial to him. How many young people follow this example today?

Holden Caulfield is not likely to go away. The echo of his voice hovers over the ubiquitous examples of phoniness whenever and wherever they dare to appear. His shadow haunts every display of obscene graffiti scrawled in millions of public places. Holden knows no generation gap. He is the super-adolescent of yesterday, today, and tomorrow.

—NANCY C. RALSTON, "Holden Caulfield: Super-Adolescent,"
Adolescence No. 24 (Winter 1971): 429–32

KEITH M. MAY

What Holden perceives from first to last is that everyone except himself is engaged in some elaborate game or other. He encounters the game of school, the game of psychoanalysis, the game of writing for films (which his brother has taken up with disgusting success), the family game, and so on. The phoniness with which Holden is surrounded and about which he makes his endless comical complaint consists only of the ordinary manoeuvres of social intercourse: people pose, strike attitudes, 'play at' being schoolmasters or doctors or mothers. It would be wrong to suppose that in this novel Salinger was attacking rich Easterners or championing the young against the middle-aged, for such factors are incidental. *The Catcher in the Rye* illustrates what Eric Berne later discussed in his work of popular psychology, *Games People Play* (1964), which amounts to a lively exposition of some common forms of bad faith.

At best Holden Caulfield is an existentialist hero in embryo. He refuses to indulge in what Heidegger called 'forgetfulness of existence' (heedlessness of the quality of what one is doing, bearing firmly in mind the fact of death), but is not mature or confident enough to do more than squirm before the ubiquitous insincerities.

—KEITH M. MAY, "Attack on the Unconscious: Sartre and the Post-War American Novel," *Out of the Maelstrom: Psychology and the Novel in the Twentieth Century* (New York: St. Martin's Press, 1977), p. 94

FRED BRATMAN

This month my fictional friend, Holden Caulfield, turns 50. For me it is an important birthday to celebrate, and yet I do not know precisely which day it falls on.

The protagonist of J. D. Salinger's *The Catcher in the Rye* first came to life as an installment in the now-defunct *Collier's* magazine in December 1945, and the entire story was published in book form six years later. In the story Holden is 16 years old, and since it was first published 34 years ago, he would be 50 years old this month. He is old enough to be my father; yet, I have always thought myself his equal or elder.

The first time I read *Catcher* I was 16 years old. That was eight years ago, and since then I have made it a point to find my tattered copy with its folded-over pages and re-read it each year. I always wonder whether it will have the same impact as it did the first time.

Then, I was simply dazzled. I thought that the book had been written especially for me. I was in a public high school, and, like Holden, flunking several of my academic courses. Just as Mr. Spencer tried to straighten Holden out, I had a teacher who tried his very best to get me to stick my nose in my books. I could not run away to New York City, as Holden did, for I was already there. But my mind drifted throughout my high school days.

The affinity that Holden evoked I am sure was not limited to me. No doubt many of the 10 million or so people who have also bought a copy since it first appeared feel the same way.

No matter where I am or what I am doing, Holden becomes my personal guide for a few hours on our annual trip. Geographically, Holden does not venture to Sumatra or to Patagonia. Instead he stays within a short commuter train ride of New York City. Yet, I always feel that I am visiting places that I have never seen before.

Holden has also been a personal savior of sorts. Once I was on a train as it crawled from Delhi to an outpost near the Nepalese border. I was ill. My stomach had not yet properly adjusted to the culinary delights of India. I gulped down a handful of tablets that I hoped would serve as a peacemaker between the warring factions in my stomach. But the only relief I experienced came from my crumpled copy of Salinger's novel. Holding my stomach with one hand and *Catcher* with the other, I followed my fictional friend through his escapades and decided that his problems were far more interesting than mine. My moans of abdominal pain were intermingled with laughs.

I often thought that Holden and I saw the world from the identical perspective, that his world was my world. However, this was not accurate. Holden had created his own world, which I was only privileged to visit. But it was ultimately his world.

Holden has a keen eye that sees the hypocrisy of what not only springs from the mouths of adults but also from his school chums. Early on in the book, for instance, Holden's roommate, Stradlater, asks Holden to write a descriptive composition for him because he is too busy with his Saturday night date. He warns Holden: "Don't stick all the commas and stuff in the right place." Holden doesn't say anything but knows that good writing is not simply about commas.

Holden has a special meaning for me because I realized that I was not unique in feeling restless. Holden felt the same way. He became my friend because we thought alike.

Realizing that Holden would be 50 years old this month, I had this thought: Where is Holden today?

J. D. Salinger lives a quiet life in New Hampshire, but did Holden get killed during the Korean War? Did he once drink too much and drive his car into a wall? Of course he could still be alive. Maybe he became a writer like his older brother. Or did he attend law school and now work for a Wall Street firm?

Maybe none of these things happened to Holden. Multitudes of possible variations often come to mind, but finally I must reject them. None of them would completely satisfy Holden's character.

I refuse to imagine my fictional friend in a gray pin-striped suit with a leather attaché case reading the morning newspaper as the 7:09 from Armonk heads toward New York. On the other hand, I cannot picture Holden as a fast-talking Hollywood screenwriter.

For me, Holden will always remain a teenager who sees people for what they are, and can laugh at his own problems.

Happy birthday, Holden.

—FRED BRATMAN, "Holden, 50, Still Catches," New York Times,
December 21, 1979, Sec. A, p. 35

⚜ JOHN S. MARTIN

J. D. Salinger's *Catcher in the Rye* contains several interesting and oblique parallels to *David Copperfield*. In the novel's first sentence, for example, Holden informs us that he is not going to tell us about his parents, his early life, and "all that David Copperfield kind of crap."

Holden, of course, goes on anyway, and, like Copperfield, gives us his life story. The fact that he does so not only reinforces the parallel to *Copperfield*, but actually establishes an important connection between the two novels. More specifically, in choosing the name Holden Caulfield for his protagonist, Salinger gives us the focal point of a substantial Dickensian frame of reference for *Catcher*.

Holden only mentions Dickens once, in describing a movie that follows the Christmas show at Radio City Music Hall. Typically, Holden scoffs at the conventional notion of Christmas, which is commonly associated with Dickens as the author of *A Christmas Carol:*

> Then he meets this nice, homey, sincere girl getting on a bus. Her goddam hat blows off and he catches it, and then they go upstairs and sit down and start talking about Charles Dickens. He's both their favorite author and all. He's carrying this copy of *Oliver Twist* and so's she. I could've puked. Anyway, they fall in love right away, on account they're both so nuts about Charles Dickens. . . .

With varying degrees of success, critics have hinted at the Salinger/Dickens parallel—but at best in only a limited way. For example, Carl F. Stauch ("in passing") sees Stradlater as the counterpart of James Steerforth in *Copperfield*. And it is well worth noting that, as Robert B. Kaplan has stated,

> Holden Caulfield does not inhabit a literary vacuum. . . . Salinger has created a world in the same sense that Dickens created a world, and the reference to David Copperfield in the fourth line of the novel is no accident. Dickens [sic] incidental characters are grotesques of the urban world of the Industrial Revolution; Salinger's are grotesques of the urban world of the Atomic Age.

In *Copperfield*, furthermore, David encounters Agnes at the theatre while he is roaring drunk; in *Catcher*, Holden calls Sally Hayes while he is in a similar condition—after a theater date with her.

Finally, near the end of each novel, the protagonist weeps with happiness over the central female character. While David Copperfield sheds tears of rapture at his union with Agnes, "never to be divided more," Holden stands in the rain and watches Phoebe ride the carrousel: "I was damn near bawling, I felt so damn happy . . ." He has just told her that he is "not going away anywhere."

Critical explication of the name Holden Caulfield has been somewhat nearsighted; none of the critics seem to be fully aware of the Dickensian background in *Catcher* or of the existence or the extent of the Caulfield/Copperfield connection. Nevertheless, reaching well beyond the "field" that appears in both names, the connection can hardly be accidental—and is in fact centered in Holden Caulfield's name. Robert G. Jacobs nearly stumbles onto it thus:

> "Caul" [i.e., in Caulfield] is a reference to the superstition that luck attends one born with part of the membrane of the foetal sack on his head, or merely to the process of birth itself. . . .

Unfortunately, Jacobs gives no further explanation of Salinger's choice—nor does he recognize the source or significance of the "caul" reference he has just elucidated. The connection that Jacobs misses appears early in *David Copperfield*, when David says: "I was born with a caul." In this context, Holden's last name assumes considerable literary significance, for it reveals Copperfield as Caulfield's ancestor in fictional autobiography.

With this connection in mind, we may examine *Catcher*, confident that "something of an extraordinary nature will turn up"—and, like Mr. Micawber, we are not disappointed. In two separate scenes, for no apparent reason, Holden expresses obvious dissatisfaction when people wish him good luck. The first passage appears early, as Holden is leaving Mr. Spencer's bedroom—and Pencey Prep:

> After I shut the door and started back to the living room, he yelled something at me, but I couldn't exactly hear him. I'm pretty sure he yelled "Good luck!" at me. I hope not. I hope to hell not. I'd never yell "Good luck!" at anybody. It sounds terrible, when you think about it.

The second incident occurs in the second-to-last chapter, as Holden leaves the aging secretary at Phoebe's high school:

> It was funny. She yelled "Good luck!" at me the same way old Spencer did when I left Pencey. God, how I hate it when somebody yells "Good luck!" at me when I'm leaving somewhere. It's depressing.

The otherwise unexplainable fact that Holden is uncomfortable in both cases is now given definite context in the "caul" reference. If we take Holden's advice and "think about it," we recognize that his virtually identical responses are not arbitrary, particularly in light of the other Dickensian links in the novel. Holden now has a "reason" for rejecting the good luck wishes as "depressing"—for in fact, he already possesses the good luck that people wish onto him.

The numerous *Copperfield* parallels establish an important thematic relationship between the phony world Holden is rejecting and that of his Victorian counterpart. Holden is continually disgusted with the phony world around him; that very phoniness is a lineal descendant of the stuffy Victorian morality of a century earlier. (Thus, Holden is actually dismissing both "phony" societies—along with autobiography—as "all that David Copperfield kind of crap.") In Dickens' Victorian world, we have a concrete image that is symbolic of all that Holden rebels against—and the Radio City movie now takes on more than coincidental importance as a microcosm of Holden's chronic disillusionment.

In short, the ubiquitous Dickens links in *Catcher*—Holden's direct allusions, the abundant incidental parallels, and, most importantly, the "caul" implications—give us a point at which Holden's disillusionment becomes more clearly defined. The Dickensian frame of reference in *Catcher,* discernible throughout the novel's background, structure, theme, and particularly in the name of its protagonist, defines and clarifies an important part of the inimitable world of Holden Caulfield.

—JOHN S. MARTIN, "Copperfield and Caulfield: Dickens in the Rye," *Notes on Modern American Literature* 4, No. 4 (Fall 1980): Item 29

CRITICAL ESSAYS

Donald P. Costello

THE LANGUAGE OF
THE CATCHER IN THE RYE

A study of the language of J. D. Salinger's *The Catcher in the Rye* can be justified not only on the basis of literary interest, but also on the basis of linguistic significance. Today we study *Adventures of Huckleberry Finn* (with which many critics have compared *The Catcher in the Rye*) not only as a great work of literary art, but as a valuable study in 1884 dialect. In coming decades, *The Catcher in the Rye* will be studied, I feel, not only as a literary work, but also as an example of teenage vernacular in the 1950s. As such, the book will be a significant historical linguistic record of a type of speech rarely made available in permanent form. Its linguistic importance will increase as the American speech it records becomes less current.

Most critics who looked at *The Catcher in the Rye* at the time of its publication thought that its language was a true and authentic rendering of teenage colloquial speech. Reviewers in the Chicago *Sunday Tribune*, the London *Times Literary Supplement*, the *New Republic*, the New York *Herald Tribune Book Review*, the New York *Times*, the *New Yorker*, and the *Saturday Review of Literature* all specifically mentioned the authenticity of the book's language. Various aspects of its language were also discussed in the reviews published in *America*, the *Atlantic*, the *Catholic World*, the *Christian Science Monitor*, the *Library Journal*, the Manchester *Guardian*, the *Nation*, the *New Statesman and Nation*, the New York *Times Book Review*, *Newsweek*, the *Spectator*, and *Time*.[1] Of these many reviews, only the writers for the *Catholic World* and the *Christian Science Monitor* denied the authenticity of the book's language, but both of these are religious journals which refused to believe that the 'obscenity' was realistic. An examination of the reviews of *The Catcher in the Rye* proves that the language of Holden Caulfield, the book's sixteen-year-old narrator, struck the ear of the contemporary reader as an accurate rendering of the informal speech of an intelligent, educated, Northeastern American adolescent.[2]

From *American Speech* 34, No. 3 (October 1959): 172–81.

In addition to commenting on its authenticity, critics have often remarked—uneasily—the 'daring,' 'obscene,' 'blasphemous' features of Holden's language. Another commonly noted feature of the book's language has been its comic effect. And yet there has never been an extensive investigation of the language itself. That is what this paper proposes to do.

Even though Holden's language is authentic teenage speech, recording it was certainly not the major intention of Salinger. He was faced with the artistic task of creating an individual character, not with the linguistic task of reproducing the exact speech of teenagers in general. Yet Holden had to speak a recognizable teenage language, and at the same time had to be identifiable as an individual. This difficult task Salinger achieved by giving Holden an extremely trite and typical teenage speech, overlaid with strong personal idiosyncrasies. There are two major speech habits which are Holden's own, which are endlessly repeated throughout the book, and which are, nevertheless, typical enough of teenage speech so that Holden can be both typical and individual in his use of them. It is certainly common for teenagers to end thoughts with a loosely dangling 'and all,' just as it is common for them to add an insistent 'I really did,' 'It really was.' But Holden uses these phrases to such an overpowering degree that they become a clear part of the flavor of the book; they become, more, a part of Holden himself, and actually help to characterize him.

Holden's 'and all' and its twins, 'or something,' 'or anything,' serve no real, consistent linguistic function. They simply give a sense of looseness of expression and looseness of thought. Often they signify that Holden knows there is more that could be said about the issue at hand, but he is not going to bother going into it:

> ... how my parents were occupied and all before they had me (5.)[3]

> ... they're *nice* and all (5.)

> I'm not going to tell you my whole goddam autobiography or anything (5.)

> ... splendid and clear-thinking and all (6.)

But just as often the use of such expressions is purely arbitrary, with no discernible meaning:

> ... he's my *brother* and all (5.)

> ... was in the Revolutionary War and all (6.)

> It was December and all (7.)

> ... no gloves or anything (7.)

> ... right in the pocket and all (7.)

Donald Barr, writing in the *Commonweal*, finds this habit indicative of Holden's tendency to generalize, to find the all in the one:

Salinger has an ear not only for idiosyncrasies of diction and syntax, but for mental processes. Holden Caulfield's phrase is 'and all'—'She looked so damn *nice*, the way she kept going around and around in her blue coat and all'—as if each experience wore a halo. His fallacy is *ab uno disce omnes;* he abstracts and generalizes wildly.[4]

Heiserman and Miller, in the *Western Humanities Review,* comment specifically upon Holden's second most obvious idiosyncrasy: 'In a phony world Holden feels compelled to reenforce his sincerity and truthfulness constantly with, "It really is" or "It really did." '[5] S. N. Behrman, in the *New Yorker,* finds a double function of these 'perpetual insistences of Holden's.' Behrman thinks they 'reveal his age, even when he is thinking much older,' and, more important, 'he is so aware of the danger of slipping into phoniness himself that he has to repeat over and over "I really mean it," "It really does." '[6] Holden uses this idiosyncrasy of insistence almost every time that he makes an affirmation.

Allied to Holden's habit of insistence is his 'if you want to know the truth.' Heiserman and Miller are able to find characterization in this habit too:

> The skepticism inherent in that casual phrase, 'if you want to know the truth,' suggesting that as a matter of fact in the world of Holden Caulfield very few people do, characterizes this sixteen-year-old 'crazy mixed up kid' more sharply and vividly than pages of character 'analysis' possibly could.[7]

Holden uses this phrase only after affirmations, just as he uses 'It really does,' but usually after the personal ones, where he is consciously being frank:

> I have no wind, if you want to know the truth. (8.)
> I don't even think the bastard *had* a handkerchief, if you want to know the truth. (34.)
> I'm a pacifist, if you want to know the truth. (44.)
> She had quite a lot of sex appeal, too, if you really want to know. (53.)
> I was damn near bawling, I felt so damn happy, if you want to know the truth. (191.)

These personal idiosyncrasies of Holden's speech are in keeping with general teenage language. Yet they are so much a part of Holden and of the flavor of the book that they are much of what makes Holden to be Holden. They are the most memorable feature of the book's language. Although always in character, the rest of Holden's speech is more typical than individual. The special quality of this language comes from its triteness, its lack of distinctive qualities.

Holden's informal, schoolboy vernacular is particularly typical in its 'vulgarity' and 'obscenity.' No one familiar with prep-school speech could seriously contend that Salinger overplayed his hand in this respect. On the contrary, Holden's restraints help to characterize him as a sensitive youth who avoids the most strongly forbidden terms, and who never uses vulgarity in a self-conscious or phony way to help him be 'one of the boys.' *Fuck,* for example, is never used as a part of Holden's speech. The word appears in the novel four times, but only when Holden disapprovingly discusses its wide appearance on walls. The Divine name is used habitually by Holden only in the comparatively weak *for God's sake, God,* and *goddam.* The stronger and usually more offense *for Chrissake* or *Jesus* or *Jesus Christ* are used habitually by Ackley and Stradlater; but Holden uses them only when he feels the need for a strong expression. He almost never uses *for Chrissake* in an unemotional situation. *Goddam* is Holden's favorite adjective. This word is used with no relationship to its original meaning, or to Holden's attitude toward the word to which it is attached. It simply expresses an emotional feeling toward the object: either favorable, as in 'goddam hunting cap'; or unfavorable, as in 'ya goddam moron'; or indifferent, as in 'coming in the goddam windows.' *Damn* is used interchangeably with *goddam;* no differentiation in its meaning is detectable.

Other crude words are also often used in Holden's vocabulary. *Ass* keeps a fairly restricted meaning as a part of the human anatomy, but it is used in a variety of ways. It can refer simply to that specific part of the body ('I moved my ass a little'), or be a part of a trite expression ('freezing my ass off'; 'in a half-assed way'), or be an expletive ('Game, my ass.'). *Hell* is perhaps the most versatile word in Holden's entire vocabulary; it serves most of the meanings and constructions which Mencken lists in his *American Speech* article on 'American Profanity.'[8] So far is Holden's use of *hell* from its original meaning that he can use the sentence 'We had a helluva time' to mean that he and Phoebe had a decidedly pleasant time downtown shopping for shoes. The most common function of *hell* is as the second part of a simile, in which a thing can be either 'hot as hell' or, strangely, 'cold as hell'; 'sad as hell' or 'playful as hell'; 'old as hell' or 'pretty as hell.' Like all of these words, *hell* has no close relationship to its original meaning.

Both *bastard* and *sonuvabitch* have also drastically changed in meaning. They no longer, of course, in Holden's vocabulary, have any connection with the accidents of birth. Unless used in a trite simile, *bastard* is a strong word, reserved for things and people Holden particularly dislikes, especially 'phonies.' *Sonuvabitch* has an even stronger meaning to Holden; he uses it only in the deepest anger. When, for example, Holden is furious with Stradlater over his treatment of Jane Gallagher, Holden repeats again and again that he 'kept calling him a moron sonuvabitch' (43).

The use of crude language in *The Catcher in the Rye* increases, as we should expect, when Holden is reporting schoolboy dialogue. When he is directly addressing the reader, Holden's use of such language drops off almost entirely. There is also an increase in this language when any of the characters are excited or angry. Thus, when Holden is apprehensive over Stradlater's treatment of Jane, his *goddams* increase suddenly to seven on a single page (p. 39).

Holden's speech is also typical in his use of slang. I have catalogued over a hundred slang terms used by Holden, and every one of these is in widespread use. Although Holden's slang is rich and colorful, it, of course, being slang, often fails at precise communication. Thus, Holden's *crap* is used in seven different ways. It can mean foolishness, as 'all that David Copperfield kind of crap,' or messy matter, as 'I spilled some crap all over my gray flannel,' or merely miscellaneous matter, as 'I was putting on my galoshes and crap.' It can also carry its basic meaning, animal excreta, as 'there didn't look like there was anything in the park except dog crap,' and it can be used as an adjective meaning anything generally unfavorable, as 'The show was on the crappy side.' Holden uses the phrases *to be a lot of crap* and *to shoot the crap* and *to chuck the crap* all to mean 'to be untrue,' but he can also use *to shoot the crap* to mean simply 'to chat,' with no connotation of untruth, as in 'I certainly wouldn't have minded shooting the crap with old Phoebe for a while.'

Similarly Holden's slang use of *crazy* is both trite and imprecise. 'That drives me crazy' means that he violently dislikes something; yet 'to be crazy about' something means just the opposite. In the same way, to be 'killed' by something can mean that he was emotionally affected either favorably ('That story just about killed me.') or unfavorably ('Then she turned her back on me again. It nearly killed me.'). This use of *killed* is one of Holden's favorite slang expressions. Heiserman and Miller are, incidentally, certainly incorrect when they conclude: 'Holden always lets us know when he has insight into the absurdity of the endlessly absurd situations which make up the life of a sixteen-year-old by exclaiming, "It killed me." '[9] Holden often uses this expression with no connection to the absurd; he even uses it for his beloved Phoebe. The expression simply indicates a high degree of emotion—any kind. It is hazardous to conclude that any of Holden's slang has a precise and consistent meaning or function. These same critics fall into the same error when they conclude that Holden's use of the adjective *old* serves as 'a term of endearment.'[10] Holden appends this word to almost every character, real or fictional, mentioned in the novel, from the hated 'old Maurice' to 'old Peter Lorre,' to 'old Phoebe,' and even 'old Jesus.' The only pattern that can be discovered in Holden's use of this term is that he usually uses it only after he has previously mentioned the character; he then feels free to append the familiar *old*. All we can conclude from Holden's slang is that it is typical teenage slang: versatile yet narrow, expressive yet unimaginative, imprecise, often crude, and always trite.

Holden has many favorite slang expressions which he overuses. In one place, he admits:

> 'Boy!' I said. I also say 'Boy!' quite a lot. Partly because I have a lousy vocabulary and partly because I act quite young for my age sometimes. (12.)

But if Holden's slang shows the typically 'lousy vocabulary' of even the educated American teenager, this failing becomes even more obvious when we narrow our view to Holden's choice of adjectives and adverbs. The choice is indeed narrow, with a constant repetition of a few favorite words: *lousy, pretty, crumby, terrific, quite, old, stupid*—all used, as is the habit of teenage vernacular, with little regard to specific meaning. Thus, most of the nouns which are called 'stupid' could not in any logical framework be called 'ignorant,' and, as we have seen, *old* before a proper noun has nothing to do with age.

Another respect in which Holden was correct in accusing himself of having a 'lousy vocabulary' is discovered in the ease with which he falls into trite figures of speech. We have already seen that Holden's most common simile is the worn and meaningless 'as hell'; but his often-repeated 'like a madman' and 'like a bastard' are just about as unrelated to a literal meaning and are easily as unimaginative. Even Holden's nonhabitual figures of speech are usually trite: 'sharp as a tack'; 'hot as a firecracker'; 'laughed like a hyena'; 'I know old Jane like a book'; 'drove off like a bat out of hell'; 'I began to feel like a horse's ass'; 'blind as a bat'; 'I know Central Park like the back of my hand.'

Repetitious and trite as Holden's vocabulary may be, it can, nevertheless, become highly effective. For example, when Holden piles one trite adjective upon another, a strong power of invective is often the result:

> He was a goddam stupid moron. (42.)

> Get your dirty stinking moron knees off my chest. (43.)

> You're a dirty stupid sonuvabitch of a moron. (43.)

And his limited vocabulary can also be used for good comic effect. Holden's constant repetition of identical expressions in countless widely different situations is often hilariously funny.

But all of the humor in Holden's vocabulary does not come from its unimaginative quality. Quite the contrary, some of his figures of speech are entirely original; and these are inspired, dramatically effective, and terribly funny. As always, Salinger's Holden is basically typical, with a strong overlay of the individual:

> He started handling my exam paper like it was a turd or something. (13.)

> He put my goddam paper down then and looked at me like he'd just beaten hell out of me in ping-pong or something. (14.)

> That guy Morrow was about as sensitive as a goddam toilet seat. (52.)

> Old Marty was like dragging the Statue of Liberty around the floor. (69.)

Another aspect in which Holden's language is typical is that it shows the general American characteristic of adaptability—apparently strengthened by his teenage lack of restraint. It is very easy for Holden to turn nouns into adjectives, with the simple addition of a -y: 'perverty,' 'Christmasy,' 'vomity-looking,' 'whory-looking,' 'hoodlumy-looking,' 'show-offy,' 'flitty-looking,' 'dumpy-looking,' 'pimpy,' 'snobby,' 'fisty.' Like all of English, Holden's language shows a versatile combining ability: 'They gave Sally this little blue butt-twitcher of a dress to wear' (117) and 'That magazine was some little cheerer upper' (176). Perhaps the most interesting aspect of the adaptability of Holden's language is his ability to use nouns as adverbs: 'She sings it very Dixieland and whorehouse, and it doesn't sound at all mushy' (105).

As we have seen, Holden shares, in general, the trite repetitive vocabulary which is the typical lot of his age group. But as there are exceptions in his figures of speech, so are there exceptions in his vocabulary itself, in his word stock. An intelligent, well-read ('I'm quite illiterate, but I read a lot'), and educated boy, Holden possesses, and can use when he wants to, many words which are many a cut above Basic English, including 'ostracized,' 'exhibitionist,' 'unscrupulous,' 'conversationalist,' 'psychic,' 'bourgeois.' Often Holden seems to choose his words consciously, in an effort to communicate to his adult reader clearly and properly, as in such terms as 'lose my virginity,' 'relieve himself,' 'an alcoholic'; for upon occasion, he also uses the more vulgar terms 'to give someone the time,' 'to take a leak,' 'booze hound.' Much of the humor arises, in fact, from Holden's habit of writing on more than one level at the same time. Thus, we have such phrases as 'They give guys the ax quite frequently at Pency' and 'It has a very good academic rating, Pencey' (7). Both sentences show a colloquial idiom with an overlay of consciously selected words.

Such a conscious choice of words seems to indicate that Salinger, in his attempt to create a realistic character in Holden, wanted to make him aware of his speech, as, indeed, a real teenager would be when communicating to the outside world. Another piece of evidence that Holden is conscious of his speech and, more, realizes a difficulty in communication, is found in his habit of direct repetition: 'She likes me a lot. I mean she's quite fond of me' (141), and 'She can be very snotty sometimes. She can be quite snotty' (150). Sometimes the repetition is exact: 'He was a very nervous guy—I mean he was a very nervous guy' (165), and 'I sort of missed them. I mean I sort of missed them' (169). Sometimes Holden stops specifically to interpret slang terms, as when he wants to communicate the fact that Allie liked Phoebe: 'She killed Allie, too. I mean he liked her, too' (64).

There is still more direct evidence that Holden was conscious of his speech. Many of his comments to the reader are concerned with language. He was aware, for example, of the 'phony' quality of many words and phrases, such as 'grand,' 'prince,' 'traveling incognito,' 'little girls' room,' 'licorice stick,' and 'angels.' Holden is also conscious, of course, of the existence of 'taboo words.' He makes a point of mentioning that the girl from Seattle repeatedly asked him to 'watch your language, if you don't mind' (67), and that his mother told Phoebe not to say 'lousy' (160). When the prostitute says 'Like fun you are,' Holden comments:

> It was a funny thing to say. It sounded like a real kid. You'd think a prostitute and all would say 'Like hell you are' or 'Cut the crap' instead of 'Like fun you are.' (87.)

In grammar, too, as in vocabulary, Holden possesses a certain self-consciousness. (It is, of course, impossible to imagine a student getting through today's schools without a self-consciousness with regard to grammar rules.) Holden is, in fact, not only aware of the existence of 'grammatical errors,' but knows the social taboos that accompany them. He is disturbed by a schoolmate who is ashamed of his parents' grammar, and he reports that his former teacher, Mr.

Antolini, warned him about picking up 'just enough education to hate people who say, "It's a secret between he and I" ' (168).

Holden is a typical enough teenager to violate the grammar rules, even though he knows of their social importance. His most common rule violation is the misuse of *lie* and *lay,* but he also is careless about relative pronouns ('about a traffic cop that falls in love'), the double negative ('I hardly didn't even know I was doing it'), the perfect tenses ('I'd woke him up'), extra words ('like as if all you ever did at Pencey was play polo all the time'), pronoun number ('it's pretty disgusting to watch some-body picking their nose'), and pronoun position ('I and this friend of mine, Mal Bros-sard'). More remarkable, however, than the instances of grammar rule violations is Holden's relative 'correctness.' Holden is always intelligible, and is even 'correct' in many usually difficult constructions. Grammatically speaking, Holden's language seems to point up the fact that English was the only subject in which he was not failing. It is interesting to note how much more 'correct' Holden's speech is than that of Huck Finn. But then Holden is educated, and since the time of Huck there had been sixty-seven years of authoritarian schoolmarms working on the likes of Holden. He has, in fact, been overtaught, so that he uses many 'hyper' forms:

> I used to play tennis with he and Mrs. Antolini quite frequently. (163).

> She'd give Allie or I a push. (64.)

> I and Allie used to take her to the park with us. (64.)

> I think I probably woke he and his wife up. (157.)

Now that we have examined several aspects of Holden's vocabulary and grammar, it would be well to look at a few examples of how he puts these elements together into sentences. The structure of Holden's sentences indicates that Salinger thinks of the book more in terms of spoken speech than written speech. Holden's faulty structure is quite common and typical in vocal expression; I doubt if a student who is 'good in English' would ever create such sentence structure in writing. A student who showed the self-consciousness of Holden would not *write* so many fragments, such afterthoughts (e.g., 'It has a very good academic rating, Pencey' [7]), or such repetitions (e.g., 'Where I lived at Pencey, I lived in the Ossenburger Memorial Wing of the new dorms' [18]).

There are other indications that Holden's speech is vocal. In many places Salinger mildly imitates spoken speech. Sentences such as 'You could tell old Spen-cer'd got a big bang out of buying it' (10) and 'I'd've killed him' (42) are repeated throughout the book. Yet it is impossible to imagine Holden taking pen in hand and actually writing 'Spencer'd' or 'I'd've.' Sometimes, too, emphasized words, or even parts of words, are italicized, as in 'Now, *shut up,* Holden. God damn it—I'm *warning* ya' (42). This is often done with good effect, imitating quite perfectly the rhythms of speech, as in the typical:

> I practically sat down in her *lap,* as a matter of fact. Then she *really* started to cry, and the next thing I knew, I was kissing her all over—*anywhere*—her

eyes, her *nose,* her forehead, her eyebrows and all, her *ears*—her whole face except her mouth and all. (73.)

The language of *The Catcher in the Rye* is, as we have seen, an authentic artistic rendering of a type of informal, colloquial, teenage American spoken speech. It is strongly typical and trite, yet often somewhat individual; it is crude and slangy and imprecise, imitative yet occasionally imaginative, and affected toward standardization by the strong efforts of schools. But authentic and interesting as this language may be, it must be remembered that it exists, in *The Catcher in the Rye,* as only one part of an artistic achievement. The language was not written for itself, but as a part of a greater whole. Like the great Twain work with which it is often compared, a study of *The Catcher in the Rye* repays both the linguist and the literary critic; for as one critic has said, 'In them, 1884 and 1951 speak to us in the idiom and accent of two youthful travelers who have earned their passports to literary immortality.'[11]

NOTES

[1] See reviews in *America,* LXXV (August 11, 1951), 463, 464; *Atlantic,* CLXXXVIII (1951), 82; *Catholic World,* CLXXIV (1951), 154; Chicago *Sunday Tribune,* July 15, 1951, Part 4, p. 3; *Christian Science Monitor,* July 19, 1951, p. 9; *Library Journal,* LXXVI (1951), 1125; *Times* [London] *Literary Supplement,* September 7, 1951, p. 561; Manchester *Guardian,* August 10, 1951, p. 4; *Nation,* CLXXIII (September 1, 1951), 176; *New Republic,* CXXV (July 16, 1951), 20, 21; *New Statesman and Nation,* XLII (August 18, 1951), 185; New York *Herald Tribune Book Review,* July 15, 1951, p. 3; New York *Times Book Review,* July 15, 1951, p. 5; New York *Times,* July 16, 1951, p. 19; *New Yorker,* XXVII (August 11, 1951), 71–76; *Newsweek,* XXXVIII (July 16, 1951), 89, 90; *Saturday Review of Literature,* XXXIV (July 14, 1951), 12, 13; *Spectator,* CLXXXVII (August 17, 1951), 224; *Time,* LVIII (July 16, 1951), 96, 97.

[2] If additional evidence of the authenticity of the book's language is required, one need only look at the phenomenal regard with which *The Catcher in the Rye* is held by today's college students, who were about Holden's age at the time the book was written. In its March 9, 1957, issue, the *Nation* published a symposium which attempted to discover the major influences upon the college students of today. Many teachers pointed out the impact of Salinger. Carlos Baker, of Princeton, stated: 'There is still, as there has been for years, a cult of Thomas Wolfe. They have all read J. D. Salinger, Wolfe's closest competitor.' Stanley Kunitz, of Queens College, wrote: 'The only novelist I have heard praised vociferously is J. D. Salinger.' Harvey Curtis Webster, of the University of Louisville, listed Salinger as one of the 'stimulators.' R. J. Kaufman, of the University of Rochester, called *The Catcher in the Rye* 'a book which has complexly aroused nearly all of them.' See 'The Careful Young Men,' *Nation,* CLXXXIV (March 9, 1957), 199–214. I have never heard any Salinger partisan among college students doubt the authenticity of the language of their compatriot, Holden.

[3] Whenever *The Catcher in the Rye* is substantially quoted in this paper, a page number will be included in the text immediately after the quotation. The edition to which the page numbers refer is the Signet paperback reprint.

[4] Donald Barr, 'Saints, Pilgrims, and Artists,' *Commonweal,* LXVII (October 25, 1957), 90.

[5] Arthur Heiserman and James E. Miller, Jr., 'J. D. Salinger: Some Crazy Cliff,' *Western Humanities Review,* X (1956), 136.

[6] S. N. Behrman, 'The Vision of the Innocent,' *New Yorker,* XXVII (August 11, 1951), 72.

[7] Heiserman and Miller, op. cit., p. 135.

[8] See H. L. Mencken, 'American Profanity,' *American Speech,* XIX (1944), 242.

[9] Heiserman and Miller, op. cit., p. 136.

[10] Ibid.

[11] Charles Kaplan, 'Holden and Huck: The Odysseys of Youth,' *College English,* XVIII (1956), 80.

Arvin R. Wells

HUCK FINN AND HOLDEN CAULFIELD: THE SITUATION OF THE HERO

As three fairly recent articles have testified, Mark Twain's *Huckleberry Finn* and J. D. Salinger's *The Catcher in the Rye* are two books with strong affinities.[1] Yet—what is less insisted upon but equally true—even as these two books are drawn together in the mind, each in relation to the other asserts its own uniqueness.

The similarities between them are readily perceived. In both novels the immediate interest is the personality of the teen-age protagonist, whose colloquial language and moral sensibility give the reported events their color. In both the narrator-protagonist goes upon a semi-comic odyssey through the heart of darkness as this is manifested in his time and place. In both the central conflict is an ethical and emotional one within the narrator-protagonist. But more important than any of these similarities is the fact that both Huck Finn and Holden Caulfield are in some sense pariahs in the society to which they belong by birth—outsiders uncertain about the necessity and desirability of becoming insiders. Moreover, their pariah status suits them for the role of social critic which each more or less unconsciously assumes and to which each brings a fine moral instinct. Their critical responses spring from the same fund of assumed values—sincerity, simple decency, and respect for whatever survives of inherent dignity in human beings.

There is finally, however, a great difference between these books, and it is one which goes far beneath stylistic matters of idiom and colloquial structure and far beneath the contrasting details of life in the backwaters of a still moving frontier and of life in mid-twentieth-century Manhattan. It is a difference in point of view, in underlying assumptions, that ultimately amounts to a difference in kind. Whatever one may think of the concluding horseplay, *Huckleberry Finn* gives us a truly comic resolution; it leaves us laughing and rejoicing over Huck's moral triumph. On the other hand, for all the laughter it provokes, *The Catcher in the Rye* approaches tragedy; it brings us to the verge of despair.

From *Ohio University Review* 2 (1960): 31–42.

It is significant that in writing these novels Mark Twain and J. D. Salinger use dissimilar means for solving the same technical problem. The problem is this. Granted that a young boy may bring to his observations of the world that adults have made a freshness of viewpoint and an uncompromising moral responsiveness which the adults themselves have lost through attrition, and granted that these qualities make his point of view critically valuable—how after all is his point of view to be articulated without destroying the reality of his character? Even an intelligent adolescent tends to respond spontaneously rather than analytically, and he is far more likely to express his deepest feelings in gesture than in words. To impose upon him the burden of saying coherently and fully what he feels is to make him unreal. Both Twain and Salinger found solutions; that these solutions are different doubtless reflects changing literary fashions and unlike temperaments, but it also implies that the two authors saw the character of the adolescent and his relationship to the society in which he grows up in the light of a different set of assumptions.

Mark Twain solves the problem largely by exploiting the assumed naïveté of the child. His chief device is that of naïve comment, innocently uttered but tipped with truth. The device is an old but an appropriate one. Huck, an underbred country boy living on the periphery of civilization and ostensibly deferential toward the attitudes and opinions of the adults who compose that civilization, yet ultimately guided by his own instinctive reactions, may be expected to misinterpret a great deal of what he observes and feels. That his misunderstandings happen to illuminate the deficiencies and the barbarousness of so much of society as comes under his eyes need not be attributed to any unlikely precociousness in him.

Though Salinger too draws a considerable fund of humor from the device of naïve comment, his primary means of solving the problem of inarticulateness are symbolism and what is perhaps best called verbal gesture. Because of the nature of his inner conflict, Holden Caulfield is even less able than Huck to analyze and articulate his own predicament. His confession that he has a "lousy vocabulary" glances obliquely at the real problem: he necessarily lacks the power to conceptualize either his experiences or the inner conflict which gives those experiences their significance. He does, however, have at his disposal a range of vulgar, obscene and profane words, which, while in themselves lacking all expressive subtlety, are readily made to serve a complex expressive function. Not only is Holden's addiction to this sort of language appropriate to his age, but it serves also to keep constantly before the reader's attention Holden's inner turmoil and his quietly aggressive, antisocial attitude which extends to the reader himself. As Holden tells his story, the language in which he tells it expresses more of defiance and conflict than he can possibly know; yet, at the same time it establishes a curious sort of intimacy between Holden and the reader—an intimacy based not on trust but upon apparent indifference to the reactions and judgments of the reader. Holden's refusal to censor his language for the reader as he does for the woman on the train[2] and for the nuns at the lunch counter (pp. 142–145) implies that he neither wishes to impress the reader nor expects anything from him. The immediate impression given is that Holden speaks without a mask—thus the intimacy. But it turns out not to be quite so simple a matter as that. For the reader gradually comes to realize that Holden's apparent indifference is itself a disguise, a kind of mask. Holden at the beginning of the novel is so far from having a statable motive for telling his story, which he himself does not understand, that he simultaneously assumes an interest on the part of the reader and belittles that interest. The motive is there, however. Behind the verbal gesture of defiance is the covert appeal to the reader's capacity for sympathetic understanding, an appeal that becomes almost overt at the end of the carrousel episode—"God, I wish you could've been there."

However, though the style of *The Catcher in the Rye* is useful in exposing Holden's character—his reluctant yet willful isolation; his contradictory fears and longings—it does not reveal the precise terms of Holden's conflict. Upon an intimate understanding of this conflict depend the moral and social implications of Holden's story, and for the purpose of focusing these implications Salinger makes use of a carefully built-in symbolism. At least for the reader aware of the assumptions of twentieth-century literature and psychology, there is nothing unexpected in the fact that Holden without understanding himself or his predicament should nonetheless be able to cast up in his imagination an image that illuminates his sense of the world about him and at the same time casts light into the even darker world within him. And nothing unexpected either in the fact that Holden's memory should cling to scenes charged with symbolic implications—implications which Holden himself both sees and does not see. Thus, by means of the integral central image of "the catcher in the rye" (p. 225) and of Holden's obsession with the dispossessed ducks in Central Park (pp. 106–107) and by means of such symbolic gestures as Holden's fight with Stradlater (pp. 56–59) and Phoebe's grab for the golden ring (pp. 273–274), Salinger manages to bring the central conflict and the theme of his novel into sharp focus without distorting the character of his narrator-protagonist and without disturbing the carefully wrought intimacy between protagonist and reader.

If we ask why these differences in technique, the answer comes back simply enough—different interests, different needs. Too simple, indeed. What after all was the nature of Mark Twain's absorption in the character of Huck Finn and of Salinger's in the character of Holden Caulfield? If the question is taken to apply, not to the psychology of the writer, but to the nature of his book, to the inferable assumptions and point of view, it is possible to arrive at some at least partial answers that illuminate the special qualities and the total effect of the book.

In reading *Huckleberry Finn* it is almost impossible to escape the impression that the novel grows spontaneously and casually and achieves greatness almost by accident. The beginning and end are, in fact, so different from the body of the novel in tone and substance as to argue a difference in intention. The episodes which they contain and the quality of their humor belong to the nostalgic comedy of childhood which Mark Twain had so successfully exploited in *Tom Sawyer*. From this alone it seems clear that Huck's original attraction for Mark Twain was the possibility of a repeat performance, but then at some fairly early point as Twain built up Huck's character, endowed him with an abundance of common sense and a fine moral instinct, and started him on a strange odyssey through a barbarous and corrupt world, he seems to have discovered in that character more serious possibilities. Huck in his innocence became the judge of a society and of human nature in general, and he became too, without ever wholly ceasing to be himself, a satirical mask for Mark Twain.

By way of contrast, *The Catcher in the Rye,* though its structure is not so very far removed from the picaresque structure of *Huckleberry Finn,* gives the impression of being closely controlled throughout by a unifying intention. Moreover, Salinger has effaced himself from the novel; he never undermines the integrity of his narrator-protagonist, never in any way intrudes upon the scene. We recall, of course, that though Mark Twain was a contemporary of Henry James, he belonged to an older and different tradition—the tradition of the raconteur and the public entertainer—and that one of the things that emphatically separates *Huckleberry Finn* from *The Catcher in the Rye* is the now generally accepted concept of the novel as a work of art—that is, as something independent of the personality of its creator, complete and unified in itself.

Uncertainty of intention, then, and a different concept of the job to be done—these do go a considerable way toward explaining the comparative looseness and casualness of the structure of *Huckleberry Finn.* They are not, however, the whole explanation. Whereas the events in *Huckleberry Finn* are disposed and bound together primarily by their relationship to the river down which Huck is carried on his adventures, those in *The Catcher in the Rye* are selected and arranged by their relevance to Holden's inner conflict. It is this inner conflict, its nature and its implications, that wholly absorb Salinger's attention in *The Catcher in the Rye.* Holden, consequently, is never simply a satirical mask, never merely a casual observer; he is the burning focus of a violent conflict between chastity, in the broadest sense, and a pervasive and insidious corruption.

To be sure Huck also has his inner conflict which arises out of the opposition between his instinctive moral decency and the example and dictates of his society and which is intensified by his social experience. But his conflict is markedly different from Holden's; it is less absorbing, less deeply rooted. For though Huck is unable to judge accurately the terms of the ethical dilemma expressed in his conflict, he is at least able to state these terms—the betrayal of a friend or damnation—and to make his choice. This conflict involves what is unconscious and impulsive in Huck's character, but it is in no sense subconscious. Conflict is in fact foreign to Huck's essential nature, and this particular conflict arises simply because Huck naïvely assumes the faulty premises of his society in judging his own behavior; thus, the very existence of the conflict calls the values of the society into question.

The case with Holden is quite otherwise. Whereas Huck's age is left uncertain, Holden's age is significantly fixed for us at sixteen—late adolescence, the verge of adulthood. Twentieth-century psychology has conditioned us to look upon this

period in the psychological history of the individual as one of more or less aggra-
vated emotional conflict, a period when an emotional vortex is likely to be set in
motion within the individual by the clash between his desire to retain the relative
security of childhood and the contrary thrust toward the supposedly unhampered
self-expression of adulthood. This awareness, which does not enter at all into Mark
Twain's conception of Huck Finn, is, so to speak, the very root of *The Catcher in
the Rye*. Not, of course, that *The Catcher in the Rye* is simply a case history of
adolescent maladjustment; nothing could be more perverse than such an approach
to the novel. It is simply that the reader is aware of the acuteness of Holden's
conflict long before he is aware of its moral and social implications and that the
terms in which he first grasps the conflict are the familiar and anticipated terms of
adolescent maladjustment; throughout the novel Holden's thoughts and feelings, like
the vast majority of his experiences, swing upon a short tether about the central
pivot of sexual awareness.

The contrast between *Huckleberry Finn* and *The Catcher in the Rye* in the
matters of language and of sexual awareness is obvious. Huck professes to have the
gift of profanity, but the reader is given no example of it; as narrator Huck
consciously censors his own language. And of sexual awareness there is scarcely a
trace. It is true, of course, that Mark Twain wrote within the limits of something
called "the genteel tradition" (which he sufficiently outraged) and that Salinger, on
the other hand, is writing not only in a less squeamish literary period but in a world
that has felt to its very roots the impact of Freudianism. But it is also worth pointing
out that Mark Twain's novel does not really suffer from the obvious censorship.
Mark Twain, with his pre-Freudian assumptions, did not see adolescence and
conflict as inevitably going together; the conflict which he develops in the novel
arises through extraordinary circumstances in a rather extraordinary personality
and is totally unrelated to sexuality. Moreover, given the manifest purposes which
we have already examined in the novel, there is no real need either for the inclusion
of sexual awareness or for greater realism in language. The humor might thereby
have been broadened but hardly the vision.

In *The Catcher in the Rye*, on the other hand, Salinger's achievement consists
in taking the commonplace elements of adolescent conflict and rebelliousness and
gradually probing their ramifications through the character of Holden until in their
outcome they have acquired some of the overtones and moral implications of
tragedy. Holden's anguished confusion about sex gives us the measure of both the
depth and complexity of his conflict. Sexual awareness is conspicuously absent from
the innocent and sincerely responsive world of children which Holden values.
Phoebe may have seen the words scratched on the schoolhouse wall, but she
would not, Holden assumes, understand (p. 260). Sex belongs to the adult world
which Holden deeply distrusts. Yet, Holden's own sex drive is very much alive; it
is part of the irresistible thrust toward adulthood. He does not want to deny it; in
this respect he wants to be "grown up." But at the same time, he is aware that it
can upset all of his values, suspending his will and forcing him to depart from the

basis of mutual decency and respect which he feels should prevail in human relationships. Thus, Holden's conflict, emotionally and ethically, involves the very core
of his character, setting him against the forces of growth within him and filling him
with disgust for society and fear of himself. Whereas Huck Finn's instinctive moral
goodness leads him fearfully to violate the mores of his particular time and place,
Holden's leads him to reject adulthood itself because in his time and place adulthood seems to imply a falling away into phoniness and insensitivity. To be sure
Huck's dilemma is not trifling; it is sufficiently timeless and fundamental in human
experience, but it is free, at least as Mark Twain presents it, of the complications
that make such a hopeless snarl of Holden's problem.

Still, it is not simply the differences in the nature of the central conflict that
account for the ultimate difference in the effects of the two novels. Nor is this
ultimate difference in effect accounted for by the observation that Huck Finn has
that generous fund of common sense and those astonishing recuperative powers
typical of the comic protagonist, whereas Holden Caulfield has the single-
mindedness typical of the tragic protagonist. The conditions under which the protagonist experiences his conflict and struggles to resolve it also play an important
part in preparing the total effect of the novel. An author, after all, selects and shapes
the circumstances of his story to meet his needs in projecting his particular vision
(comic or tragic or whatever), just as, anteriorly, similar though possibly less personal circumstances have helped to shape the vision itself. Consequently, the vast
dissimilarity between the conditions of Huck's world and those of Holden's is
significant. In fact, when *Huckleberry Finn* and *The Catcher in the Rye* are examined together, this dissimilarity more than any other reminds us forcibly of how
much history, social and literary, intervenes between them, reminds us that not only
Salinger but the major portion of contemporary literature looks out, if not upon a
different world, at least through different windows from those familiar to the Mark
Twain who wrote *Huckleberry Finn.*

In the matter of circumstances Huck Finn is, so to speak, far more fortunate
than Holden. Huck exists on the periphery of his society; he can and does at any
moment escape its egregious demands and corrupt example by the simple expe-
dient of taking to the river which, like Huck's own instincts, flows unrestrained and
largely untainted by the scattered civilization along its banks. Even on the river, of
course, the King and the Duke can reach Huck, but in the midst of the natural
isolation imposed by the river and compared with what is to be met on shore, their
viciousness seems almost innocuous. Moreover, Huck always has a final resource in
the open West. Having judged his own behavior according to the preconceptions
of his society and having accepted his own damnation, he is nonetheless free to
declare his practical independence of that society by moving beyond its pale. There
are no such openings in Holden Caulfield's world. Like the dreaming lieutenant at
the end of Graham Greene's *The Power and the Glory,* Holden seems to move
along a corridor without doors; he moves to the sound of laughter, but he moves
all the same toward some inevitable disaster. He cannot move about the edge of

society as if it were an island; rather he is trapped within its midst where the only isolation possible for him is the cruelly lonely isolation of withdrawal within himself. For Huck's frontier refuge, he can substitute only the improbable fantasy of a hermitical life led as a pretended deaf-mute in a cabin out West. Furthermore, while Huck Finn enjoys the companionship of an adult in whom a primitive but essential moral goodness has persisted, Holden ultimately fails to find a single adult who seems to him worthy of trust or emulation. Consequently, though Holden must live in the world in which he is placed, he is utterly unable to define for himself a realistic, adult role in that world.

The result of these contrasting circumstances is, on the one hand, for Huck that his inner conflict is intermittent. Again and again the pressures of society are assuaged and the image of irrationality and violence effaced by the serene flow of the river. When society's representatives or society's voice speaking through Huck's "conscience" intrude upon this serenity, the conflict is reawakened to new crisis, but nonetheless the conflict remains realistically and even ideally resolvable. For there are realistic choices to be made and new worlds to move on to. The result, on the other hand, for Holden is that he is driven back upon fantasy and upon impossible, desperate solutions. Unable to accept adulthood on society's terms, he clings to childhood: that is, to what is dead or dying in himself. He loves the changeless calm of the museum, but fears the irresistible change within himself that this changeless-ness reveals (p. 159). He feels betrayed by his older brother, D.B., who is pros-tituting his talents in Hollywood, and returns obsessively to the memory of his dead younger brother, Allie. Feeling that he himself is beyond childhood, he would like at least to be able to preserve other children in their rye field, their Eden, to prevent their fall from grace. But this too he knows is desperate, fantastic, impossible—"If they fall off, they fall off, but it's bad if you say anything to them" (p. 274); and he is aware that, unless he can find some exit from his narrow corridor, his own fall is imminent. (Note the large number of references to and images of falling in the last five or six chapters of the novel.) In the background there remains always the figure of Jane Gallagher, an image of ideal purity, but this image has already been slightly soiled by Stradlater, and Holden is afraid to approach her for fear she like everyone else may have grown feet of clay. At the last only Mr. Antolini seems to afford a practical refuge; and when Holden, compelled by his accumulated distrust, puts the worst possible interpretation upon Mr. Antolini's ambiguous gestures, he has reached the end of his corridor. The prophecy of that early scene in which Holden fights in impotent rage against the archetypal "phony," Stradlater, is fulfilled. There seems to remain for Holden only one narrow gate— what the psychologists somewhat glibly call adjustment. And this is no happy ending. For given Holden's world and Holden's character, adjustment implies a tragic waste of moral sensibility.

Is this after all simply to say that Holden Caulfield is neurotic and Huck Finn is not? Perhaps, but the point is that Holden's neuroticism is not self-generated; it is a by-product of the discrepancy between what Holden implicitly demands of society in the way of sincerity and decency and what society actually can or will afford. The fact is that *Huckleberry Finn* and *The Catcher in the Rye* rest upon very different assumptions about what might be called the situation of the hero—about the relationship of the individual to his society. Huck shares Holden's moral instinct and sensibility, and his society too produces its neurotic types—for example, Pap and Mrs. Watson and Emmeline Grangerford; but Huck's world is actually larger than the society to which he finds himself in opposition. There is room in it for self-determination because there are doors opening onto other possibilities. That is why *Huckleberry Finn* for all its undertone of cynicism, its quick barbs shot at "the damned human race," impresses us as an optimistic book expressing an optimistic age. On the other hand, if Huck Finn is reborn in Holden Caulfield, he is reborn to a far more implacable fate, a far more inflexible and debilitating set of circumstances; Holden must somehow live in his house of rotten timbers. That is why *The Catcher in the Rye* brings us to the verge of despair, so that if while we are still in its power, we glance at the literature that has come after it, we feel no surprise at the steady emergence of the passively nihilistic hero in American literature or at the abortive "beatnik" attempt to build a world and a literature purely out of kicks.

NOTES

[1] See Edgar Branch, "Mark Twain and J. D. Salinger: A Study in Literary Continuity," *American Quarterly*, IX (1957), 144–85; Arthur Heisman and James E. Miller, Jr., "J. D. Salinger: Some Crazy Cliff," *Western Humanities Review*, X (1956), 129–37; and Charles Kaplan, "Holden and Huck: Odysseys of Youth," *College English*, XVIII (1956), 76–80. The first and third of these three articles, while recognizing dissimilarities, are primarily concerned with similarities of characterization and ethical viewpoint, with the artistic and thematic continuity that clearly exists between *Huckleberry Finn* and *The Catcher in the Rye*. The second article is only incidentally concerned with the parallels between the two novels; its primary purpose is to examine *The Catcher in the Rye* in relation to "the tradition of the Quest." As for this present article, its purpose is to examine the marked dissimilarities as contributory to the ultimately very different effects produced by these two novels. This shift in emphasis, I believe, results in bringing the essential qualities and fundamental attitudes found in each into much sharper focus and at the same time gives weight to the fact that these novels are, after all, the products of two unique creative imaginations responding to quite different milieux.
[2] J. D. Salinger, *The Catcher in the Rye* (New York: Modern Library, 1951), pp. 71–76. All other references to *The Catcher in the Rye* are to this edition.

Vera Panova

ON J. D. SALINGER'S NOVEL

The Catcher in the Rye reaches the reader's heart in extremely subtle, secret ways. Why should the confused wanderings of ill-fated, infantile Holden Caulfield so concern us? No extreme David Copperfield calamities have befallen him. He does not wander on the highways of the American West like John Steinbeck's heroes, but in New York where his parents, sister, aunt, "and all my crummy relatives" and his numerous friends live. He does not ride the rails—he hires taxis. Holden Caulfield has never had to worry about a piece of bread. He is from a solid intelligentsi family, he studies in the most respectable educational institutions in the United States. Four times a year his ancient grandmother sends him money "for his birthday." And by a number of signs we gather that Holden is handsome, which of course is not unimportant for happiness, especially at sixteen. In a word, he is a rich man's kid, a loafer, and it would not seem that the reader has any reason to worry about him.

Besides, Holden has so many traits and does so many things which the reader simply cannot approve of. Holden tells his own story—and what language, replete with slang expressions and swear words! Holden has no respect for anything—not his school, or the teachers, or his studies, or his nation's history. "This crazy cannon that was in the Revolutionary War and all," he notes casually telling where he is during the football game. His infantile behavior makes an unpleasant impression: the scene in the washroom where Holden does a tap dance in front of the shaving Stradlater is so repulsive—we are used to sixteen-year-olds conducting themselves decently, and not making faces. Readers also become indignant because Holden is so stubborn about not wanting to study. Literature interests him; he reads a lot and writes excellent papers on literature. But when he has to write a paper on history, about ancient Egypt, he writes a few disdainful, parodistic lines. He does not know anything about ancient Egypt and does not want to. That does not interest him.

From *Soviet Criticism of American Literature in the Sixties: An Anthology*, edited by Carl R. Proffer (Ann Arbor, MI: Ardis, 1972), pp. 4–10. First published in Russian in 1960.

Holden has been expelled from four schools for his failures. "What are you doing to yourself, boy?" they ask, and he sits with a red hunting cap on, bill backwards, and reads Isak Dinesen's *Out of Africa*. And when a kind old teacher tries to persuade him he should think about his future, Holden answers patiently, "Yes, sir. I know. I know all that,"—but he is wondering where the ducks in New York's Central Park go in the winter. "I was wondering where the ducks went when the lagoon got all icy and frozen over."

That's the kind of impossible, unreasonable person this Holden is.

He makes the rounds of New York bars (very worried about getting alcoholic beverages which they do not want to serve him since he is a minor), dances with a woman of some sort, proposes to a girl he knows that she go away with him to "live somewhere by a river," and when the hotel elevator operator asks him, "Do you want a girl for the night?" Holden answers, after the initial embarrassment, "Okay."

And, in addition to all this, he is a liar! He himself says, "I'm the most terrific liar you ever saw in your life." How adroitly he lies to the poor sympathetic Mrs. Morrow on the train . . .

But this novel about a loafer, a petty liar, a swaggering dandy, a strange, unlucky young creature, a novel outwardly so simple, but so complex in its inner structure, creates a whirlwind of feelings and thoughts . . . This is the hallmark of a really important book.

It develops before us gradually; line by line each page of the novel strikes us by revealing new aspects, new secrets of a young human soul. Salinger strives to unveil all of these secrets. It is important to him that he tell everything about his hero, including that which literature often passes over in hypocritical silence. However, in baring the sores of contemporary American life, Salinger frequently resorts to the devices of decadence. We have in mind the selection of facts, details, the choice of situations, and finally, the misuse of slang.

This tribute to a fashion which is widespread in the West somewhat weakens the impact of the novel on the reader. However, on the whole the novel is truthful and realistic.

Holden is taken at a time in his life when he is surrounded by minor and major unpleasantnesses, when nothing is going right for him: his coat has been stolen, he forgot the fencing foils in the subway, and he has been expelled from school for the fourth time—he is afraid to go home—and the self-satisfied, experienced flirt Stradlater has started dating the girl who was once dear to him, and Holden comes out of a fight with Stradlater cut and bleeding . . . It is all disgusting; in his heart there is melancholy and depression. Is it not because of all this that Holden is deliberately rude on the first pages of the novel? It is characteristic of youth to hide its disillusionment and despair underneath rudeness. Yes, the reader becomes convinced as he learns more about Holden's pure and tender soul. This is all superficial, and affectation.

In a soulless barracks—the dormitory of a respectable school called Pencey—
there are only two things left which console Holden: *Out of Africa* and the red hat
which Holden bought for a dollar. But in these circumstances this is too little
consolation, and Holden runs away from school. Driven by a number of annoy-
ances, large and small, especially poisonous because they are insignificant, he "simply
flies away" like a duck from a frozen pond where it is no longer possible to live. He
plans to spend a few days in New York without showing up at home until
Wednesday—to "live quietly" in an inexpensive hotel until that fateful Wednesday
about which he speaks as if casually, but in reality he tries not to think about it.

We, the readers, cannot wait for this Wednesday either. But the narration
stops at its threshold. We can only guess what happened that Wednesday in the
Caulfield intelligentsi family. "My mother gets very hysterical," says Holden, in the
main commenting on his parents correctly and with restraint ("of course, they're
good people"), and on his mother with sad, tender pity . . . "Daddy will kill you, he'll
kill you," Phoebe keeps saying. "I could probably tell you what I did after I went
home, and how I got sick and all, and what school I'm supposed to go to next fall
. . . but I don't feel like it. I really don't. That stuff doesn't interest me too much right
now."

But however condescendingly tender Holden is to his mother, or proper to
his father, they are part of the world which does not suit him, in which it is bad to
live, where a person has no place to shelter his soul. And it is not by chance that
Salinger's novel, along with Hemingway's *Fiesta* and Saroyan's *The Human Comedy*,
was banned from the high school library in the California city of San Jose.

However, with his skepticism and unconscious cynicism Holden is an intrinsic
part of this world. He would probably be indignant if he were told this. But it is
unquestionably so. Whether Holden likes it or not he is a prisoner of this world, its
tastes, its customs; and basically his "revolt" leads to nothing.

Holden does not stop to think that this world can and should be changed, that
he, Holden, should overcome much in himself, that his own passivity and lack of will
hang on his legs like chains. Holden just rejects with repugnance a reality which
maintains itself through force, "phoniness," and hypocrisy.

Six curs, six young Fascists torture the schoolboy James Castle, and "all they
did with the guys . . . was expel them." Sated boa constrictors like Ossenburger get
rich on poor people who die. "Pencey was full of crooks. Quite a few guys came
from these very wealthy families, but it was full of crooks anyway. The more
expensive a school is, the more crooks it has." The art with which they stuff people
in America is vulgar, phony, poison, not food for the spirit. With scorn and hate
Holden summarizes the content of these phony plays and films. He talks about the
war with even more hate, and not he alone: "My brother D.B. was in the Army for
four goddam years . . . All he had to do was drive some cowboy general around all
day in a command car. He once told Allie and I that if he'd had to shoot anybody,
he wouldn't've known which direction to shoot in. He said the Army was practically
as full of bastards as the Nazis were."

Holden loiters in this world sadly and senselessly, alone and helpless before a life which is no good for him, trying to conceal his helplessness by being compulsively talkative and reckless.

They accuse him (and we have accused him) of behaving like a twelve-year-old boy. However, "sometimes I act a lot older than I am—I really do—but people never notice it. People never notice anything," says Holden tiredly. He knows disappointingly much about people; he knows, for example, that a grown-up looks at a sixteen-year-old from his grown-up tower and completely refuses even to attempt to comprehend what is happening in a sixteen-year-old's infinitely wounded soul, which is so full of ferment and confusion.

To whom can he go with this confusion? "I don't even like . . . cars. I mean they don't even interest me. I'd rather have a goddam horse. A horse is at least *human,* for God's sake. A horse you can at least—"

When Holden lies, people listen to him. But who listens to him when he tells the truth? When he talks about what interests him? "You ought to go to a boy's school sometime. Try it sometime . . . It's full of phonies, and all you do is study so that you can learn enough to be smart enough to be able to buy a goddam Cadillac someday . . . And I'd be working in some office, making a lot of dough, . . . Reading newspapers, and playing bridge all the time, and going to movies . . . Well, I hate it. Boy, do I hate it. But it isn't just that. It's everything."

Thus he speaks to Sally, asking her to "live somewhere with a brook and all." But what does Sally answer? "Stop screaming at me, please."

"Stop hollering like that, for God's sake," Louis says to him too.

And poor Holden searches for someone with whom he can speak! The three days during which the novel takes place are filled with these muddled, clumsy, unsuccessful efforts. Feverishly he telephones everyone in whom there is even the slightest hope in this regard. In the middle of the night he wakes up a woman with whom he is totally unacquainted, the friend of a friend. For a moment Mrs. Morrow's maternal affectionateness breathes on him. Two grey nuns pass by before him fleetingly, and their humble, quiet existence, their desire to do all the good in their power touch Holden, and he remembers them with respect and warmth. Warmth is essential to him. Occasionally, he has to warm himself a little somewhere. Even ducks retreat somewhere away from the frozen pond . . .

Some people who have temporarily lost all hope disappear in the bustling city without a trace. Others cause nothing but disillusionment.

During his wanderings and searchings Holden hears a song sung by a little boy on the street: "If a body catch a body coming through the rye." [In Russian translation: "If a body call a body. . ."—C.P.]

This line could stand as the epigraph to the novel. To the story of how someone has gone astray, who feels lost calls for someone . . . and there is no reply.

It is considered that at sixteen it is obligatory for a person to be in love. Holden is not in love with anyone, even though many people think of love in the hardest days of their life. He is not in love with Sally—he simply tries to hold on sincerely to this life-loving creature who is satisfied with everything. His relation to "old Jane" is unclear to Holden himself. Something in her attracts and touches him; maybe their unhappy childhoods bring them together. But this is not all-consuming youthful amorousness. Is Jane the reason for his fight with Stradlater? Or was it really Stradlater calling the sacred baseball mitt of the late little Allie "a goddam baseball mitt" ["some stupid baseball mitt" in the Russian version—C.P.] which made Holden lose his temper. Or had he simply gotten tired, in his mood, of watching the brazen successes of the lucky Stradlater? For Holden love is still in the future, and he is not a profligate—"if you want to know the truth, I'm a virgin."

We know how the incident with the prostitute ended and how Holden had to pay for his virginity not only with extra dollars but also with blood. Yes, that is the way things are in the world in which Holden lives—they make you bleed for purity and virtue! The girl for whom he feels sorry goes away with her protector, the elevator operator. Holden is alone in the room again, cursed and beat up. One more insult has been added to the long series. And it seems to Holden that there will never be anything else—nothing good. And a strange delirium begins in his feverish mind: "I started that stupid business with the bullet in my guts again. I was the only guy at the bar with a bullet in their guts. I kept putting my hand under my jacket, on my stomach and all, to keep the blood from dripping all over the place. I didn't want anybody to know I was even wounded. I was con*cealing* the fact that I was a wounded sonuvabitch." Here the essence of Holden's tragedy is concentrated in a few words.

The symbolic bullet, symbolic blood dripping onto the floor... The father's house where there is no place for his own son is symbolic too. But the symbolism is done extremely cautiously, so that it does not ruin the whole fabric of the novel. Take just the multiple significant line from the song: "If a body call a body..." Initially Holden hears it incorrectly, he hears: "If a body catch a body..." Only many pages later does Phoebe correct him, and he agrees, "She was right... I didn't know it then, though." And only by the extensiveness and detail of the conversation in which the words of the song are made precise does the author give the reader to understand that these words are important for his idea.

If people exist who reconcile Holden to life, whom he accepts without reservation, for whom he is ready to go through fire and water, they are children. And not only his warmly loved ten-year-old sister Phoebe, not only his deceased brother Allie, but all the children: the boy who sings the song, the kid in the movie, and two little ones in the museum, and the boys and girls studying in Phoebe's school. When he gets to the school, Holden notices that someone has written an obscenity on the wall: "It drove me damn near crazy. I thought how Phoebe and all the other little kids would see it, and how they'd wonder what the hell it meant, ... I kept wanting to kill whoever'd written it." And Holden wipes out the graffito. But then he sees an obscenity on another wall too. "I tried to rub it off with my hand again, but this one was *scratched* on, with a knife... It wouldn't come off."

"You know what I'd like to be?" says Holden to his sister Phoebe. "I keep picturing all these little kids playing some game in this big field of rye and all. Thousands of little kids, and nobody's around—nobody big, I mean—except me. And I'm standing on the edge of some crazy cliff. What I have to do, I have to catch everybody if they start to go over the cliff—I mean if they're running and they don't look where they're going I have to come out from somewhere and *catch* them. That's all I'd do all day. I'd just be the catcher in the rye and all. I know it's crazy, but that's the only thing I'd really like to be."

He wants to save the children from falling off the cliff, but is he himself being saved? "You're riding for some kind of a terrible, terrible fall," Mr. Antolini says to him, "It may be the kind where . . . you sit in some bar . . . Or you may end up in some business office, throwing paper clips at the nearest stenographer."

Antolini doesn't know what will happen to his pupil. And Holden does not know what is ahead for him. But even the author does not see anything good for his hero in the future. The novel is tragically hopeless; everything is as if enclosed in a small space which is suffocating, gloomy, and without exit. But still we are sorry to think that Holden could start heading in the same direction as the vile Ossenburger or the murderers of James Castle, that he will accept life as a game which must be played according to the rules of Ossenburger and James' murderers.

The novel is not long—anything bulky which might hinder the clear expression of central matters has been omitted. Very great precision. Very great sincerity. The maturity of a strong and witty talent is felt in every scene. Everything seems to be written almost casually, but examine it carefully and you will see the subtlest, most masterful fine-finishing. It is as if nothing is described, "drawn"; everything is conveyed as if casually—but you see Pencey, and Phoebe's school, and the hotel, and the beautifully-done Museum of Natural History.

There are hardly any colors or painted tones, therefore those few objects which are colored cut into the memory like bright spots: the green dress of the prostitute, her pink dress on "narrow narrow" shoulders, Phoebe's blue coat, and especially, the bright red cap with the long bill which is mentioned repeatedly throughout the novel.

One could enumerate many felicitous discoveries, magnificent details, and brilliant dialogue.

Its best pages are the meeting of Holden and Phoebe in front of the museum, their wanderings around the city, the walk around the zoo, and Phoebe's ride on the carrousel during the rainstorm . . . ". . . I stuck around on the bench for quite a while. I got pretty soaking wet . . . I didn't care, though. I felt so damn happy all of a sudden, the way old Phoebe kept going around and around. I was damn near bawling, I felt so damn happy . . . It was just that she looked so damn *nice,* the way she kept going around and around, in her blue coat and all. God, I wish you could've been there."

When Holden's heart matures and the chaos of confusion abates in him, may he find that elevated goal, the one in the name of which one wants to live and for the sake of which it is not frightening to die.

Jonathan Baumbach

THE SAINT AS
A YOUNG MAN

J. D. Salinger's first and only novel, *The Catcher in the Rye* (1951), has undergone in recent years a steady if overinsistent devaluation. The more it becomes academically respectable, the more it becomes fair game for those critics who are self-sworn to expose every manifestation of what seems to them a chronic disparity between appearance and reality. It is critical child's play to find fault with Salinger's novel. Anyone can see that the prose is mannered (the pejorative word for stylized); no one actually talks like its first-person hero Holden Caulfield. Moreover, we are told that Holden, as poor little rich boy, is too precocious and specialized an adolescent for his plight to have larger-than-prep-school significance. The novel is sentimental; it loads the deck for Holden and against the adult world; the small but corrupt group that Holden encounters is not representative enough to permit Salinger his inclusive judgments about the species. Holden's relationship to his family is not explored: we meet his sister Phoebe, who is a younger version of himself, but his father never appears, and his mother exists in the novel only as another voice from a dark room. Finally, what is Holden (or Salinger) protesting against but the ineluctability of growing up, of having to assume the prerogatives and responsibilities of manhood? Despite these objections to the novel, *Catcher in the Rye* will endure both because it has life and because it is a significantly original work, full of insights into at least the particular truth of Holden's existence. Within the limited terms of its vision, Salinger's small book is an extraordinary achievement; it is, if such a distinction is meaningful, an important minor novel.

Like all of Salinger's fiction, *Catcher in the Rye* is not only about innocence, it is actively for innocence—as if retaining one's childness were an existential possibility. The metaphor of the title—Holden's fantasy-vision of standing in front of a cliff and protecting playing children from falling (Falling)—is, despite the impossibility of its realization, the only positive action affirmed in the novel. It is, in Salinger's Manichean universe of child angels and adult "phonies," the only moral alternative—

From *Modern Language Quarterly* 25, No. 4 (December 1964): 461–72.

otherwise all is corruption. Since it is spiritually as well as physically impossible to prevent the Fall, Salinger's idealistic heroes are doomed either to suicide (Seymour) or insanity (Holden, Sergeant X) or mysticism (Franny), the ways of sainthood, or to moral dissolution (Eloise, D.B., Mr. Antolini), the way of the world. In Salinger's finely honed prose, at once idiomatically real and poetically stylized, we get the terms of Holden's ideal adult occupation:

> Anyway, I keep picturing all these little kids playing some game in this big field of rye and all. Thousands of little kids, and nobody's around—nobody big, I mean—except me. And I'm standing on the edge of some crazy cliff. What I have to do, I have to catch everybody if they start to go over the cliff—I mean if they're running and they don't look where they're going I have to come out from somewhere and *catch* them. That's all I'd do all day. I'd just be the catcher in the rye and all. I know it's crazy, but that's the only thing I'd really like to be. I know it's crazy.[1]

Apparently Holden's wish is purely selfless. What he wants, in effect, is to be a saint—the protector and savior of innocence. But what he also wants, for he is still one of the running children himself, is that someone prevent *his* fall. This is his paradox: he must leave innocence to protect innocence. At sixteen, he is ready to shed his innocence and move like Adam into the fallen adult world, but he resists because those no longer innocent seem to him foolish as well as corrupt. In a sense, then, he is looking for an exemplar, a wise-good father whose example will justify his own initiation into manhood. Before Holden can become a catcher in the rye, he must find another catcher in the rye to show him how it is done.

Immediately after Holden announces his "crazy" ambition to Phoebe, he calls up one of his former teachers, Mr. Antolini, who is both intelligent and kind—a potential catcher in the rye.

> He was the one that finally picked up that boy that jumped out the window I told you about, James Castle. Old Mr. Antolini felt his pulse and all, and then he took off his coat and put it over James Castle and carried him all the way over to the infirmary. (p. 226)

Though Mr. Antolini is sympathetic because "he didn't even give a damn if his coat got all bloody," the incident is symbolic of the teacher's failure as a catcher in the rye. For all his good intentions, he was unable to catch James Castle or prevent his fall; he could only pick him up after he had died. The episode of the suicide is one of the looming shadows darkening Holden's world; Holden seeks out Antolini because he hopes that the gentle teacher—the substitute father—will "pick him up" before he is irrevocably fallen. Holden's real quest throughout the novel is for a spiritual father (an innocent adult). He calls Antolini after all the other fathers of his world have failed him, including his real father, whose existence in the novel is represented solely by Phoebe's childish reiteration of "Daddy's going to kill you." The fathers in Salinger's child's-eye world do not catch falling boys—who have been thrown out of prep school—but "kill" them. Antolini represents Holden's last chance to find a catcher-father. But his inability to save Holden has been prophesied in his failure to save James Castle; the episode of Castle's death provides an anticipatory parallel to Antolini's unwitting destruction of Holden.

That Antolini's kindness to Holden is motivated in part by a homosexual interest, though it comes as a shock to Holden, does not wholly surprise the reader. Many of the biographical details that Salinger has revealed about him through Holden imply this possibility. For example, that he has an older and unattractive wife whom he makes a great show of kissing in public is highly suggestive; yet the discovery itself—Holden wakes to find Antolini sitting beside him and caressing his head—has considerable impact. We experience a kind of shock of recognition, the more intense for its having been anticipated. The scene has added power because Antolini is, for the most part, a good man, whose interest in Holden is genuine as well as perverted. His advice to Holden is apparently well-intentioned. Though many of his recommendations are cleverly articulated platitudes, Antolini evinces a prophetic insight when he tells Holden, "I have a feeling that you're riding for some kind of a terrible, terrible fall"; one suspects, however, that to some extent he is talking about himself. Ironically, Antolini becomes the agent of his "terrible, terrible fall" by violating Holden's image of him, by becoming a false father. Having lost his respect for Antolini as a man, Holden rejects him as an authority; as far as Holden is concerned, Antolini's example denies the import of his words. His disillusionment with Antolini, who had seemed to be the sought-for, wise-good father, comes as the most intense of a long line of disenchantments; it is the final straw that breaks Holden. It is the equivalent of the loss of God. The world, devoid of good fathers (authorities), becomes a soul-destroying chaos in which his survival is possible only through withdrawal into childhood, into fantasy, into psychosis.

The action of the novel is compressed into two days in which Holden discovers through a series of disillusioning experiences that the adult world is unreclaimably corrupt. At the start of the novel, we learn from Holden that he has flunked out of Pencey Prep for not applying himself; he has resisted what he considers foolish or "phony" authority. Like almost all of Salinger's protagonists, Holden is clearly superior to his surroundings; he functions by dint of his pure sight, his innocence and sensibility, as initiate in and conscience of the world of the novel. Allowing for the exaggerations of innocence, we can generally accept Holden's value judgments of people and places as the judgments of the novel. For example, when Holden observes about his seventy-year-old, grippe-ridden history teacher that

> Old Spencer started nodding again. He also started picking his nose. He made out like he was only pinching it, but he was really getting the old thumb right in there. I guess he thought it was all right to do because it was only me that was in the room. I didn't *care,* except that it's pretty disgusting to watch somebody pick their nose. (pp. 13–14)

he is not being gratuitously malicious; he is passing what amounts to a moral judgment, although he is consciously doing no more than describing his reactions. Whereas the adult observer, no matter how scrupulous, censors his irreverent or unpleasant responses because he is ashamed of them, the child (Holden is sixteen) tells all.

Like Jane Austen, Salinger treats fools, especially pretentious ones, mercilessly. Though Spencer is seventy years old and for that reason alone may be worthy of respect, he is nevertheless platitudinous and self-indulgent, interested less in Holden than in pontificating before a captive audience. In a world in which the child is the spiritual father of the man, old age represents not wisdom but spiritual blindness and physical corruption. Spencer is not only foolish and "phony" ("Life *is* a game, boy"), but in his self-righteous way also actively malicious. Though Holden's is ostensibly a social visit, the old man badgers the boy about having failed history ("I flunked you in history because you knew absolutely nothing") and then insists on reading aloud Holden's inadequate exam.

> He put my goddam paper down then and looked at me like he'd just beaten hell out of me in ping-pong or something. I don't think I'll ever forgive him for reading me that crap out loud. I wouldn't've read it out loud to *him* if *he'd* written it—I really wouldn't. (p. 17)

In this confrontation between Holden and Spencer, there is an ironic inversion of the traditional student-teacher, son-father relationship which extends throughout the novel and throughout Salinger's fictional world. While Spencer, out of a childish need for personal justification, insensitively embarrasses Holden (already wounded by his expulsion from Pencey), the boy is mature enough to be kind to his conspicuously vulnerable antagonist. Holden accepts the full burden of responsibility for his scholastic failure so as to relieve Spencer of his sense of guilt.

> Well, you could see he really felt pretty lousy about flunking me. . . . I told him I was a real moron, and all that stuff. I told him how I would've done exactly the same thing if I'd been in his place, and how most people didn't appreciate how tough it is being a teacher. That kind of stuff. The old bull. (p. 17)

In protecting his teacher's feelings, Holden performs the role of wise father; he is here a kind of catcher in the rye for a clumsy old child. His compassion is extensive enough to include even those he dislikes, even those who have hurt him. As he tells Antolini later in the novel:

> But you're wrong about that hating business. . . . What I may do, I may hate them for a *little* while, like this guy Stradlater I knew at Pencey, and this other boy, Robert Ackley. I hated *them* once in a while—I admit it—but it doesn't last too long, is what I mean. After a while, if I didn't see them, if they didn't come in the room . . . I sort of missed them. (p. 243)

Both Antolini and Spencer are too corrupt to notice that Holden is unable to cope with the world not because he hates, but because he loves and the world hates.

Spencer symbolizes all the stupid and destructive teacher-fathers at Pencey Prep, which is in microcosm all schools—the world. In the short scene between Holden and Spencer, Salinger evokes a sense of Holden's entire "student" experience in which flunking out is an act of moral will rather than a failure of application. Here, as throughout the novel, the wise son resists the initiatory knowledge of the false ("phony") father and, at the price of dispossession, retains his innocence. Holden is not so much rebelling against all authority, or even false authority, as he is searching for a just one. That there are no good fathers in the world is its and Holden's tragedy. It is the tragedy of Salinger's cosmos that the loss of innocence is irremediable. Ejected from the fallow womb of the prep school, Holden goes out alone into the world of New York City in search of some kind of sustenance. His comic misadventures in the city, which lead to his ultimate disillusion and despair, make up the central action of the novel.

Holden not only suffers as a victim from the effects of the evil in this world, but for it as its conscience—so that his experiences are exemplary. In this sense, *Catcher in the Rye* is a religious or, to be more exact, spiritual novel. Holden is Prince Mishkin as a sophisticated New York adolescent; and like Mishkin, he experiences the guilt, unhappiness, and spiritual deformities of others more intensely than he does his own misfortunes. This is not to say that Holden is without faults; he is, on occasion, silly, irritating, thoughtless, irresponsible—he has the excesses of innocence. Yet he is, as nearly as possible, without sin.

The most memorable love affair Holden has experienced had its fruition in daily checker games with Jane Gallagher, an unhappy, sensitive girl who was his neighbor one summer. She has become the symbol to him of romantic love, that is, innocent love. When Holden discovers that his "sexy" roommate Stradlater has a date with her, he is concerned not only about the possible loss of Jane's innocence, but about the loss of his dream of her—the loss of their combined checker-playing, love-innocence. Holden has had one previous emotional breakdown at thirteen when his saint-brother, Allie,[2] died of leukemia. In Allie's death, Holden first recognized the fact of evil—of what appears to be the gratuitous malevolence of the universe. Allie, who was, Holden tells us, more intelligent and nicer than anyone else, has become for Holden a kind of saint-ideal. By rejecting an English theme on Allie's baseball glove that Holden has written for him, and by implying that he has "given Jane Gallagher the time," Stradlater spiritually maims Holden. Holden's sole defense, a belief in the possibility of good in the world, collapses: "I felt so lonesome, all of a sudden. I almost wished I was dead" (p. 62).

It is in this state of near-suicidal despair that Holden leaves for New York. That Stradlater may have had sexual relations with Jane—the destruction of innocence is an act of irremediable evil in Holden's world—impels Holden to leave Pencey immediately (but not before he quixotically challenges the muscular Stradlater, who in turns bloodies his nose). At various times in New York, Holden is on the verge of phoning Jane, and actually dials her number twice—that he is unable to reach her is symbolic of his loss of her innocence. The sexually experienced Stradlater, who is one of Holden's destructive fathers in the novel, has destroyed not Jane's innocence so much as Holden's idealized notion of her.[3]

Obliquely searching for good in the adult world, or at least something to mitigate his despair, Holden is continually confronted with the absence of good. On his arrival in the city, he is disturbed because his cabdriver is corrupt and unsociable and, worst of all, unable to answer Holden's obsessional question: where do the Central Park ducks go when the lake freezes over? What Holden really wants to know is whether there is a benevolent authority that takes care of ducks. If there is one for ducks, it follows that there may be one for people as well. Holden's quest for a wise and benevolent authority, then, is essentially a search for a God-principle. However, none of the adults in Holden's world has any true answers for him. When he checks into a hotel room, he is depressed by the fact that the bellboy is an old man ("What a gorgeous job for a guy around sixty-five years old"). As sensitized recorder of the moral vibrations of his world, Holden suffers the indignity of the aged bellhop's situation for him, as he had suffered for Spencer's guilt and Ackley's self-loathing. Yet, and this is part of his tragedy, he is an impotent saint, unable either to redeem the fallen or to prevent their fall.

If the world of Holden's school was a muted purgatory, the world of his New York hotel is an insistent Hell. The window of his room provides him with a view of the other rooms in the hotel. In one, he sees a man dress himself in women's clothes, and in another, a man and woman who delight (sexually) in squirting water at each other from their mouths. This is the "real" world, with its respectable shade lifted, which fascinates and seduces Holden by its prurience. Having lost the sense of his innocence, he seeks sexual initiation as a means of redemption. His attraction to older women suggests that his quest for a woman is really a search for a mother whose love will protect him against the corrupt world as well as initiate him into it. Where the father-quest is a search for wisdom and spirit (God), the mother-quest is a search not for sex but ultimately for Love. They are different manifestations, one intellectual, the other physical, of the same spiritual quest. His search for sexual experience, Salinger indicates, is the only love alternative left Holden after he loses Jane. Once the possibility of innocent love ceases to exist, sexual love seems the next best thing, a necessary compensation for the loss of the first. However, Holden is only mildly disappointed when he is unable to arrange a date with a reputedly promiscuous girl whose telephone number he has inherited from a Princeton acquaintance. For all his avowed "sexiness," he is an innocent, and his innocence-impelled fear dampens his desire. Though the women he meets are by and large less disappointing than the men, they too fail Holden and intensify his despair. That they are not as good as he would like them to be seems to him *his* fault, *his* responsibility, *his* failure.

If Jane represents sacred love profaned, the prostitute who comes to Holden's room represents profane love unprofaned. After he has agreed to have her come to his room (the elevator operator, Maurice, is go-between), he refuses to make love to her once she is there. The scene is a crucial one in defining Holden's nontraditional sainthood. Holden refuses the prostitute not because of moral principle, but because the condition of her existence (she is about Holden's age and a kind of lost-innocent) depresses him.

> I took her dress over to the closet and hung it up for her. It was funny. It made me feel sort of sad when I hung it up. I thought of her going in a store and buying it, and nobody in the store knowing she was a prostitute and all. The salesman probably just thought she was a regular girl when she bought it. It made me feel sad as hell—I don't know why exactly. (p. 125)

He would save her if he could, but she is far too fallen for any catcher in the rye. But as child-saint, Holden is quixotic. In not sleeping with her, he means to protect her innocence, not his own; he is spiritually, hence physically, unable to be a party to her further degradation. The consequences are ironic. Holden as saint refuses to victimize the prostitute, but he is victimized by the girl and her accomplice, Maurice. Though Holden has paid the girl without using her, Maurice beats Holden and extorts an additional five dollars from him. This episode is a more intense recapitulation of the Stradlater experience. In both cases Holden is punished for his innocence. If the hotel is a symbolic Hell, Maurice, as far as Holden is concerned, is its chief devil. In offering Holden the girl and then humiliating him for not accepting his expensive gift, Maurice is another of Holden's evil fathers.

After his disillusionment with Antolini, who is the most destructive of Holden's fathers because he is seemingly the most benevolent, Holden suffers an emotional breakdown. His flight from Antolini's house, like his previous flights from school and from the hotel, is an attempt to escape evil. The three are parallel experiences, except that Holden is less sure of the justness of his third flight and wonders if he has not misjudged his otherwise sympathetic teacher.

> And the more I thought about it, the more depressed I got. I mean I started thinking maybe I *should've* gone back to his house. Maybe he *was* only patting my head just for the hell of it. The more I thought about it, though, the more depressed and screwed up about it I got. (p. 253)

The ambivalence of his response racks him. If he has misjudged Antolini, he has wronged not only his teacher, but he has wronged himself as well; he, not Antolini, has been guilty of corruption. Consequently, he suffers both for Antolini and for himself. Holden's guilt-ridden despair manifests itself in nausea and in an intense sense of physical ill-being, as if he carries the whole awful corruption of the city inside him. Walking aimlessly through the Christmas-decorated city, Holden experiences "the terrible, terrible fall" that Antolini had prophesied for him.

> Every time I came to the end of a block and stepped off the goddam curb, I had this feeling that I'd never get to the other side of the street. I thought I'd

just go down, down, down, and nobody'd ever see me again. Boy, did it scare me. You can't imagine. I started sweating like a bastard—my whole shirt and underwear and everything. . . . Every time I'd get to the end of a block I'd make believe I was talking to my brother Allie. I'd say to him, "Allie, don't let me disappear. Allie, don't let me disappear. Allie, don't let me disappear. Please, Allie." And then when I'd reach the other side of the street without disappearing, I'd *thank* him. (pp. 256–57)

Like Franny's prayer to Jesus in one of Salinger's later stories, Holden's prayer to Allie is not so much an act of anguish as an act of love, though it is in part both. Trapped in an interior hell, Holden seeks redemption, not by formal appeal to God or Jesus, who have in the Christmas season been falsified and commercialized, but by praying to his saint-brother who in his goodness had God in him.

Like so many heroes of contemporary fiction—Morris' Boyd, Ellison's Invisible Man, Malamud's Frank, Salinger's Seymour—Holden is an impotent savior. Because he can neither save his evil world nor live in it as it is, he retreats into fantasy—into childhood. He decides to become a deaf-mute, to live alone in an isolated cabin, to commit a kind of symbolic suicide. It is an unrealizable fantasy, but a death wish nevertheless. However, Holden's social conscience forces him out of spiritual retirement. When he discovers an obscenity scrawled on one of the walls of Phoebe's school, he rubs it out with his hand to protect the innocence of the children. For the moment he is a successful catcher in the rye. But then he discovers another such notice, *"scratched* on, with a knife or something," and then another. He realizes that he cannot possibly erase all the scribbled obscenities in the world, that he cannot catch all the children, that evil is ineradicable.

This is the final disillusionment. Dizzy with his terrible awareness, Holden insults Phoebe when she insists on running away with him. In his vision of despair, he sees Phoebe's irrevocable doom as well as his own, and for a moment he hates her as he hates himself—as he hates the world. Once he has hurt her, however, he realizes the commitment that his love for her imposes on him; if he is to assuage her pain, he must continue to live in the world. When she kisses him as a token of forgiveness and love and, as if in consequence, it begins to rain, Holden, bathed by the rain, is purified—in a sense, redeemed.

A too literal reading of Holden's divulgence that he is telling the story from some kind of rest home has led to a misinterpretation of the end of the novel. Holden is always less insane than his world. The last scene, in which Holden, suffused with happiness, sits in the rain and watches Phoebe ride on the merry-go-round, is indicative not of his crack-up, as has been assumed, but of his redemption. Whereas all the adults in his world have failed him (and he, a butter-fingered catcher in the rye, has failed them), a ten-year-old girl saves him—becomes his catcher. Love is the redemptive grace. Phoebe replaces Jane, the loss of whom had initiated Holden's despair, flight, and quest for experience as salvation. Holden's pure communion with Phoebe may be construed as a reversion to childlike innocence, but this is the only way to redemption in Salinger's world—there is no other good. Innocence is all. Love is innocence.[4]

The last scene, with Holden drenched in Scott Fitzgerald's all-absolving rain,[5] seems unashamedly sentimental. Certainly Salinger overstates the spiritually curative powers of children; innocence can be destructive as well as redemptive. Yet Salinger's view of the universe, in which all adults (even the most apparently decent) are corrupt and consequently destructive, is bleak and somewhat terrifying. Since growing up in the real world is tragic, in Salinger's ideal world time must be stopped to prevent the loss of childhood, to salvage the remnants of innocence. At one point in the novel, Holden wishes that life were as changeless and pure as the exhibitions under glass cases in the Museum of Natural History. This explains, in part, Holden's ecstasy in the rain at the close of the novel. In watching Phoebe go round and round on the carrousel, in effect going nowhere, he sees her in the timeless continuum of art on the verge of changing, yet unchanging, forever safe, forever loving, forever innocent.

Salinger's view of the world has limited both his productivity and his range of concerns. In the last nine years, he has published only four increasingly long and increasingly repetitive short stories, all of which treat some aspect of the mythic life and times of the Glass family, whose most talented member, Seymour, committed suicide in an early story, "A Perfect Day for Bananafish." But though Salinger may go on, as Hemingway did, mimicking himself, trying desperately to relocate his old youthful image in some narcissistic internal mirror, his achievement as a writer cannot be easily discounted. All his stories, even the least successful, evince a stunning and original verbal talent, despite some stylistic debt to Fitzgerald and Lardner. Like *The Great Gatsby,* which both Holden and Salinger admire, *Catcher in the Rye* is, as far as the human eye can see, a perfect novel; it is self-defining, that is, there seems to be an inevitability about its form. Although the craft of the author is unobtrusive, everything of consequence that happens in the novel has been in some way anticipated by an earlier episode or reference. The rain that baptizes Holden at the end is, in symbol, the same rain that had fallen on Allie's gravestone and had depressed Holden; the scurrying of the visitors as they left the cemetery to seek shelter in their cars had emphasized Allie's immobility, his deadness. In praying to Allie, Holden implicitly accepts the fact of his brother's immortality which his earlier response had denied. Through association, Salinger suggests that the purifying rain is a manifestation of Allie's blessed and blessing spirit. Like Phoebe's kiss, Allie's rain is an act of love.

NOTES

[1] J. D. Salinger, *The Catcher in the Rye* (Boston, 1951), pp. 224–25; all page references are to this edition.
[2] Holden's relationship to Allie, though less intense, is the equivalent of Buddy's to Seymour in the several Glass family stories.
[3] Another destructive father is Ackley, who refuses Holden solace after Holden has been morally and

physically beaten by Stradlater. (The father concern is intentional on Salinger's part.) Both Ackley and Stradlater are two years older than Holden, and at one point Ackley reproves Holden's lack of respect, telling him, "I am old enough to be your father."

[4] Like the narrator in "For Esmé—with Love and Squalor," Holden is redeemed by the love of an innocent girl. In both cases the protagonist is saved because he realizes that if there is any love at all in the world—even the love of one child—Love exists.

[5] At the graveside service for Gatsby, as rain falls on his coffin, Nick hears someone say, "Blessed are the dead that the rain falls on." I suspect that Salinger had the Fitzgerald passage in mind.

Clinton W. Trowbridge

CHARACTER AND DETAIL IN
THE CATCHER IN THE RYE

Once we recognize that J. D. Salinger's depiction of Holden Caulfield as symbolizing the plight of the idealist in the modern world provides the primary structural framework of *The Catcher in the Rye,* we can see every other aspect of this concise, symbolically compressed novel as reinforcing that design. Whether we look at the significance of the briefly drawn but highly individualized minor characters or at the use of concrete details, whether we consider the major or the minor emphases, we recognize each in turn as symbolic extensions of the protagonist. Thus *The Catcher in the Rye* stands on every count as one of the masterpieces of symbolist fiction.

By utilizing many of his secondary characters so purposively, as exaggerated or distorted forms of Holden himself, Salinger succeeds in rendering the character of his "hero" more objectively than he could otherwise. In fact, it is largely this technique that makes Holden the extraordinarily "round" character that he is. We see him not merely from the highly limited first person point of view, but also in a series of dramatic self-portraits.

Some of the characters, like Stradlater and Carl Luce, dramatize Holden's man-of-the-world image of himself. The paradoxical attitude that he adopts toward these—he both admires and despises them—is resolved when we realize that these are really attitudes that he has adopted toward images of himself. Others, like Antolini, Allie, Phoebe, and, to some extent, Mr. Spencer, are Catcher figures, symbols, that is, of Holden in his imagined role of protector of innocence and goodness.[1] James Castle represents the apparent inflexibility of Holden's idealism and thus dramatizes for us the fearful image that Antolini has of Holden—that of his dying nobly for some highly unworthy cause. Not only does Holden say he admires Castle's behavior, but he and Castle are symbolically identified through Holden's sweater. But the genuineness of Holden's admiration is tested and found to be wanting when he refuses to jump out of the window after the Maurice

From *Cimarron Review* No. 4 (June 1968): 5–11.

episode. That Holden's idealism is anything but inflexible is further shown by the fact that Maurice himself represents another and completely different ideal of behavior to Holden: that of the tough guy who gets what he wants when he wants it. By being an extension of the assertive personality that Holden would like to have, Maurice dramatizes both the phoniness of that ideal and the fact that Holden actually despises it.

With some of the characters a recognition that they are symbolic extensions of Holden himself is absolutely necessary if we are fully to understand his attitude toward them. His treatment of Sunny, for instance, is not just the result of adolescent inexperience; he cannot treat her as a prostitute because she is too close to being a pathetic image of himself; she so depresses him because his pity for her amounts to self-pity, because she contributes to the gradually encroaching vision of himself as the homeless wanderer, alienated from man and society. So, too, his admiration for the drummer at Radio City Music Hall can only be fully understood when we recognize that to Holden he represents a kind of saintliness. If the aim of life is to retain, or regain, youthful innocence and goodness, the drummer, with his total absorption in perfecting a relatively simple and uninteresting task, has achieved a kind of beatific state.

We fail to see the significance that Holden attaches to Jane Gallagher's keeping her kings on the back row unless we realize that both Holden and Jane are scared of the adult world into which they are plunging and that her behavior symbolizes her unwillingness to risk the loss of innocence and goodness by confronting life, by using instead of hoarding whatever powers she might possess. Stradlater's date with Jane so upsets Holden not just because he knows what a lady's man Stradlater is but because he would like to approach her romantically himself but no more dares to upset their childish relationship than she to move her kings from the back row. That Stradlater symbolizes Holden's romantic ideal of himself in this scene is underlined by the fact that Stradlater is actually wearing Holden's jacket. It is significant that only after Holden feels momentarily secure at the Antolinis' does he actually decide to call Jane on the telephone. His failure to call her is a symbolic reminder to us of two things: that he cannot reestablish contact with what he believes to be goodness and innocence; and secondly, that he is experiencing a growing alienation from his world. That he never does call her and that there is no specific mention of her at the end also reminds us that, although he has been saved from figurative and perhaps literal death, he is still far from being "romantically" adjusted to the adult world.

Salinger's method of using other characters to dramatize various images that Holden has of himself does more than just increase the "roundness" of his character, however. It reinforces the structural pattern of the novel in that it allows Holden to sort out the true from the false images of himself through direct confrontation with them. He thinks he admires James Castle, for instance, but he cannot act like him. Actually, he comes to the final stages of his quest by discovering whom he can and cannot act like, and the person he most acts like at the end is Mr. Spencer.

At first glance, Mr. Spencer does not seem to embody any of Holden's ideals. He is old, sickly, and generally pathetic; he is phony enough to laugh at the headmaster's jokes; in the lecture he gives Holden, he is by turns blunt, sarcastic, and woe-begone about Holden's future. In marked contrast to Antolini's sympathetic understanding of Holden's condition, all Mr. Spencer can offer is to underline the headmaster's observation that life is a game and must be played according to the rules. Perhaps his parting cry: "Good Luck!" sounds so terrible to Holden because taken literally it puts the outcome of Holden's quest wholly on the level of chance, whereas what Holden is so desperately seeking is a plan whereby he can control his life. But behind all this is Mr. Spencer's loving concern for Holden and the fact that Mr. and Mrs. Spencer both seem to get a bang out of life. Holden's whole treatment of Phoebe at the Museum is similar to Mr. Spencer's treatment of him (it is in fact much harsher); and, at the end, he is getting a bang out of the counterpart to Mr. Spencer's Navajo Indian blanket: Phoebe's blue coat.

That Mr. Spencer represents the nearest thing to a dramatization of Holden's final image of himself is suggested in several other ways by Salinger. They are both tall and stooped in posture. Like Mr. Spencer, Holden constantly uses the term "boy," nods his head, repeats himself, and is often sarcastic. While he criticises Mr. Spencer bitterly for his phony laughing at the headmaster's jokes, one of the most obvious things about Holden's behavior is that he is outwardly conventional. Though he hates saying "Glad to've met you" to someone he is not glad to have met, he is constantly doing so. As he recognizes early in the novel, "If you want to stay alive, you have to say that stuff, though."[2] Not only does the special subject that Holden has been studying with Mr. Spencer, the Egyptians, take on a tremendous symbolic significance for him, but in the scene with the two boys outside the Natural History Museum, Holden both acts the part of the history teacher and shows us how much more he had learned from Mr. Spencer than his exam paper indicated.

Many of the characters in the novel can be understood as exaggerated portraits of Holden as he is. All of these characters are treated with a greater or lesser degree of pity, scorn, or annoyance by Holden, and, as we have seen to be the case with two of these—Sunny and, to some degree, Mr. Spencer—his attitudes are only fully understood when we see that Holden is really concerned with these traits in himself. Again Salinger's method is to take one of the traits or attitudes that Holden deplores in himself, exaggerate it, and dramatically portray it in the form of another character. The three "grools" from Washington who are going to get up early to go to Radio City Music Hall are pathetic examples of tourism and of the hold that phony values, as epitomized by Hollywood, have on Americans; but not only does Holden himself go to two movies and a play in the course of the action of the novel, he goes to Radio City Music Hall as well. What he says about the movie that he sees there expresses succinctly the dilemma he is in, the manner in which he is trapped in the very world he is so hostile to: "It [the picture] was so putrid I couldn't take my eyes off it." (125) Holden does not look for his initials on the bathroom doors, as does the old alumnus of Pencey Prep, but the smells of the

Natural History Museum and of his old public school make him just as nostalgic and sentimental, and what he does find engraved on the walls of both places symbolize not a romanticized version of lost youth—the initials—but a crass reminder of the defeat of innocence. Just as Stradlater represents, in part, a phony ideal, so does Ackley dramatize a depressing reality. Stradlater, the "secret slob," and Ackley, the repulsive pimple-squeezer, serve as obverse images of Holden himself. Stradlater bloodies his nose as Maurice is later to crush the wind from his belly; Ackley, an extension of all that is friendless and pathetic in Holden, refuses Holden's plea for sanctuary just as Sunny greets Holden's attempt to treat her with compassion with the devastating "So long, crumb bum."

While many of the characters in *The Catcher in the Rye* take on an additional interest and importance once their symbolic connection to Holden is seen, Salinger's deepest and most suggestive symbols are found not in them but in some of the apparently minor details of the novel. Of these the most important is Holden's red hunting hat. The effectiveness of this symbol lies in its great suggestiveness. Not only does it operate on several different levels of meaning, but Salinger is so careful to make it unobtrusive as a symbol that to most readers it is simply a funny hat, just the sort of thing that a rebellious adolescent would wear. Even the circumstances of Holden's buying the hat, however, suggest that we must go beyond this understanding of it. Holden purchases it just *after* he notices that he has lost all the fencing foils. As manager of the fencing team he is immediately ostracized by the other boys, and thus, from the very beginning, the hat is comforter, a consolation prize for failure. He feels comfortable in it when he is reading alone in his room; but partly because he likes to wear it with its long peak toward the back of his head, he does not feel at ease wearing it in public. On its surface level the hat is simply a detail by which Salinger dramatizes an important part of Holden's character.

Yet there is a deeper meaning. Holden is outwardly conventional in manner and particularly in dress; but, as we discover when he ruminates about his Gladstone bags from Mark Cross, he sees this conventionality as a sign of phoniness in himself. Through his conventional dress and manner he dimly sees himself as supporting the very world that he is so hostile to. Thus, wearing the cap also symbolizes his desire to break through the phony conventions of his world; not wearing the cap dramatizes his failure to destroy what is phony, either in himself or in his world, as well as reminds us of the power that the conventions have over him. His ideas are unconventional but his behavior, except for his running away from school, is remarkably like that of any well brought-up boy.

The hunting hat, then, is closely associated with the basic structural pattern of the novel: Holden's quest for truth. In fact, it is even more intimately connected to it than we have so far indicated. To Ackley the hat is simply a hunting hat, a deer shooting hat, as he calls it. Holden's response is: " 'Like hell it is.' I took it off and looked at it. I sort of closed one eye, like I was taking aim at it. 'This is a people shooting hat,' I said. 'I shoot people in this hat.' " (24) At the core of Holden's personality lies the double vision, and therefore double nature, of the idealist. The essential paradox of his being is his love-hate for humanity. He sees with frightening clarity the difference between what is and what ought to be, and that vision is the basic motivation for whatever he does. Though he finally learns that he must love man and the world in spite of their faults, the major portion of the novel charts his progress towards world-weariness and the triumph of hate, not love. Through his jocular remark to Ackley, made early in the novel, Holden unwittingly reveals the degree of his hatred for man as he is. He would like to kill him.

But before Holden's remark can be fully understood, we must consider one other important aspect of the hat: the fact that Holden likes to wear it backwards. This detail leads us to the full richness of the symbol. With the peak to the back, he looks far more like what he really is, a catcher rather than a killer. Nor is the literal image of a baseball catcher inappropriate to consider here. One of Holden's most prized possessions is his brother Allie's fielder's mitt. In the fact that it is a left-handed mitt and that Allie had covered it with poems so that he could read them when no one was up at bat, the mitt is a rich symbol in its own right. Holden idealizes Allie as by far the brightest as well as the nicest member of his family. When Allie died Holden so damaged his hand by breaking out the garage windows that, as he tells us, it still hurts him when it rains and he can no longer make a proper fist. Part of what is suggested here is that Holden, equipped by his brother with a means of catching the good and the innocent, has, because of his love for his brother, made himself ineffective as a hater (the broken fist) and, like his brother, has dedicated himself to an impossible ideal. When the impossibility, and more importantly, the undesirability of the ideal is finally grasped (as it is by Holden while watching Phoebe on the merry-go-round), the idealist is saved from self-destruction and uselessness and led back to man and the world by means of love.

The fact that Holden likes to wear his cap with the peak reversed not only provides us with an ironic visual picture of the catcher ideal but also dramatizes for us the very direction of Holden's search. In many senses of the phrase, Holden is trying to go backwards. He is between childhood and adulthood, a condition that is symbolically represented in the fact that the hair on one side of his head is grey. More than anything else he wants to keep for himself and others what he imagines to be the untarnished goodness and innocence of the child. The reversed peak, then, suggests his idealization of and yearning for the childhood condition. It also, both literally and figuratively, emphasizes his own childishness, for it is partly be-cause Allie had died while still a child that death is associated with goodness and innocence in Holden's mind. Thus the reversed peak also reminds us of what must be the outcome if Holden continues to look to the past—his own death. As he comes nearer to literal as well as figurative death in the course of the novel, the death images predominate. The peak of his cap points to the dead civilization of the Egyptians, to the death in life image that Holden imagines for himself in the form of his deaf-mute ideal, and to the mummies that symbolize that state. His fainting spell after visiting the tombs is a figurative death; his meeting with Phoebe outside the museum is the beginning of his re-birth.

Phoebe is wearing Holden's hat; she has accepted his quest as her own. When she meets him she throws the hat at him in fury because she recognizes that his refusal to accept her as a companion is really an admission of phoniness, both in himself and in his plan. In reality, of course, she has saved him by symbolically showing her willingness to die with him. Instead of looking to the past, he is now going to try to deal with the future. This is the affirmation with which the novel ends, and Salinger has very unobtrusively underlined it by the use he makes of the hunting cap in this final scene. He has forced the hat upon her—given up the quest, that is; and her forgiveness of him for disappointing her is again symbolically portrayed in her giving him back his hat, his identity as an idealist. That he has changed the direction of his quest and that she is the person responsible for his doing so is told us by her putting on his hat for him and putting it on his head with the peak facing the front. It is clear that she does so place the hat on his head, but Salinger is clever enough not to force the symbol on us in so direct a manner. Rather he chooses that we discover it. While Holden watches Phoebe ride around on the carrousel, it begins to rain. He sits there in the rain and Salinger tells us: "I got pretty soaking wet, especially my neck and my pants. My hunting hat really gave me quite a lot of protection, in a way, but I got soaked anyway." (191) The "especially my neck" is Salinger's master stroke in the use of symbolic technique, a technique that so often in modern fiction results in lifeless allegory. Holden has thus been re-born into at least a partial acceptance of life. His direction has been radically changed. It seems to be no mere happenstance, then, that Salinger should set this final scene in the Zoo, the place of life, after leading Holden from the Egyptian tombs, the place of death. Nor, particularly as we know that Salinger himself is deeply interested in Zen, does it seem improbable that Salinger means us to see the carrousel as symbolic of the wheel of life, the constantly changing pattern of the Eternal One.

NOTES

[1] Clinton W. Trowbridge, "The Symbolic Structure of *The Catcher in the Rye,*" *Sewanee Review,* Summer, 1966.
[2] J. D. Salinger, *The Catcher in the Rye,* New York, The New American Library, 1948, p. 81. All future references are to this edition.

David J. Burrows
ALLIE AND PHOEBE

Literary passions were not easily formed among America's youth in the 1950's. But during those years many students in high schools and colleges discovered, through J. D. Salinger's *The Catcher in the Rye,* that "literature" need not mean the, to them, dull poetry and fiction of their textbooks. After the novel's appearance in 1951, its fame began to spread by word-of-mouth, until something of an underground "Catcher cult" existed throughout the country. The speech mannerisms of Holden Caulfield, the book's protagonist and narrator, were carefully imitated, and a generation of young Americans perceived through Holden the extent to which the world was divided between the "phonies" and the "nice" people, the former comprising the vast majority of the population. Then, in the late 1950's, young college and high school teachers, themselves having been deeply affected by the book six or eight years earlier, introduced it formally into the classroom, and thus within a decade of its publication it reached the stature of an American "classic."

Many of the attempts to explain the book's appeal have been sociological in nature. Critics have concentrated on the disparity between the society which Holden realizes he must conform to and his own adolescent vision of innocence which, he is coming to realize, is for him no longer an effective means of coping with that society. He fears that his life will become a boring routine of "working in some office, making a lot of dough . . . reading newspapers, and playing bridge all the time, and going to the movies. . . ."[1] Or, as a teacher of his warns, it may be that at age thirty, Holden will "end up in some business office, throwing paper clips at the nearest stenographer" (pp. 242–243).

Such a critical emphasis, however, does not sufficiently explain the deep and lasting effect the book has had on so many readers. Certainly every reader, no matter how young, has at least begun to make his own compromise with the adult society he is entering, and still may identify his own plight very strongly with

From *Private Dealings: Modern American Writers in Search of Integrity,* edited by David J. Burrows, Lewis M. Dabney, Milne Holton, and Grosvenor E. Powell (Rockville, MD: New Perspectives, 1969), pp. 106–14.

Holden's, feel compassion for him, and have brought to the surface while reading the book great reservoirs of wistfulness and nostalgia for an innocence perhaps quite recently lost. Nonetheless, the profoundest level of the book's power lies deeper, at that level where we sense that there is little of significance in life except the necessity of death, and that the motivation of most religion, philosophy, and art—literature especially—is in some way related to man's attempt to understand the fact of death. The death by leukemia of his brother Allie, three years earlier, is Holden's obsessive concern in this book; his fear of growth and change, expressed throughout the novel, is the result of his realization that one grows toward death and that death is the ultimate change.

It is by means of a series of related images that Salinger makes clear the nature and the extent of the anxieties besetting Holden. This imagery, dealing mainly with the act of falling, functions to suggest the fear of the loss of wholeness of mind, and more traditionally, the fear of aging, of loss of innocence of vision, and finally, of death.

The book's title comes, it will be remembered, from Holden's formulation of his desire to act as a savior for little children:

> I keep picturing all these little kids playing some game in this big field of rye and all. Thousands of little kids, and nobody's around—nobody big, I mean— except me. And I'm standing on the edge of some crazy cliff. What I have to do, I have to catch everybody if they start to go over the cliff—I mean if they're running and they don't look where they're going I have to come out from somewhere and *catch* them. That's all I'd do all day. I'd just be the catcher in the rye and all (pp. 224–225).

By the time Holden comes to the point of expressing this desire to his sister Phoebe, the reader understands well that there is one character in the book greatly in need of such "catching"—Holden himself; his vision of the cliff develops out of his own desire to be saved. What he wishes to be saved from is, one senses, not completely clear in his own mind. Certainly it is more than simply the "phoniness" which he sees displayed by the majority of people he comes in contact with; and it is more than the violence which he suffers at the hands of his roommate and the hotel elevator operator.

Not even Mr. Antolini, the perceptive English teacher Holden visits near the end of the book, is quite accurate when he tells Holden that he is "riding for some kind of a terrible, terrible fall". It is, Antolini explains, a fall in which the "man falling isn't permitted to feel or hear himself hit bottom. He just keeps falling and falling. The whole arrangement's designed for men who, at some time or other in their lives, were looking for something their own environment couldn't supply them with. Or they thought their own environment couldn't supply them with. So they gave up looking" (pp. 243–244). Antolini's analysis of Holden's predicament, though valid in many ways, is too much a description of Antolini's own situation; he has, Holden notes, to a great extent "sold out", married a wealthy woman, moved to an exclusive address, joined the right tennis club, and turned heavily to drink. When Holden awakes to find the teacher stroking his head, it is not, as the boy fears, a perverted pass; rather it is Antolini's gesture of mourning for his own loss of integrity and youthful purpose. To say that Holden is seeking something his environment cannot provide him is certainly true; but the implications of Holden's inability to accept reality are greater than Antolini's summation of the problem indicates.

The significance of the imagery of falling becomes clearer in the scene following the one with Antolini. Having spent the night in Grand Central Station, Holden begins walking up Fifth Avenue. As he walks, "something very spooky" begins happening. Holden explains: "Every time I came to the end of a block and stepped off the goddam curb, I had this feeling that I'd never get to the other side of the street. I thought I'd just go down, down, down, and nobody'd ever see me again. Boy, did it scare me" (p. 256).

To save himself from this deathlike falling, he begins, at the end of each block, to make believe he is talking to his dead brother Allie: "'Allie, don't let me disappear. Please Allie.' And then when I'd reach the other side of the street without disappearing, I'd *thank* him" (p. 257). This continues from street corner to street corner until he is far uptown.[2] Finally, sweating and out of breath, he sits on a bench and makes his decision to go West, find a cabin, and lead a life of quiet simplicity. The fear of death and the appeal to Allie to save him from it become understandable in the light of what Holden discloses elsewhere in the novel about his dead brother.

He describes Allie as having been two years younger than he, but "about fifty times as intelligent". Unlike Holden, with his history of academic failure, Allie was the kind of boy whose teachers wrote letters telling Mrs. Caulfield "what a pleasure it was having . . . Allie in their class". Holden sums up Allie's character and his feeling for him when he exclaims, "God, he was a nice kid, though." Thirteen years old when his brother died, Holden's reaction to the death was such that his parents considered having him psychoanalysed: "I slept in the garage the night he died, and I broke all the goddam [garage] windows with my fist, just for the hell of it." He adds: "I even tried to break all the windows on the station wagon . . . but my hand was already broken and everything by that time, and I couldn't do it. It was a very stupid thing to do, I'll admit, but I hardly didn't even know I was doing it, and you didn't know Allie" (pp. 49–50).

The glimpses Holden gives us of his brother are enough, however, to prove to us Allie's "niceness". He was the kind of boy who wrote poems on his baseball glove, to be able to read them when he was out in the field; he "never got mad at anybody"; and he "used to laugh so hard at something he thought of at the dinner table that he just about fell off his chair". He also had the sensitivity to know intuitively what it means to say that Emily Dickinson is a better war poet than Rupert Brooke.

In chapter 20, Holden, at his most depressed moment, is walking at night in

for example, never brushes his teeth. And most people, unconsciously or indiffer-
ently, breathe their tainted breath on others, such as the "very Cuban-looking guy"
mentioned earlier, or Charlene, the Caulfield maid, who, as Phoebe says, "always
breathes on me whenever she puts something down. She breathes all over the
food and everything. She *breathes* on *everything.*" Unlike these other people,
Holden tries to remain conscious of the state his breath is in by blowing it up into
his own nostrils; he tries to keep his breath clean whenever he thinks that it may
smell bad; and he is deeply upset whenever he breathes his tainted breath on
anyone else, especially if he believes that the other person is untainted, as is
illustrated by the following incident, which occurs at the end of Holden's breakfast
with the nuns:

> When they got up to go, the two nuns, I did something very stupid and
> embarrassing. I was smoking a cigarette, and when I stood up to say good-by
> to them, by mistake, I blew some smoke in their face. I didn't mean to, but I
> did it. I apologized like a madman. . . .

Holden's earlier references to himself as a "madman" were based on the irrationality he manifested within his life because of his emotions predominating over his
thought. In this instance, however, Holden apologizes to the nuns "like a madman"
because of the tainted state of his breath. This additional basis for the comparison
is established when Holden refers to his next-to-favorite character in the Bible: "If
you want to know the truth, the guy I like best in the Bible, next to Jesus, was that
lunatic and all, that lived in the tombs and kept cutting himself with stones." To
understand how the term "madman" is also equated with one whose breath is
tainted, one must pursue Holden's Biblical allusion to the opening verses of St.
Mark:

> And they came over unto the other side of the sea, into the country of
> the Gad-a-renes.
> And when he was come out of the ship, immediately there met him out
> of the tombs a man with an unclean spirit,
> Who had his dwelling among the tombs. . . .
> And always, day and night, he was in the mountains, and in the tombs,
> crying, and cutting himself with stones.

This particular madman is described as "a man with an unclean spirit." Holden
apparently identifies with this man because he feels himself to be existing in a similar
state: his "unclean spirit," as noted above, is manifested by his breath, tainted by
cigarettes and alcohol. This correlation of *tainted breath–unclean spirit–madman* is
maintained throughout the novel: Holden, for example, makes such statements as
"I went right on smoking like a madman" and "When I'm drunk, I'm a madman" (an
effective combination of tainted breath and loss of rationality). Furthermore, the
Biblical madman, unlike most of the people in the novel, is trying to keep his

Central Park. His hair is wet, and he feels ice particles on the back of his head. He starts thinking that he will perhaps die of pneumonia, and in that moment recalls Allie's death and the horror of his funeral; and then he thinks about people "coming and putting a bunch of flowers on your stomach on Sunday, and all that crap. Who wants flowers when you're dead? Nobody." He continues:

> When the weather's nice, my parents go out quite frequently and stick a bunch of flowers on old Allie's grave. I went with them a couple of times, but I cut it out. In the first place, I certainly don't enjoy seeing him in that crazy cemetery. Surrounded by dead guys and tombstones and all. It wasn't too bad when the sun was out, but twice—*twice*—we were there when it started to rain. It was awful. It rained on his lousy tombstone, and it rained on the grass on his stomach. It rained all over the place. All the visitors that were visiting the cemetery started running like hell over to their cars. That's what nearly drove me crazy. All the visitors could get in their cars and turn on their radios and all and then go someplace nice for dinner—everybody except Allie. I couldn't stand it. I know it's only his body and all that's in the cemetery, and his soul's in Heaven and all that crap, but I couldn't stand it anyway. I just wish he wasn't there. You didn't know him. If you'd known him, you'd know what I mean. It's not too bad when the sun's out, but the sun only comes out when it feels like coming out (pp. 201–202).

Holden tries to stop thinking about pneumonia and dying, but cannot; and his next thought is of how his own death would affect his young sister Phoebe. He considers this childish thinking, but realizes that she would "feel pretty bad if something like that happened. She likes me a lot. I mean she's quite fond of me. She really is." What Holden means, of course, but is too embarrassed to state, is that she loves him, as he loved Allie, and realizing how deeply he feels Allie's death, his concern for the little girl is spontaneous. It is at that moment that he decides, supposedly for her sake but as importantly for his own, to sneak into their apartment to see her. From this point in the book to the end, the role of Phoebe will become increasingly important, as Holden, in his concern for the youngster, begins to accept responsibly the reality of becoming a "catcher in the rye". This indeed seems to be the implication of Holden's watching Phoebe on the carrousel as she tries to grab for the gold ring; he, though afraid she will fall from the horse, does not interfere, but with maturer wisdom than he might have been capable of previous to the weekend, thinks, "The thing with kids is, if they want to grab for the gold ring, you have to let them do it, and not say anything. If they fall off, they fall off, but it's bad if you say anything to them" (pp. 273–274). Holden seems to be learning the limits within which the "catcher", the guardian of innocence, the defender against phoniness, violence, corruption, and death, must work.

From the book's opening to the very end, Salinger has provided the reader with a series of episodes which portray the difference between what Holden would have the world be and the world's reality. And, it is important to note, as many critics do not, that it is more than just the hypocrisy of man which troubles Holden; it is more than meretricious movies and the fact that talented young men like D.B. are lured into selling their talent to Hollywood. Indeed, the ways in which the world does not meet Holden's specifications for it are many, covering practically all the areas of human foible and failing, including that most unavoidable of all failings, death. Holden is, in a limited, instinctual way, a Platonist, though with no meaningful perfect realm to contemplate except as his memory, imagination, and feelings are capable, at certain instants, of providing.

One of the best descriptions of such an instant occurs in chapter 5 when Holden is waiting for Ackley to get ready to go to town. He looks out of the window of his room, opens it, and packs a snowball from the snow on the window ledge. He begins to throw it at a parked car, but doesn't because the car "looked so nice and white". Then he aims at a fire hydrant, but stops again because that also looks "too nice and white". Finally he decides not to throw it at anything and closes the window. This brief and simple episode illustrates—almost symbolizes—Holden's compulsive longing for perfection. The scene suggests not only that his refusal to blemish the landscape is a simultaneous refusal to endanger that which is pure and innocent—snow, of course, being traditionally a symbol of purity and innocence: the vision of the snow-covered object satisfies the boy's desire for some state which is perfect, silent, uncorrupted, aesthetically and emotionally complete. What Holden sees through the window is for him a visual embodiment of what he unconsciously seeks: a state of Being which is distinct from the flux of this world of Becoming, with its corruption, violence, noise, decay, and death.

One thinks too of the importance to Holden of the Museum of Natural History. It functions in his mind in much the same way as the landscape of snow, and it is one of the few things about which he remarks in a positive manner: "I get very happy when I think about it. . . . I loved that damn museum." It contains, he tells us, stuffed and mounted animals seemingly in their original habitat, and life-like figures of humans engaged in normal everyday activities. What pleases him most is that "everything always stayed right where it was. Nobody'd move. You could go there a hundred thousand times" and the animals and human figures would not have changed in any way. "The only thing that would be different would be *you*"(p. 158). He tells how each time he visited the museum as a schoolchild he was aware that in some way he was a bit different from the last time he was there; and, during the weekend, not having been there for a long time, he suddenly feels that he "wouldn't have gone inside for a million bucks" (p. 159). Perhaps he fears that the exhibits will have been changed; or perhaps he thinks of how much different he will sense he is from the boy he was when he used to visit with his grammar school classes. The images of the figures in the museum, at least, like the snowscape, will remain inviolate in his mind.

It is against the images of the museum, the snowscape, and the memories of his childhood and of Allie alive, that Holden measures the reality about him, where social adjustment demands phoniness, where children become grownups, and grownups become infirm and decrepit like Mr. Spencer, the history teacher, and where ugliness and violence in the form of people like Stradlater and Maurice, the elevator operator, are constant threats to his innocence and integrity.

Holden's reaction to his awareness of the world's imperfection and mutability is the formulation of the dream to be the "catcher" of small children, saving them from the knowledge and the dangers of what he is slowly coming to realize is the "given" of life. That he is coming to such a realization, perhaps even beginning to accept those facts of existence, is suggested by Salinger, although certainly not insisted upon. Holden knows, for instance, that even though he and others are constantly forced to say "Glad to've met you" to people they are not at all glad to have met, that such hypocrisy is a vital social necessity: "If you want to stay alive," he suggests, "you have to say that stuff." And as for the existence of such boors as Stradlater, Ackley, and Maurice, one has the feeling that by the end of the novel Holden has sensed their importance to his experience and perhaps has even begun to understand them, and feel some compassion for them, when he claims that he "misses" them. In the same way, in his refusal to intervene and stop Phoebe from trying to grasp the gold ring on the carrousel, he is demonstrating that he realizes that children do grow up, must take risks—even of falling—and that they cannot be shielded from life's dangers, at least not in the quixotic way he had envisaged; balancing seesaws and tightening roller skates have shown him that children prefer and need to cope with difficulties independently, that they might rather not be "caught in the rye."

Phoebe's importance to the process of Holden's adjustment to the reality of a world of change is suggested symbolically by the phonograph record he buys for her during the weekend. Buying it makes him feel "so happy all of a sudden". He carries it about with him throughout the day, but when, in chapter 20, he visits Central Park to search for the ducks, "something terrible happened" as he entered the park: "I dropped old Phoebe's record. It broke into about fifty pieces. . . . I took the pieces out of the envelope and put them in my coat pocket. They weren't good for anything, but I didn't feel like just throwing them away" (pp. 199–200). The shattering of the record seems to represent the failure of Holden's attempt to exist in the world on the terms of his idealism: in the park, lonely, depressed, and fearful of illness and possibly even death, the tension between reality and his ideal version of it bring him to the point of nervous breakdown.

He carries the fragments of the record to Phoebe and shows them to her: " 'Gimme the pieces,' she said. 'I'm saving them.' She took them right out of my hand and then she put them in the drawer of the night table" (p. 212). Phoebe takes from him the remnants of his idealism and the fragments of his personality and accepts the burden of "saving the pieces". Mature in her own way, and at home in the world, she will, through her love, be the means by which Holden will begin to move towards maturity. Her affection allows him to relinquish his plan of escaping to the West, and to return home; and her love creates for him a bridge to the environment from which he has been running.

Unable to realize for himself a function in life other than saving children from Allie's fate, and acutely aware of the relatedness of change to decay and death, Holden can, through his sister's love, find an alternative to those moments of memory and imagination, themselves static, cold, and deathlike. The responsibility he assumes toward her, as well as the freedom he realizes she requires, provides a starting point from which he can learn to accept the world's pervasive mutability.

NOTES

[1] J. D. Salinger, *The Catcher in the Rye* (Boston: Little, Brown and Co., 1951), pp. 172–173. Further citations within the text are to this edition.

[2] The death by falling of James Castle (related in chapter 22) no doubt contributes to this manifestation of Holden's fear.

William Glasser

THE CATCHER IN THE RYE

Uring the course of his adventures in *The Catcher in the Rye*, Holden Caulfield undergoes a startling transformation: from an existence in which his nature is dangerously divided, to a remarkably integrated state of being. To perceive this transformation, one must examine closely the particular dilemma in which Holden finds himself, his various failures to cope with this dilemma, and the peculiar solution he attains by the end of the novel.

Holden introduces his narrative by stating his intention of telling the reader "about this madman stuff that happened to me around last Christmas. . . ." Throughout the book, whenever he acts in an apparently inexplicable manner, Holden repeatedly asserts that he is a "madman" or that he is "crazy." For example, after telephoning Sally Hayes and making a date, Holden says, when she finally appears, "I felt like marrying her the minute I saw her. I'm crazy. I didn't even *like* her much, and yet all of a sudden I felt like I was in love with her and wanted to marry her. I swear to God I'm crazy. I admit it." Later, after getting "fed up" with her and leaving, he recalls asking her to run away with him "to Massachusetts and Vermont" to live by a brook:

> If you want to know the truth, I don't even know why I started all that stuff with her. I mean about going away somewhere. . . . I probably wouldn't've taken her even if she'd wanted to go with me. She wouldn't have been anybody to go with. The terrible part, though, is that I *meant* it when I asked her. That's the terrible part. I swear to God I'm a madman.

Although frequently referring to himself as a "madman," Holden does so without realizing the basis of the comparison: that his nature, which should be developing towards maturity, has stalled within an early state of childhood. A child, at birth, is able to perceive and to feel, but is not yet capable of thinking rationally. He remains an essentially irrational creature—like a "madman"—until he develops

From *Michigan Quarterly Review* 15, No. 4 (Fall 1976): 432–57.

the capability of exerting his rational thought over his random feelings. Holden says, "I'm the only dumb one in the family." Although he is a boy of uncommonly deep sensibilities, his nature is still childishly one-sided, for his feelings, like a child's, still predominate over his inadequately developed intellect. Thus, one consistently finds Holden's thoughts being either suppressed by, or occurring as a result of, his feelings. For example, after he arrives in New York and checks into a hotel, his sense of loneliness starts him "toying with the idea . . . of giving old Jane a buzz" at her college. After figuring out the excuse he would use to get her to the phone so late at night, he doesn't call her: "The only reason I didn't do it was because I wasn't in the mood"—a "reason" which he offers repeatedly throughout his narrative. Later, when he accepts the elevator boy's proposition to send a whore to his room, Holden remarks: "It was against my principles and all, but I was feeling so depressed I didn't even *think*. That's the whole trouble. When you're feeling very depressed, you can't even think."

Holden's feelings also predominate over his experiences of things outside himself. Each of his experiences generally arouses within him an immediate emotional response, over which he exerts no rational control, as is illustrated, for example, by his reaction to Stradlater's statement that his ex-date is "too old" for Holden: "All of a sudden—for no good reason, really, except that I was sort of in the mood for horsing around—I felt like jumping off the washbowl and getting old Stradlater in a half nelson." Because Holden generally reacts to things outside himself in this manner, with no conception of the causal relationship between his experiences and his emotional responses, he views his world as a place where things usually *happen* to him *all of a sudden* as immediate occurrences—or, one might stress, they *hap*pen to him as though by *chance:* "Then all of a sudden, something very spooky started happening"; "Then something terrible happened just as I got in the park"; "Then, all of a sudden, I got in this big mess." It is important to realize that this sense of immediacy accompanying everything that happens to Holden divides his existence into a temporal sequence of seemingly isolated instances occurring one after the other, as is manifested on almost every page of the novel—in his thoughts: "Then, all of a sudden, I got this idea," "Then I thought of something, all of a sudden," "But all of a sudden, I changed my mind"; and in his actions: "All of a sudden I looked at the clock," "Then, all of a sudden, I yawned," "Then, all of a sudden, I started to cry."

Holden's sense of immediacy within each thing that happens to him also leads to his sense of transiency. Because he experiences his world temporally, with the present moment always becoming a segment of the past, Holden views his life as being in a state of continual change. Since a developed intellect is needed to realize immutable conceptions, and since Holden's "thinking," as illustrated below, is limited to his sense of the mutability of life. Holden remains trapped within time, unable to recognize anything permanent in human existence. For example, as he walks through the park, he recalls the Museum of Natural History from his grammar school days as a place in which everything displayed in the glass cases stays the same, and mentions how he and the other children, by contrast, changed from visit to visit. Then he remembers Phoebe:

> I kept walking and walking, and I kept thinking about old Phoebe going to that museum on Saturdays the way I used to. I thought how she'd see the same stuff I used to see, and how *she'd* be different every time she saw it. . . . Certain things they should stay the way they are. You ought to be able to stick them in one of those big glass cases and just leave them alone. I know that's impossible, but it's too bad anyway. Anyway, I kept thinking about all that while I walked.

Holden would like to keep Phoebe a child because he is troubled by the differences he sees between children and adults, both in their physical appearances and in their personalities. Holden finds children physically acceptable under any conditions, but not adults, as he reveals when he sneaks home and finds Phoebe in bed:

> She was laying there asleep, with her face sort of on the side of the pillow. She had her mouth way open. It's funny. You take adults, they look lousy when they're asleep and they have their mouths way open, but kids don't. Kids look all right. They can even have spit all over the pillow and they still look all right.

Adults become more physically repulsive to Holden the older they get, as his reaction to old Spencer, his history teacher, illustrates. Spencer, as Holden says, "was all stooped over, and he had very terrible posture. . . ." As Holden enters Spencer's room, he notices that "there were pills and medicine all over the place, and everything smelled like Vicks Nose Drops." After remarking that Spencer was wearing "this very sad, ratty old bathrobe," Holden comments:

> I don't much like to see old guys in their pajamas and bathrobes anyway. Their bumpy old chests are always showing. And their legs. Old guys' legs, at beaches and places, always look so white and unhairy.

The personality of a child is also preferable to Holden: "God, I love it when a kid's nice and polite. . . . Most kids are. They really are." Phoebe typifies all that Holden likes about a child's nature. For example, she is "very affectionate" towards him. She is also able to converse with him: "I mean if you tell old Phoebe something, she knows exactly what the hell you're talking about." And she is capable of discriminating between the "good" and the "lousy" things existing in her world: "If you take her to a lousy movie, for instance, she knows it's a lousy movie. If you take her to a pretty good movie, she knows it's a pretty good movie."

However, as the child grows toward adulthood, its nature changes. This inevitable consequence of existence is caused, not simply by aging, but by the child's accumulated experiences of its world—as Holden tries to explain when talking about the museum:

The best thing, though, in that museum was that everything always stayed right where it was. Nobody'd move. . . . Nobody'd be different. The only thing that would be different would be *you*. Not that you'd be so much older or anything. It wouldn't be that, exactly. You'd just be different, that's all. You'd have an overcoat on this time. Or the kid that was your partner in line the last time had got scarlet fever and you'd have a new partner. Or you'd have a substitute taking the class, instead of Miss Aigletinger. Or you'd heard your mother and father having a terrific fight in the bathroom. Or you'd just passed by one of those puddles in the street with gasoline rainbows in them. I mean you'd be *differ*ent in some way—I can't explain what I mean.

This change occurring within the developing child as he experiences his world proves to be, in part, a corrupting one—as is manifested throughout the novel in a variety of ways, but most consistently, perhaps, by the change occurring in the state of one's breath as he matures. Holden remarks in particular whenever anyone has bad breath, such as his "stupid aunt with halitosis," or Ackley, who had "halitosis" and "sinus trouble and he couldn't breathe too hot when he was asleep," or the "very Cuban-looking guy" who asked where the subway was and then, says Holden, "kept breathing his stinking breath in my face while I gave him directions." The significance of these recurrent references to breath may at first remain elusive, for, as is often the case in this novel, a symbol introduced early in the work may not be understood until a later clarifying passage is reached. In this instance, Holden comments as he is waiting in his hotel room for Sunny, the prostitute: "Then I tested to see if my breath stank from so many cigarettes and the Scotch and sodas I drank at Ernie's. All you do is hold your hand under your mouth and blow your breath up towards the old nostrils." One is reminded by this seemingly casual statement of another act of blowing breath into nostrils: "And the Lord God formed man of the dust of the ground, and breathed into his nostrils the breath of life; and man became a living soul." An examination of additional evidence will further substantiate that this Biblical association of man's breath with his spirit or soul has been established in the novel. Holden's act of blowing his own breath up into his nostrils "to see if my breath stank from so many cigarettes and the Scotch and sodas I drank" must therefore be looked upon as a more meaningful test than simply one of determining if his breath smells. In other words, the extent to which Holden's breath has been tainted, in this case by the adult acts of drinking and smoking, is, by implication, the extent to which Holden's spirit has been corrupted.

After Holden tests his breath, he says, "It didn't seem to stink much, but I brushed my teeth anyway." To brush one's teeth, or, to make one's breath smell better, thus becomes equivalent, in symbolic terms, to cleansing one's spirit. As a result, spiritual significance is given to bathrooms, where one cleanses not only his body, but also his soul, a view which is emphasized when Phoebe's mother asks, "Did you say your prayers?" and Phoebe answers, "I said them in the bathroom."

Most people in the novel, however, do not keep their breath clean: Ackley,

corrupted spirit isolated from the rest of the world—a point that also appeals to Holden, as will later be discussed.

As one's breath continues to be tainted, a loss of breath results. Holden repeatedly makes such comments as "I was sort of out of breath. I was smoking so damn much, I had hardly any wind." The older one grows, the more one experiences this loss, as is illustrated by the Pencey Prep alumnus who returns for a visit on Veteran's Day:

> You should've seen this one old guy that was about fifty.... What he did, he carved his goddam stupid sad old initials in one of the can doors about ninety years ago, and he wanted to see if they were still there.... Maybe it wouldn't have been so bad if he hadn't been all out of breath. He was all out of breath from just climbing up the stairs, and the whole time he was looking for his initials he kept breathing hard....

Apparently, one finally reaches a state of existence similar to that of Holden's history teacher, old Spencer, who has the grippe, a disease of the lungs, and who must rely on Vicks Nose Drops to get breath into his nostrils.

Most of the people encountered by Holden in the novel have already experienced, to varying degrees, the corrupting influence of this world, people whose behavior Holden generally labels as *phony,* for they do not even realize that they have been corrupted. For example, after Holden sees Ernie, the snobbish piano player, make his "humble" bow to the applauding crowd, he says, "I felt sort of sorry for him when he was finished. I don't even think he *knows* any more when he's playing right or not. It isn't all his fault. I partly blame all those dopes that clap their heads off—they'd foul up *any*body, if you gave them a chance." Watching the Christmas Show at Radio City, Holden remarks, "I can't see anything religious or pretty, for God's sake, about a bunch of actors carrying crucifixes all over the stage. When they were all finished and started going out the boxes again, you could tell they could hardly wait to get a cigarette or something." Later, as he is walking along the street, he says, "I passed these two guys that were unloading this big Christmas tree off a truck. One guy kept saying to the other guy, 'Hold the sonuvabitch *up!* Hold it *up,* for Chrissake!' It certainly was a gorgeous way to talk about a Christmas tree." Even Mr. Antolini, an adult who has earlier gained Holden's respect, behaves in a way that causes Holden to run from his apartment, thinking of him as a "flit."

Considering his many contacts with spiritually deficient adults, one can see why Holden likes children so much, for the individual most likely still to have breath would be the one who has least experienced this world, or, in other words, the child—a role obviously fulfilled by Phoebe. When Holden sneaks home and dances with Phoebe, he says afterwards, "I sat down next to her on the bed again. I was sort of out of breath. I was smoking so damn much. I had hardly any wind. She wasn't even out of breath." Phoebe uses the pseudonym Hazel Weatherfield. Holden says that Phoebe misspells the first name as Hazle, an archaic word meaning "dry," which can be joined with the initial part of the second name to form a meaningful phrase: Hazle Weather. This phrase, which implies, as part of Phoebe's pseudonym, that she is to be associated with "dry weather," helps clarify the meaning of wet weather, or rain, which is used throughout the novel to symbolize what the child has not yet been altered by: the inevitably corrupting experiences of this world. Holden's repeatedly stated preference for weather that is "sunny" and "dry" reflects his desire to exist in a climate which, unlike damp weather, would not be detrimental to his already impaired lungs. Phoebe's association with dry weather suggests that she has yet to experience the world to the point where her breath is affected.

Holden can remember when he, too, as a small child, was also out of the rain. He recalls the auditorium in the museum: "the inside of that auditorium had such a nice smell. It always smelled like it was raining outside, even if it wasn't, and you were in the only nice, dry, cosy place in the world. I loved that damn museum." But Holden is no longer a small boy. Finding himself now on the brink of adulthood, he will soon be sitting in a pouring rain, as one sees him doing at the end of the novel. Holden's dilemma, therefore, throughout the book, is that he is unable to prevent his impending loss of that uncorrupted spirit possessed by children, such as Phoebe, before they have been immersed in the experiences of this world.

Holden's sense of this inevitable loss of childhood spirit is further manifested by his feeling that he might disappear whenever he crosses a street, that he might step from the curb, as though from a cliff, and fall out of sight, as is illustrated by his walk up Fifth Avenue near the end of the novel:

> Then all of a sudden something very spooky started happening. Every time I came to the end of a block and stepped off the goddam curb, I had this feeling that I'd never get to the other side of the street. I thought I'd just go down, down, down, and nobody'd ever see me again. Boy, did it scare me. . . . Then I started doing something else. Every time I'd get to the end of a block I'd make believe I was talking to my brother Allie. I'd say to him, "Allie, don't let me disappear. Allie, don't let me disappear. Allie, don't let me disappear. Please, Allie." And then when I'd reach the other side of the street without disappearing, I'd *thank* him. Then it would start all over again as soon as I got to the next corner. But I kept going and all. . . . I know I didn't stop till I was way up in the Sixties, past the zoo and all. . . . Then I sat down on this bench. I could hardly get my breath. . . .

To understand why childhood might "disappear" in a street, one must realize the symbolic significance of movement. In this particular instance, the numbers of the streets crossed by Holden are suggestively correlated with chronological stages in an individual's life. For example, old Spencer may be recalled here for an explanation of why Holden does not stop crossing streets until he "was way up in the Sixties." When Holden goes to visit his history teacher, he mentions having seen on an earlier visit "this old beat-up Navajo blanket that he and Mrs. Spencer'd bought off some Indian in Yellowstone Park." He then adds, "You take somebody old as hell, like old Spencer, and they can get a big bang out of buying a blanket." The point he is making is clarified when he arrives at the house and asks Mrs. Spencer, "How's Mr. Spencer. He over his grippe yet?" and she answers, "Over it! Holden, he's behaving like a perfect—I don't know *what.*" Mr. Spencer is behaving like a perfect—child, one may add, for what Holden finds appealing about old Spencer, and the reason that Holden is able to stop crossing streets when he is "way up in the Sixties," is that a man of old Spencer's age has reached his *second* childhood.

However strained this last correlation may be, the important idea to be derived from this material is that *movement,* usually in a straight line, becomes symbolic, not only of aging, but of proceeding from one state of existence to another. Various colloquial expressions are used in the novel to strengthen this idea, such as Mrs. Hayes's criticism that Holden "had no direction in life," or Mr. Antolini's advice to Holden about the "first move" to be taken "once you have a fair idea where you want to go. . . ." This symbolic conception of movement functions consistently throughout the novel to clarify such points as (1) why Holden always wants to feel a goodbye, to *know* he is leaving a place, or a state such as childhood, rather than discovering one day that it is no longer there, or that it has disappeared; (2) why Holden always wants to know where he is going, as seen when he keeps getting up from his seat on the subway to look at the map, and loses all the fencing foils, or when he admits that sex is something he does not understand because "You never know *where* the hell you are"; (3) why Holden is persistently concerned with taxis, trains, buses, suitcases, hotels—anything suggestive of traveling, of proceeding out of one place or state into another.

A second kind of movement, up and down, is also developed symbolically. Any downward movement—towards earth, one might say—suggests a deeper immersion into the experiences of this world. Thus, any kind of fall, from a cliff, into a street, out of a window, implies a loss of childhood spirit, which Holden would prefer to keep up, on a cliff, above any involvement with the world below. Throughout his entire narrative, Holden feels increasingly "depressed," until, just before the resolution to the novel, he says, "I think I was more depressed than I ever was in my whole life." This word denotes both an emotional state: "to lower in spirits," and a physical movement: "to press down, lower." One can understand, therefore, why Holden is "depressed" by such thoughts as having "to go downstairs in elevators with suitcases and stuff," for a combination of depressing movements is suggested in this act: downward in the elevator, and forward on a trip to another place.

Faced with his impending movement into the spiritually impaired state of adulthood, Holden considers various means of escaping from the world's influences to preserve his childhood. For example, he attempts at times to close himself off from these influences. This particular means of escape is reflected in the peculiar name which the author has given him: Holden Caulfield. The division noted earlier in Phoebe's pseudonym, Hazle Weather/field, directs one's attention to a similar division in the name Holden Caul/field. Holden is an archaic past participle of "hold," and Caul, traced back to Old French *cale,* a kind of cap, is a membrane sometimes enveloping the head of a child at birth. Within the limits of Holden's narrative, that which is "held" by him as a "caul," a kind of a cap, is obviously his red hunting hat: "I pulled the old peak of my hunting hat around to the front, then pulled it way down over my eyes. That way I couldn't see a goddam thing"; and later, "That hat I bought had earlaps in it, and I put them on. . . ." Just as a membrane enveloping the head of a child at birth would temporarily keep the child from perceiving the world into which it is born, Holden's red hunting hat functions at times to close him off from his world.

Holden would also like to stop his development toward adulthood by physically preserving his body from change, as is illustrated by his interest in the Egyptian mummies, who were treated with "secret ingredients . . . so that their faces would not rot for innumerable centuries," and by his interest in what happens to the ducks in the lagoon in Central Park "when that whole little lake's a solid block of ice." The significance of the ducks is clarified when Holden encounters Horwitz, the taxi driver, who turns their conversation away from the ducks to tell what the fish do during the winter: "They live right *in* the goddam ice. It's their nature, for Chrissake. They get frozen right in one position for the whole winter." Horwitz thus establishes that the fish are by nature capable of achieving a complete lack of movement—by a method, however, of no use to Holden, as Horwitz reveals when he adds: "If you was a fish, Mother Nature'd take care of *you,* wouldn't she? Right? You don't think them fish just *die* when it gets to be winter, do ya?" Unfortunately, Holden is not a fish. Mother Nature has not fulfilled his need. Being warm-blooded, he shares the plight of the ducks; his getting "frozen right in one position for the whole winter" is no solution to his dilemma. On the contrary, when Holden, with wet hair, begins to feel ice forming on the back of his head, he realizes that he could catch pneumonia, a disease of the lungs.

Holden also tries to escape the influences of this world by forming a fantasy: he attempts to create a "make believe" substitute for the actual world, one in which, even though he has become "big," he is capable of preserving the state of childhood. Thus, he mentally fashions for himself the role of the catcher in the rye:

> I keep picturing all these little kids playing some game in this big field of rye and all. Thousands of little kids, and nobody's around—nobody big, I mean—except me. And I'm standing on the edge of some crazy cliff. What I have to do, I have to catch everybody if they start to go over the cliff—I mean if they're running and they don't look where they're going I have to come out from somewhere and *catch* them.

The peculiar setting of this fantasy is recollective of two actual settings Holden would like to avoid, since they are not as beneficial to the preservation of childhood. The first setting, analogous to the cliff, is any street-curb from which, as noted earlier, a child may step and fall down in the street, possibly ending his childhood. Holden removes this danger in his fantasy by giving himself the role of the catcher. The second setting, analogous to the big field, is the park. In contrast with the city, with its concentrated gathering of corrupted adults, its hotels "full of perverts and morons. Screwballs all over the place," the park is a setting more often associated, in the context of Holden's experiences, with children. However, unlike the big field in Holden's "make believe" world, in which children can play without falling from childhood, the park too clearly reflects those corrupting influences of the actual world from which Holden wishes to escape: "It was lousy in the park. . . . there didn't look like there was anything in the park except dog crap and globs of spit and cigar butts from old men, and the benches all looked like they'd be wet if you sat down on them. . . ."

Holden's fantasy, however, proves to be no practical solution to the dilemma he faces in the actual world. And so, in desperation, as the novel nears its conclusion, Holden decides to attempt a compromise withdrawal from the world, a withdrawal similar to the kind he considered early in the novel when he asked Ackley, "What's the routine on joining a monastery?" He decides that he will go out West, where it is dry and sunny (an escape from rain), and live there as a deaf-mute (an escape from people).

Shortly after reaching this decision, an incident occurs which illustrates for Holden the futility of attempting any retreat from this world. As he is waiting for Phoebe at the museum to return her Christmas money before starting out West, he meets two small boys who ask where the mummies are. As they near the tomb of the mummies, the two boys become frightened and run off, leaving Holden by himself in a setting recollective of the Biblical madman, who withdrew from the world to live "in the tombs":

> I was the only one left in the tomb then. I sort of liked it, in a way. It was so nice and peaceful. Then, all of a sudden, you'd never guess what I saw on the wall. Another "Fuck you."

As Holden now learns, "That's the whole trouble. You can't ever find a place that's nice and peaceful, because there isn't any." Not even within a tomb or a grave—in other words, in death—as Holden also realizes now, can he fully escape this corrupting world:

> I think, even, if I ever die, and they stick me in a cemetery, and I have a tombstone and all, it'll say "Holden Caulfield" on it, and then what year I was born and what year I died, and then right under that it'll say "Fuck you." I'm positive, in fact.

The obscenity is particularly meaningful to Holden's dilemma, for not only does it express an adult act which confuses Holden—"You never know *where* the hell you are"—the crude statement also suggests a corruption of that act, another worldly influence to be experienced by growing children, as Holden comments when he first sees the obscenity on the school wall:

> I thought how Phoebe and all the other little kids would see it, and how they'd wonder what the hell it meant, and then finally some dirty kid would tell

them—all cockeyed, naturally—what it meant, and how they'd all *think* about it and maybe even *worry* about it for a couple of days.

Once Holden realizes that he cannot escape the world's corrupting influences, he leaves the tomb, goes into the bathroom in the museum, and falls: "When I was coming out of the can, right before I got to the door, I sort of passed out. I was lucky, though. I mean I could've killed myself when I hit the floor, but all I did was sort of land on my side." This event, one assumes, since it occurs in a bathroom (a place which has earlier been given spiritual significance), is meant to signify the fall of Holden's childhood spirit, as is also suggested by the ensuing change in his relationship with Phoebe after he leaves the bathroom and meets her out in front of the museum. The evening before he fell, Holden went home to see Phoebe, a warm and tenderly sad meeting between a child and a boy who was leaving childhood. Now, when Phoebe arrives and asks Holden if she can go with him out West, he responds to her almost abusively: he tells her to "shut up," grabs the suitcase she is carrying, and makes her cry. As a result, Phoebe gets so mad at him that she, in turn, tells him to "shut up," and then runs across the street, leaving Holden on the opposite side—an act which strengthens the sense of separation now existing between them. After this crucial moment, however, in which Holden appears to have been defeated in his desire to remain close to childhood, the sequence of events which end the novel shows the breach between them being repaired. And as a result of their moving slowly back together into another warm relationship, Holden finally experiences a resolution to the dilemma he has faced throughout the novel.

Holden experiences this resolution at the moment his previously one-sided nature becomes complete. As mentioned earlier, Holden's feelings, like a child's, have predominated over his inadequately developed intellect. Although a variety of happenings contribute to the awakening of Holden's intellect, one might look closely at two in particular. When Holden sneaks home to visit Phoebe, and she guesses that he has been "kicked out" of school, her reaction illustrates, and thus allows Holden to gain a better perspective of, the one-sided nature of the irrational child:

> "Daddy'll *kill* you!" she said. Then she flopped on her stomach on the bed and put the goddam pillow over her head. She does that quite frequently. She's a true madman sometimes.
> "Cut it out, now," I said. . . . "C'mon, Phoebe, take that goddam thing off your head. . . .
> "Nobody's gonna kill me. Use your head." . . .
> She wouldn't come out, though. You can't even reason with her sometimes.

Holden goes next to Mr. Antolini's apartment, where Mr. Antolini advises him that, in the subsequent direction his life will take, his intellect will play a necessary role:

> "I think that once you have a fair idea where you want to go, your first move will be to apply yourself in school. You'll have to. You're a student—whether the idea appeals to you or not. You're in love with knowledge."

An important point is then clarified by Mr. Antolini. Holden's nature has thus far remained one-sided because, in his response to his perceptions of the world, his emotions have prevailed within him; but the other side of human nature, the intellect, can be equally delimiting to one's life. One might recall Carl Luce, who "had the highest I.Q. of any boy at Whooton." The narrow self-satisfaction and the lack of any meaningful feelings for others he manifests during his conversation with Holden at the Wicker Bar dramatically illustrates that intellect, by itself, is as distorting to one's life as irrational emotion. Mr. Antolini now clarifies for Holden that a human being must fulfill both sides of his nature. Thus, says Mr. Antolini, the "educated and scholarly men" he admires "usually have a *passion* for following their *thoughts* through to the end." Furthermore, as he says, if Holden continues searching for knowledge, "you're going to start getting closer and closer . . . to the kind of *information* that will be very, very dear to your *heart.*" (Italics added.) In other words, Mr. Antolini is asserting that within the complete human being intellect and emotion, which are usually considered opposite and conflicting forces, must exist and work together.

Holden is later awakened by Mr. Antolini patting him on the head, an act which is apparently meant to signify the awakening of Holden's intellect, for after he flees from the apartment, embarrassed by Mr. Antolini's "perverty" behavior, Holden reveals that his intellect is no longer subordinated by his emotions. After his immediate emotional rejection of Mr. Antolini, Holden begins to "think" about the incident:

> I didn't want to, but I started thinking about old Mr. Antolini. . . . I mean I started thinking that even if he was a flit he certainly'd been very nice to me. . . . I mean I started thinking maybe I *should've* gone back to his house.

Holden now consciously recognizes that he need not totally reject an individual for behaving at times in a phony way, since opposite qualities can exist in the same person at the same time.

If Holden had earlier responded to everything he experienced with both sides of his nature, he would have recognized the existence of opposite qualities, not only within people, but in every single thing he perceived in his world. For example, the Museum of Natural History would have appeared to him, not only as a number of isolated glass cases in which "everything always stayed right where it was," but as a record of the whole flux of evolutionary development that has continuously changed everything existing on this earth. The solution to Holden's dilemma lies in his being able to perceive, with both sides of his nature, that everything in reality has two faces: that the ice in the lagoon in Central Park can both preserve and kill; that the "gasoline rainbows" Holden mentions are composed of "gasoline" and "rainbows"; that an old teacher can be like a child, and a child, such as Phoebe, can be "like a goddam schoolteacher sometimes"; that everyone's nature extends, at the same time, back towards childhood and forward towards adulthood. One might see Holden himself, with his hat on backwards, facing in two directions, as typifying the sense of reality established in this novel. Therefore, if something that stays the same also conveys a sense of continuous change, then something that Holden earlier saw as continuously changing, such as childhood, should also convey a sense of staying the same.

Holden gains this new awareness as a result of re-experiencing his own childhood. When he decides to leave for the West, he wishes first to return Phoebe's Christmas money. Planning to tell her, in a note, to meet him at the museum, he starts towards Phoebe's school:

> I knew where her school was, naturally, because I went there myself when I was a kid. When I got there, it felt funny. I wasn't sure I'd remember what it was like inside, but I did. It was exactly the same as it was when I went there.

Thus, when he sees a boy going toward the bathroom, he notes that "He had one of those wooden passes sticking out of his hip pocket, the same way we used to have. . . ." And when he sits on the stairs to write the note, he remarks, "The stairs had the same smell they used to have when I went there." By re-experiencing his own childhood in relationship to that of Phoebe's generation, Holden is able to associate childhood, not only with the past, as something waning and ending, but also with the future, as something beginning and becoming. Holden has thus far remained trapped in time, unable to recognize anything permanent within human existence, because of his incapability of perceiving that both the past and the future may be found in the present moment. Continuing now in this new direction, he eventually reaches such a moment: as he watches Phoebe on the carrousel, his sense of the past and his sense of the future become completely integrated, and he finally experiences an immutable conception of childhood.

One might approach this moment by starting at the point where Holden meets Phoebe in front of the museum. Her appearance at that time is recollective of Holden's earlier in the novel: she is wearing his red hunting hat and carrying his old suitcase, and, says Holden, "She was all out of breath from that crazy suitcase." When she asks to go with him out West, his initial outburst of emotion angers Phoebe and causes her to turn away from him. After he takes the suitcase into the check-room in the museum, he then comes out and tries to *reason* with her: "If I let you not go back to school this afternoon and go for a walk, will you cut out this crazy stuff?" (One might note here in passing that Holden reacts at this point first with emotion and then with reason, illustrating that though both sides of his nature are now active, they still remain divided from each other.) When he repeats his question, asking her if she will "go back to school tomorrow like a good girl," she responds to this apparently adult attempt to keep her in childhood by acting, one might say, "like a child." In a manner reminiscent of Holden's one-sided reactions to his world, she responds irrationally, like a "madman":

> "I may and I may not," she said. Then she ran right the hell across the street, without even looking to see if any cars were coming. She's a madman sometimes.

After this moment of separation, Holden and Phoebe slowly move back together again. When they reach the zoo, Phoebe crosses back to Holden's side, but stays behind, following him, until she stops to watch the sea lions. Holden then goes back and stands behind her. As they go through the zoo, Holden says, "She sort of walked on one side of the sidewalk and I walked on the other side." When they leave the zoo and head for the carrousel, Holden remarks that "she was sort of walking next to me now." Finally, she starts talking to him again, "I thought the carrousel was *closed* in the wintertime," and he asks her if she wants to go for a ride. Thus, by the time they reach the carrousel and Holden watches her going around on her first ride, he reveals that he has gained a new perspective concerning her movements and her eventual fall:

> All the kids kept trying to grab for the gold ring, and so was old Phoebe, and I was sort of afraid she'd fall off the goddam horse, but I didn't say anything or do anything. The thing with kids is, if they want to grab for the gold ring, you have to let them do it, and not say anything. If they fall off, they fall off, but it's bad if you say anything to them.

Holden has become intellectually capable of giving up his desire to be the catcher in the rye,[1] for he realizes by this point that it is "bad" to keep a child in childhood. As he learned from watching Phoebe's anger wane with the passing of time and events, Phoebe must be allowed to experience her world if her one-sided nature is to develop beyond its present state. It is "bad" to interrupt her movement forward, even though it will result in the eventual fall of her inexperienced, innocent spirit, for the only alternative to this process would be to keep her in the same state, unmoving, undeveloping, as though she were in a glass case—an eternal child, but an incomplete and lifeless human being.

Therefore, Holden becomes capable of accepting the necessity for movement within a child's existence: even though it steadily brings the child into greater contact with corrupting influences, the child will never attain a complete existence unless it continues "becoming" within this world. This change within Holden's outlook is stunningly illustrated at the end of the novel when all of the movements developed symbolically throughout Holden's narrative are brought together in a manner acceptable to Holden: that is, by the movements of Phoebe on the carrousel. One must first recall, as presented earlier, that a *forward* movement is suggestive of proceeding from one state of being to another, and that a movement *up* suggests the uncorrupting isolation of spiritual heights, and *down*, a deeper immersion into worldly experiences. As Phoebe rides upon her horse, her actions illustrate every one of these symbolic movements: she goes forward, a suggestion of her nature changing, but in a circular motion, which keeps her essentially in the same place; and, at the same time, the horse she sits on continues moving her up and down. As a result, all of these characteristic motions, with all of their opposite qualities, are harmoniously blended within the immediate moment for Holden's perception as he watches Phoebe on the carrousel riding her horse "around and around."

As the various aspects of Phoebe's ride are more closely examined, one discovers that the carrousel has been fashioned into a symbol embodying such a host of opposite qualities that it approaches, as a literary creation, the inexhaustible complexity of reality. Having noted the interplay of opposite motions established above, one might look now at a sampling of the other ambiguities associated with the carrousel. For example, as Holden approaches the carrousel with Phoebe, he remarks:

> Anyway, we kept getting closer and closer to the carrousel and you could start to hear that nutty music it always plays. It was playing "Oh, Marie!" It played that same song about fifty years ago when *I* was a little kid. That's one nice thing about carrousels, they always play the same songs. . . . There were a few kids riding on it, mostly very little kids. . . .

Within Holden's immediate perception of the carrousel, one finds a sense of the past—in Holden's remembrance and re-experience of his own particular childhood—and of the future, as suggested by the presence of "very little kids"—childhood, in other words, as a general state, continuously beginning.

Two colloquial phrases used throughout the novel establish an additional ambiguity associated with the carrousel. Early in his narration, Holden says, "I started yawning. Then I started horsing around a little bit. Sometimes I horse around quite a lot, just to keep from getting bored." And later he mentions "horsing around all over the place. It was very childish. . . ." In other words, "horsing around" is equivalent to acting "childish." Phoebe, on the carrousel, is literally "horsing around." As noted earlier, her going "around," if contrasted with movement in a straight line, suggests a permanence in the childhood state she is experiencing at that moment. But a second phrase used in the novel implies a limitation to that experience, for although she may be "horsing around," she is also, at the same time, "riding for a fall."

The song that the carrousel plays for the children as Phoebe first rides is "Smoke Gets in Your Eyes," a title which brings to mind those earlier references to the debilitating effect of cigarette smoke upon one's breath or spirit. Thus, the carrousel, as a symbol of enduring childhood, plays a song suggestive of its eventual corruption.

As noted before, Phoebe's going "around," rather than straight ahead, suggests that she exists, while on the carrousel, within an unchanging, timeless state. However, as her name establishes, Phoebe may be associated with the moon—and as the moon goes "around and around," it constantly changes, moving through phases that have been used for ages as a standard of time. Furthermore, as Hazle Weatherfield, she was associated with dry weather; as Phoebe, however, she is also related to wet weather, again through her connection with the moon, which has been traditionally viewed as having control over the rain.[2]

The carrousel, therefore, as a symbol composed of a complexity of opposite qualities and tenuous ambiguities, all existing together within a harmony of music and motion, typifies the sense of reality Holden finally perceives. As a result, the dilemma which he has faced throughout his narration is resolved, for he is capable now, as he sits in the rain, of accepting his world as it is. Furthermore, as is revealed by his concluding response to Phoebe on the carrousel, the divisive aspects of his nature, his emotions and his intellect, are finally integrated:[3]

> I felt so damn happy all of a sudden, the way old Phoebe kept going around and around. I was damn near bawling, I felt so damn happy, if you want to know the truth. I don't know why. It was just that she looked so damn *nice*, the way she kept going around and around, in her blue coat and all.

By means of these seemingly simple statements, Holden reveals that his response at this moment is an *aesthetic* one: he "felt so damn happy" because "she looked so damn *nice*." An aesthetic response is, by nature, a blending of sense perception, emotion, and intellect.[4] It is not dependent upon one's being conscious of a reason for responding so—as Holden says, "I don't know why." It is elicited only when one perceives something which gives pleasure to every aspect of his nature at the same moment—a pleasure manifested in this case when Holden, by simply watching Phoebe on the carrousel, feels "so damn happy."

Where, then, is Holden at the end of the novel? Critics have seen him as narrating his story to an analyst in a mental institution, Holden's concluding retreat from his world. But why would Holden talk *about* "this one psychoanalyst guy they have here" if he were supposedly talking *to* the analyst? And certainly at least "one psychoanalyst" is often found on the staff of various kinds of institutions. Furthermore, why would Holden have been placed in a mental institution in the West rather than near his home? One need not surmise in this manner to determine where Holden is. There is enough information in the novel to place him exactly: within a particular state of existence. On the final page, Holden says, "I could probably tell you what I did after I went home, and how I got sick and all. . . ." The nature of Holden's sickness was clarified at the beginning of the novel, for when Holden introduced his narrative from the unidentified place he is in, he said:

> I have no wind, if you want to know the truth. I'm quite a heavy smoker, for one thing—that is, I used to be. They made me cut it out. Another thing, I *grew* six and a half inches last year. That's also how I practically got t.b. and came out here for all these goddam checkups and stuff.

Having finally attained a solution to his dilemma, Holden is now attempting to recover, at least partially, from the particular physical impairment caused by his experience of growing up within a corrupting world. He is out West—but no longer wishing to isolate himself from people—because the dry and sunny climate is beneficial to his immediate condition. Avoiding the rain temporarily, apparently in a sanitarium for lung diseases, Holden is recovering from his loss of breath.

One might conclude by stressing that Holden is talking, not to an analyst, but to "you," the reader. Holden's reason for doing so was established earlier by Mr. Antolini, when he described for Holden "the kind of information that will be very, very dear to your heart":

> Among other things, you'll find that you're not the first person who was ever confused and frightened and even sickened by human behavior.... Many, many men have been just as troubled morally and spiritually as you are right now. Happily, some of them kept records of their troubles. You'll learn from them—if you want to. Just as someday, if you have something to offer, someone will learn something from you.

Holden is talking directly to anyone who might be as "troubled morally and spiritually" as Holden was about the nature of this world in which everyone exists. He offers his narration of *The Catcher in the Rye* as a record of his troubles for anyone who might wish to learn from his experiences. As Mr. Antolini says, "It's a beautiful reciprocal arrangement. And it isn't education. It's history. It's poetry."

NOTES

[1] Holden's hunting hat, at the end, reinforces the idea that Holden has given up the role of the catcher. Phoebe put the hat back on Holden's head for "a while" as it began to rain. When Holden says, as he sits in the downpour, that his neck "got pretty soaking wet," he is apparently referring to the now exposed *back* of his neck, the point being made indirectly that Phoebe has put the hat on him with the peak forward, not backwards as a catcher would wear it.

[2] One might also consider placing the following surmise within this sampling of ambiguities. Two colors are brought together as Phoebe rides the carrousel: blue and brown. Since she is still an unfallen child, the blue of her coat might possibly suggest the height at which she exists in spirit: above the earth, in the sky, or the heavens—where one would also see the moon; the "beat-up-looking old horse" she rides is brown, a color one may associate with the earth. If these two colors are, indeed, suggestive of the heavens and the earth, then they might be viewed together as another effective illustration of the dependency of human existence upon a blending of spirit and matter.

[3] In writing *The Catcher in the Rye*, Salinger may have been influenced by the writings of Carl Jung, especially *The Integration of the Personality*, as is suggested by the many parallels existing between these two works. For example, in reporting the dreams of a particular individual whose personality has yet to become integrated, Jung notes a dream in which someone asks the dreamer the following question: "Is there really a right and left part of human society?" The dreamer's answer might serve as a fitting description of Holden Caulfield's dilemma:

> The existence of the left does not contradict that of the right. Both are in every man.... There is no right and no left part of human society, but there are *symmetrical* and *crooked* persons. The crooked ones are those who can realize only the *one* side in themselves, the left *or* the right. They are still in a childhood state.

The course to be taken by such a one-sided individual, as described below by Jung, parallels the direction Holden finally takes, which leads to the integration of his divided nature:

> No one can free himself from his childhood without first generously occupying himself with it.... Nor is this freedom accomplished through mere intellectual knowledge; it can be effected only by a re-remembering, which is also a re-experiencing.

The carrousel, which plays such a central role in the completion of Holden's development, fits Jung's description of a "mandala," a symbol of integration or wholeness:

"Mandala," a Sanskrit word, means circle or magic circle. Its symbolism embraces all concentrically arranged figures, all circular or square circumferences having a center, and all radial or spherical arrangements.

As a mandala figure, the carrousel would also be included by Jung within a particular class of archtypes, which he labels *archtypes of transformation:* "typical situations, places, ways, animals, plants, and so forth that symbolize the kind of change, whatever it is." Jung continues his description as follows:

these archtypes are genuine and true symbols that cannot be taken ... as allegories, and exhaustively interpreted. They are, rather, genuine symbols just in so far as they are ambiguous, full of intimations, and, in the last analysis, inexhaustible. ... Our intellectual judgement, of course, keeps trying to establish their singleness of meaning, and so misses the essential point; for what we should above all establish, as alone corresponding to their nature, is their manifold meaning, their almost unbounded fullness of reference.

Such symbols of man's developing nature will always include ambiguities and contrarieties, but as Jung categorically states, and as Holden finally experiences: "in human life there is no totality that is not based upon the conflict of opposites." Jung further describes this central truth about human life in a passage which may be suitably applied to Holden's existence:

The paradoxical remark of Thales, that only rust gives its true value to the coin ... simply means that there is no light without shadow and no psychic completeness without imperfection. To round itself out, life calls, not for *perfection,* but for *completeness.*

Those persisting ambiguities within Holden's state of existence at the end of the novel may illustrate one of the most strongly emphasized ideas of Jung's work:

For in the adult there is hidden a child—an eternal child, something that is always becoming, is never completed, and that calls for unceasing care, attention, and fostering. This is the part of human personality that wishes to develop and to complete itself.

[4] If Salinger was indeed influenced by Jung's *The Integration of the Personality,* as has been suggested in Footnote 3, he would have found it difficult not to go on to Friedrich Schiller's letters on aesthetic education. As Jung nears the end of his book, he refers his readers to Schiller's work in a most enticing manner:

The yearning for personality has become a real problem that occupies many minds today, whereas earlier there was only one man who foresaw this question—Friedrich Schiller—and his letters on aesthetic education have lain dormant like a Sleeping Beauty of literature while more than a century has passed.

Within Schiller's letters one discovers a concern with the opposing demands made upon man by each aspect of his "sensuous-rational nature" and a method for harmonizing these contrarieties: that of making man "aesthetic." Schiller defines this term as follows:

For readers to whom the pure significance of this word—so often misused through ignorance—is not entirely familiar, what follows may serve as an explanation. Every phenomenon whatsoever may be thought of in four different connections. A thing may relate directly to our sensuous condition (our being and well-being); that is its *physical* character. Or it can relate to our reason, and furnish us with knowledge; that is its *logical* character. Or it can relate to our will, and be regarded as an object of choice for a rational being; that is its *moral* character. Or finally, it can relate to the totality of our various powers, without being a specific object for any single one of them; that is its *aesthetic* character. A man can be pleasant to us through his readiness to oblige; he can cause us to think by means of his transactions; he can instil respect into us by his high moral standards; but finally, independently of all these and without our taking into consideration any law or design in our own judgement of him, but simply contemplating him, simply by his manifesting himself—he can please us. In this last-named character we are judging him aesthetically.

See Friedrich Schiller, *On the Aesthetic Education of Man,* translated by Reginald Snell (Yale University Press, 1954), p. 99.

Duane Edwards

"DON'T EVER TELL ANYBODY ANYTHING"

Salinger's admirers have responded in a variety of ways to *The Catcher in the Rye,* but most have something in common: they idealize Holden. In order to do so, they play down the seriousness of his ambivalence, exhibitionism, and voyeurism and assign the blame for his severe depression entirely to society, to the world of perverts and bums and phonies. Failing to respond to the first-person narrator as ironic, they assume that Holden should be taken at his word; that he is right and the world wrong; that there is a sharp dichotomy between Holden and the world he loathes. Charles H. Kegel, for example, refers to Holden's "absolute hatred of phoniness."[1] Carl F. Strauch cites "the violent contrast between . . . society and Holden's world."[2] Ihab Hassan views Holden's "retreat to childhood" as "an affirmation of values."[3] What these writers ignore is that Holden shares in the phoniness he loathes; that he lives by his unconscious needs and not the values he espouses; that he withdraws from rather than faces the challenge of personal relationships.

It's not difficult to understand why readers have ignored, or have failed to perceive, Holden's grave deficiencies as a person. After all, he is very appealing—on the surface. He genuinely appreciates brief and isolated instances of kindness and accurately pinpoints phoniness in both high and low places; he is witty and his love for Phoebe is touching. But he himself is a phony at times, and he has virtually no self-awareness. Furthermore, he has no intention of gaining self-awareness. Offered good advice by the psychoanalyst Wilhelm Stekel (through Mr. Antolini), he becomes "so damned *tired* all of a sudden" and is unable to concentrate (188.)[4] Confronted with the charge that he cannot name one "thing" he likes "a lot," he again cannot "concentrate too hot" (169). Of course he can't; he's too busy repressing the truth. So he rambles on about two nuns he met briefly and will never see again, and he tries to convince Phoebe—and himself—that he likes James Castle, a boy who is dead. But he cannot name one *living* person, or even one occupation, that he likes. Nevertheless, he believes he is a lover of people in general because he wants to be the catcher in the rye.

From *ELH* 44, No. 3 (Fall 1977): 554–65.

When Holden says that he wants to be the catcher in the rye, he reveals a great deal about himself—a great deal more than he knows. He reveals that he does not seriously want to learn about himself. He simply won't make the effort. After all, he hasn't bothered to read Burns's poem; he isn't even able to quote accurately the one line he heard a small boy recite (173); he doesn't know that Burns's narrator contemplates kissing the "body" he meets in the rye field. So when Holden changes the word "meet" to "catch"[5] and talks not of love but of potential death (falling off a cliff), he reveals his willingness to distort the truth by ignoring—or even changing—the facts. He also reveals his use of displacement: he substitutes one response for another. He focuses on danger and potential death instead of love and a personal relationship. Ultimately, he reveals his unreliability as the narrator of his own life's story.

Fortunately, the fact that Holden distorts doesn't matter to anyone concerned with the *significance* of the events and dialogue recorded in *The Catcher in the Rye*. Like the psychoanalyst analyzing a dream, the reader can analyze what matters most: the distortions. What emerges from this analysis is an an awareness that Salinger's narrator is ironic: he doesn't understand (or know) himself, but he un-wittingly lets the reader know what he is like. In fact, he does so at the very beginning of the novel when he promises to give the reader none of "that David Copperfield kind of crap" about his "lousy childhood" (1).[6] Normally, such a state-ment would be innocent and unrevealing, but Holden isn't "normal": he's a severely depressed adolescent telling the story of his youth while in a mental institution. He is, by his own admission, sick (213).[7] So his refusal to talk about the incidents of his childhood signifies that he will remain ill, as does his chilling advice, "Don't ever tell anybody anything," at the end of the novel (214).

Elsewhere in the novel there is evidence that Holden will remain ill because he refuses to assume responsibility for his own actions. For example, when he is "the goddam manager of the fencing team," he leaves the "foils and equipment and stuff" on the subway. Although he admits that he left them there, he hastens to add: "It wasn't all my fault" (3).[8] Here and elsewhere he simply will not or can not let his mind rest without ambivalence or qualification on a conclusion.

Ambivalence is, in fact, characteristic of Holden and the surest evidence of his mental instability. If he loathes what he loves and does so intensely, he is by no means well. He is also not what he and many readers assume he is: an anti-establishment figure whose disgust is directed entirely at other people.

It's easy to demonstrate that Holden is ambivalent since he is ambivalent toward so many people and things. He hates movies and the Lunts but attends movies (137) and takes Sally to a play starring the Lunts (125). He is contemptuous of Pencey but is careful to emphasize that it has a "very good academic rating" (4). He claims to loathe the perverts he sees through his hotel window but makes a special effort to watch them and even admits that "that kind of junk is sort of fascinating" and that he wouldn't mind doing it himself "if the opportunity came up" (62).[9] He criticizes phony conversations but engages in them himself—with Mr.

Spencer (8) and Ernest Morrow's mother (54–55), for example. He criticizes "old Spencer" (and others) for using a phony word like "grand" (9), but he himself uses equally phony words such as "nice" (1) and "swell" (124).[10] He loathes Ackley and Stradlater but misses them as soon as they're gone. He wants to see people—Mr. Antolini, Mr. Spencer, and Carl Luce, for example—but doesn't like them when they're in his presence. Obviously, then, Holden is ambivalent, and ambivalence is a certain indication of mental instability.

What is Holden's problem? Whatever it is in specific form, it's reflected in his inability to relate sexually to females. Holden himself suggests this when he says, "My sex life stinks" (148). But even when he speaks the truth he fools himself: he believes that he cannot "get really sexy" with girls he doesn't like a lot whereas, in reality, he cannot get sexy with a girl he does like. In fact, what he likes about Jane Gallagher is that a relationship with her will not go beyond the hand-holding stage. In his other attempts to establish connections with girls or women, he fails sexually and, in fact, deliberately avoids both affection and serious sexual advances.[11] He kisses Sally Hayes—but in a cab where the relationship cannot go beyond "horsing around" (125). He consents to have a prostitute sent to his hotel room but asks her to stop when she starts "getting funny. Crude and all" (97), that is, when she proceeds from words to action. Aroused by watching the "perverts" in the hotel, he does call up Faith Cavendish (64), a woman he has never seen, but at an impossibly late hour and so ensures that she will refuse his request for a date. Clearly, Holden has a problem with females.

This problem is reflected in his response to Mercutio in *Romeo and Juliet*. Acting in character, Holden identifies with Mercutio, the character in the play he has most in common with. As Strauch has pointed out,[12] both Holden and Mercutio are associated with foils. But the two have much more in common than weapons. To begin with, Mercutio assigns the role of lover to Romeo (I.iv.17) just as Holden assigns the role of lover to Stradlater. Then, too, both young men ramble on when they talk. Mr. Antolini reminds us that this is true of Holden (183ff.); Romeo calls Mercutio's long speech (I.iv.53–94) "nothing" and Mercutio himself admits that he talks of "dreams / Which are the children of an idle brain, / Begot of nothing but vain fantasy" (I.iv.96–98). Finally, both Mercutio and Holden like to "horse around." Holden does so repeatedly; Mercutio does so even when he's dying.

What these two characters have in common at the level of speech and overt behavior reveals how they are alike in subtler ways. For example, both talk about, but do not engage in, sexual love. Both are more enamoured of words than facts. Both are victims—from Holden's point of view. Mercutio is the victim of the Capulets and of Romeo's desire to live at peace in the world; Holden sees himself as the victim of snobs, perverts, and phonies. Since Holden identifies with victims in general and, in fact, projects his suffering onto them, he has sympathy for the ducks in Central Park (13), for Selma Thurmer (3), and for the lunatic in Mark V (99). It follows logically that he likes Mercutio.

It also follows logically that he did not like "Romeo too much after Mercutio gets stabbed" (111). Clearly, Romeo is the antithesis of both Mercutio and Holden. He is passionate; he speaks without irony; he goes to bed with Juliet. He is by no means sexually shy although he, like Holden, is very young. In contrast, Holden is sexually shy; paradoxically, he also has an exhibitionistic attitude, that is, he has a *need* to attract attention to himself by attempting "to amuse, to stir, or to shock others."[13] Acting on this need, he performs for Stradlater in the men's room (29); he pretends to have a bullet in his stomach (103–04; 150); performing for Ackley, he pulls his hunting hat over his eyes and says in a hoarse voice, "I think I'm going blind" (21); he wears a red hunting cap in the streets of New York. He even calls himself an exhibitionist to attract attention to himself (29).

It's true that each of these examples of exhibitionism is, in itself, both harmless and normal, especially for a boy of Holden's age. (Holden himself would say that he was simply "horsing around.") But Holden has a need to show off, and he has more serious problems eventually. After all, he does end up in a mental institution. Consequently, his exhibitionistic attitude serves as a clue to his state of mind; it also helps to explain why Holden "got sick and all." Since he himself won't tell us, this clue is especially important.

Other important clues to Holden's problem are included in Chapter 25, the chapter following Holden's flight from Mr. Antolini and preceding the one-page concluding chapter which reveals that Holden is in a mental institution. Near the beginning of Chapter 25, Holden's mental breakdown (which is not recorded in the novel) is anticipated: Holden has a headache and feels "more depressed than [he] ever was in [his] whole life" (194). He also has the desire to catch what he assumes is "some perverty bum that'd sneaked in the school late at night to take a leak or something and then wrote [an obscenity] on the wall" (201). And, finally, he notices—and comments on—a little boy who "had his pants open" (202). Since Holden likes children more than adults and dead people more than the living, he is in character when he enters the tombs of the mummies with the little boy and his brother. He is also in character when, left alone in the tomb, he finds peace among the dead—at least temporarily. But then the words "Fuck you" written in red crayon on the wall remind him that he has not escaped from people, not even from the "perverty bums." Furthermore, he realizes that there is no escape even in death: some day someone will write this same obscenity on his tomb, he assumes. So when he leaves the tomb he is not cured but is, in fact, very ill: he "sort of had diarrhea" and finally passes out.[14]

Commenting on this scene, Strauch stresses that Holden feels better after he faints and "is reborn into a world of secure feelings and emotions, with himself fulfilling the office of catcher in his mature view of Phoebe."[15] Since Holden is reconciled with Phoebe and says that he felt "so damn happy all of a sudden" (213), there is some basis for this statement. However, Holden is not "reborn." Instead, by his own admission, he "got sick" (that is, mentally ill) *after* the fainting incident and the expression of happiness and is *subsequently* in an institution. Furthermore, his identification with the lunatic in Mark V prepares us for this.

Although Carl F. Strauch sees in Holden's response to the lunatic an anticipation of the fact that Holden "will subsequently break his morbid psychological fetters,"[16] there is too much evidence to the contrary. It's true that Holden and the lunatic have something in common: both spend time in the tombs; both suffer; both are mentally ill. But they are also unlike one another in some important ways. To begin with, the lunatic participates in his own cure by running up to Jesus, adoring him, and calling out to him. In contrast, Holden withdraws from people, including Phoebe. (Significantly, she isn't mentioned or referred to in the concluding chapter although characters peripheral to Holden's existence are.) He watches her "going around and around" on the carrousel, but he remains at a distance and stands apart from "the parents and mothers and everybody" who seek shelter from the rain under the roof of the car-rousel. It's true that he, like the lunatic, does go home, but the lunatic goes home cured while Holden goes home only to leave in order to enter an institution. Finally, whereas the lunatic tells everybody what has been done for him, Holden regrets having told anybody anything (214). So it's not surprising that when Holden says he likes the lunatic "ten times as much as the Disciples" (99), he refers to him as "the poor bastard" who "lived in the tombs and kept cutting himself with stones" (99) and does not refer to the lunatic's cure or his re-entry into the world of people, including adults. Acting consistently, he responds to Mark V the way he responds to Burns's poem: he cites what pleases him and ignores what doesn't.

This subjectivity and tendency to distort explains a great deal about Holden. Specifically, it explains his interest in the "perverty bum" and the little boy whose pants are unbuttoned. Both appeal to him because of his voyeuristic tendencies.

That Holden has voyeuristic tendencies should surprise no one. He himself admits that he finds it "sort of fascinating to watch" (62) bizarre sexual activity through his hotel window. Besides, anyone "who in the unconscious is an exhibi-tionist is at the same time a voyeur" in psychoanalytic terms.[17] So it is not surprising that Holden is interested in the "perverty bum" and the little boy. What is surprising is the degree of his response. In the first instance he responds with extreme hostility; he wants to catch the bum urinating and/or writing on the wall (Holden is a bit ambiguous here) and "smash his head on the stone steps till he was good and goddam dead and bloody" (201). In the second instance he responds with extreme concern and embarrassment; he says the boy's behavior "killed" him and adds that he wanted to laugh when the boy buttoned his pants without going behind a post, but he didn't dare to; he was afraid he'd "feel like vomiting again" (202–03).

What is happening is that looking is becoming a perversion for Holden: it is beginning to be concentrated on the genitals and associated with the function of excretion. It also does not prepare for the normal sexual act[18] and is the logical, although not "normal," outgrowth of his sexual shyness, of his reluctance to go beyond holding hands. It also follows quite naturally from the fact that Holden is sexually ambivalent; he hasn't lost interest in females and cannot acknowledge his sexual interest in males.

Most critics writing about homosexuality in *The Catcher in the Rye* assume that Holden is the victim of homosexuals, but there is a great deal of evidence to the contrary. To begin with, Holden fails to complete most of his phone calls to females, but he easily completes phone calls to two homosexuals: Mr. Antolini and Carl Luce. Secondly, *he* seeks *them* out; he is the aggressor if there is one. In fact, his first two remarks to Luce reveal his unconscious desire to make sexual contact with his former Student Adviser. "Hey, I got a flit for you," he says first of all, and then asks him, "How's your sex life?" (144). Thirdly, Salinger links Holden to the two homosexuals by letting the reader know (through the narration) that all three of them respond sexually to older women:[19] Luce is dating a woman in her late thirties (145); Antolini is married to a woman who "looked pretty old and all" (185); Holden responds sexually to Ernest Morrow's mother (56). But nothing reveals more about Holden's relationship to homosexuals than his response when he wakes up in the middle of the night in Mr. Antolini's house. Consider his exact words:

> I woke up all of a sudden. I don't know what time it was or anything, but I woke up. I felt something on my head, some guy's hand. Boy, it really scared hell out of me. What it was, it was Mr. Antolini's hand. What he was doing was, he was sitting on the floor right next to the couch, in the dark and all, and he was sort of petting me or patting me on the goddam head (191–92).

Since Holden tells us that Antolini is there in the dark touching him, we have to assume this is true; there is nothing to negate or contradict or undercut this statement. But what Antolini's intention was we cannot know since even Holden is confused. Antolini was patting *or* petting him, Holden says. But the difference between patting and petting is great: we pat children and pet lovers. Furthermore, nothing that Holden says about Antolini's response to Holden's wild flight in the night suggests that Antolini is guilty of making a sexual advance. Besides, what matters most of all in this incident is Holden's distortion of experience, specifically, his overreaction. Even if Antolini did make an improper move, Holden is safe: Mrs. Antolini is in the adjoining room; Antolini is by no means aggressive; and Antolini has agreed to go to bed.

Why, then, does Holden respond so violently? Why is he sweating and ill when he leaves the house? The answer is that he is projecting his desire for homosexual expression onto Antolini. (This does not mean that Holden is himself a homosexual but that he has not yet made a sexual choice.) In the passage cited above, this is evident. Holden assumes that "some guy's hand" is on his head before he can identify Mr. Antolini or identify the hand as his. Furthermore, in this same scene he acknowledges, as the ironic narrator, that he inspires such behavior. He says, first of all, that perverts are "always being perverty when *I'm around*" (105) and em-phasizes that this "kind of stuff's happened to me about twenty times since I was a kid" (193). Naturally. He is attracted to—and attracts—homosexuals.

Unfortunately, Holden isn't conscious of this. In fact, he works hard to repress all knowledge of his latent desires. To begin with, he doesn't seem to be conscious of the significance of his remarks to Carl Luce in the bar even though he admits that he "used to think" Luce was "sort of flitty" (143). But the patting (or petting) incident is more overt and threatens to make Holden conscious of his latent homosexual desires. He reacts by becoming ill. He has a headache, becomes anxious and depressed (194), has sore eyes (195), experiences a mild form of hypochondria when he says he has "lousy hormones" and cancer (195–96), and wishes to negate his identity by "going out West" where nobody would know him (198). But, most important of all, he wants to be unable to hear or speak; he wants to be a deaf-mute who marries and lives in isolation with a beautiful deaf-mute girl (198–99). In other words, Holden wants to live apart from men and wants to be unable to hear or speak anything. In expressing this Holden expresses his wish to have no reminders through speech or action of his unresolved sexual conflicts.

It shouldn't be surprising that Holden has severe sexual conflicts: his family situation is far from ideal. The father barely exists as far as Holden and Phoebe are concerned, and the mother is not emotionally involved in the lives of her children. This is revealed in the scene in which the Caulfields return from a party. First of all, they are indifferent to Phoebe. Although she is still a child, they have left her home alone. When they do return home late at night, only Mrs. Caulfield bothers to look in on her daughter. But she is by no means greatly concerned. She doesn't object seriously to what she assumes is smoke from a cigarette Phoebe has been smoking; she moves randomly and nervously (like Holden) from one subject to another, including Holden's return from school; she fails to react to Phoebe's statement that she couldn't sleep. In brief, she is a mother incapable of affection.

Meanwhile, the father has gone into another room without bothering to inquire about Phoebe. Since Phoebe has said that he will not attend her Christmas pageant, it's safe to assume that he is generally absent from his children's lives. He is the aloof father whose inaccessibility makes it impossible for his son to identify with him and thus to develop "normally."

But he does have a connection with Holden: he punishes him. Confirming this, Phoebe says repeatedly that Mr. Caulfield will "kill" Holden (165, 166, 172), and Holden himself acknowledges that "it would've been very unpleasant and all" if his father had found him at home (178). Since Mr. Caulfield remains a vague and powerful figure, his effect on his son is inevitably exaggerated and debilitating. He joins forces with his wife to stifle and stunt his son's sexual development.

Because Holden's home situation is so unfortunate, it's easy to sympathize with him. It's even tempting to see the conclusion (Chapter 26) as affirmative. Besides, Holden is very appealing when he criticizes bums and phonies and perverts—so appealing that it's easy to forget that he's a bum, a phony (at times), and a potential pervert. And when he expresses his love for Phoebe, his hostility and egotism seem relatively unimportant. So it's tempting to see Holden as a person who doesn't need a psychoanalyst because he has gone beyond affirmation and denial. But at the end of the novel Holden is depressed and subdued. He has lost interest in life: he doesn't want to think about the past; he isn't interested in his future. When he tells D.B. that he doesn't know what to think about "all this stuff I just finished telling you about," he reveals that he is still confused. And when he says that he misses everybody—even Stradlater and Ackley and Maurice—he reveals that he is still sentimental. Although his sentimentality has often been sentimentalized as love, it is not love at all. It is a symptom of his inability to express his feelings easily and naturally.

Nevertheless, Holden is likable. He also deserves sympathy because, as William Faulkner has said, he "tried to join the human race and failed."[20] But Faulkner is not quite accurate when he says that there was no human race for him to enter. Phoebe loves him; D.B. expresses an interest in him by visiting him in the mental institution; Mr. Antolini offers him shelter and good advice. Ultimately, people are as good to Holden as he is to them. So Holden should not be idealized. It may be true that he is "more intelligent than some and more sensitive than most,"[21] but his response to his own experience results in deep depression and may have culminated in mania.[22] Nor does Holden resist the establishment that makes it difficult for him to love and develop. His rebellion is all fantasy. He tells off no one—not even the prostitute or the phonies at Pencey. And his overt behavior is conventional except when he is acting out his exhibitionistic attitude. He doesn't become a recluse or a beatnik; instead, he returns home, enters an institution, and will *again* return to school in the fall.

He does have what Faulkner calls an "instinct" to love man,[23] but this makes him a typical, rather than extraordinary, teenager. It's what causes him to want to join the human race.

What does make him extraordinary is his special ability to detect phoniness everywhere (except in himself). Of course it's unfair to emphasize, to the exclusion of everything else, that Holden shares in the phoniness he loathes. After all, Holden conforms to phoniness because he wants so badly to join the human race. But in doing so he makes it difficult for others like himself to find a human race to join.

NOTES

[1] Charles H. Kegel, "Incommunicability in Salinger's *The Catcher in the Rye*," *Western Humanities Review*, 11 (Spring, 1957), 189.

[2] Carl F. Strauch, "Kings in the Back Row: Meaning through Structure, A Reading of Salinger's *The Catcher in the Rye*," *Wisconsin Studies in Contemporary Literature*, 2 (Winter, 1961), 11.

[3] Ihab Hassan, *Radical Innocence: Studies in the Contemporary American Novel* (Princeton Univ. Press, 1961), p. 261.

[4] Page numbers which appear parenthetically in the body of this paper refer to the Bantam Books paperback edition of *The Catcher in the Rye*.

[5] It's possible that the little boy quoted Burns's poems inaccurately and that Holden is repeating accurately what he heard. Nevertheless, my central point remains valid: Holden is not concerned enough about the truth to gather the facts. Being in the right is much more important to him than being right.

[6] In one sense, Holden keeps his promise: he doesn't tell the reader much about his childhood. However, since he reveals his "symptoms" through his speech and behavior, it's possible to infer what his childhood was like. Besides, Holden has something in common with David Copperfield: he's very sentimental. This should surprise no one since Salinger carefully links Holden to David in two ways. First of all, Holden is a Caul-*field* and David is a Copper-*field*. Secondly, both are born with a caul. Caul is the first part of Holden's surname; it is also the name of the fetal membrane David is born with (see the fourth paragraph of Dickens's novel).

[7] Unwittingly, he acknowledges this again when he says, "In my *mind*, I'm probably the biggest sex maniac you ever saw" (62). On other occasions he calls himself an exhibitionist (29) and admits that he can be sadistic (22).

[8] The significant word here is "all"; it suggests that Holden knows he is at fault but will not assume responsibility for his actions.

[9] Carl F. Strauch cites this scene to confirm that Holden contrasts the world he loathes; however, Strauch ignores the fact that Holden finds the perverse behavior attractive. In addition to admitting that indulging in perverse behavior would be "quite a lot of fun," Holden renders a long, detailed account of the women's clothing used by the transvestite (61); he also watches the "perverts" willingly, with obvious interest, and for quite a long time.

[10] Holden's use of what Strauch calls "slob" and "literate" language suggests that Holden is ambivalent toward language and toward education in general.

[11] It is important to emphasize that Holden has difficulty expressing himself either affectionately or sensually. (Sentimentality should not be mistaken for affection.) For example, he finds even Phoebe *"too* affectionate" when she puts her arms around his neck (161). This inability to express or receive affection suggests that Holden had difficulty "from the very beginning" with parents who were too cold or too aloof. Since "normal" sexual development depends on the successful fusion of the earlier "affectionate current" of love with the later "sensual current," Holden's chances of maturing "normally" are not good.

For an interesting and informative discussion of the relationship of tenderness to sensuality, see Philip Rieff's *Freud: The Mind of the Moralist* (Garden City, New York: Doubleday, 1961), pp. 174–77.

[12] Strauch, p. 15.

[13] Any of a large number of psychology or psychoanalytic texts could be used to arrive at an understanding of the term "exhibitionistic attitude." I have quoted briefly from the Laurel *Dictionary of Psychology*, ed. J. P. Chaplin (New York: Dell, 1975), p. 184 because it offers a succinct definition which applies so exactly to Holden without distorting what a more elaborate discussion of the term would include. The definition of the term helps to explain why Holden has a need to amuse Stradlater, to shock Ackley, and to stir Phoebe.

[14] If Salinger intended the reader to see Holden's diarrhea and fainting as a cure, D. H. Lawrence is right: novels cannot lie but novelists are often dribbling liars.

[15] Strauch, p. 23.

[16] Strauch, p. 17.

[17] Sigmund Freud, *Three Contributions to the Theory of Sex*, ed. A. A. Brill (New York: Random House, 1938), p. 575.

[18] It is instructive to relate what Freud says about voyeurism in *Three Contributions to the Theory of Sex* (especially on pp. 569, 575, and 593 in the Brill edition) to Holden's behavior. Freud may not present the last word on the subject, but what he says fits Holden so exactly that it is difficult not to believe that Salinger knew Freud's essay when he wrote his novel.

[19] Salinger likes to link two or more people by means of specific details. As indicated above, David Copperfield and Holden are linked by a caul; Mercutio and Holden are linked by foils; the lunatic in Mark V and Holden are linked by tombs and madness. Analogously, Carl Luce, Mr. Antolini, and Holden are linked by their sexual interest in older women.

[20] Frederick L. Gwynn and Joseph L. Blotner, eds., *Faulkner in the University* (New York: Random House, 1965), p. 244. .

[21] Gwynn, p. 244.

[22] Although Holden does not acknowledge that he was manic between Chapters 25 and 26, it is likely that he was. To begin with, he has most of the criteria "required for 'definite' depression": depression, loss of energy, agitation, feelings of self-reproach and guilt, complaints of diminished ability to concentrate, mixed-up thoughts, and recurrent thoughts of death. Furthermore, at the end of Chapter 25, when he is watching Phoebe on the carrousel, he appears to be approaching that state of euphoria characteristic of the manic. He also exhibits at least some of the symptoms which must be present in mania: distractibility, racing thoughts, and "push of speech." If Holden does become manic, the break between the last two chapters is explained: manics generally cannot remember what they said and did during the manic period.

For a professional presentation of diagnostic criteria of depression and mania, see pp. 199–200 of *Psychiatric Diagnosis* (New York: Oxford U. Press, 1974) written by Drs. Robert A. Woodruff, Jr., Donald W. Goodwin, and Samuel B. Guze.

[23] Gwynn, p. 244.

James Lundquist
AGAINST OBSCENITY

*T*he Catcher in the Rye appeared in a sober and realistic time, a period when (by comparison with the 1960s, at any rate) there was a general disenchantment with ideologies, with schemes for the salvation of the world. Salinger's novel, like the decade for which it has become emblematic, begins with the words, "If you really want to hear about it,"[1] words that imply a full, sickening realization that something has happened that perhaps most readers would not want to know about. What we find out about directly in the novel is, of course, what has happened to Salinger's hero-narrator, Holden Caulfield; but we also find out what has happened generally to human ideas on some simple and ultimate questions in the years following World War II. Is it still possible to reconcile self and society? Is it any longer possible to separate the authentic from the phony? What beliefs are essential for survival? What is the role of language in understanding the nature of our reality? Is it possible to create value and endow the universe with meaning? That Salinger deals with these questions in one way or another points to a problem with *The Catcher in the Rye* that has often been ignored or simply not taken seriously—that the climate of ideas surrounding the novel is dense, and that the book is not just the extended and anguished cries of a wise-guy adolescent whose main trouble is that he does not want to grow up.

From the start in *The Catcher in the Rye,* we are struck with the bleakness of Holden Caulfield's life. His existence seems so gratuitous and contingent, so absurd and without apparent meaning that we wonder where Salinger could possibly go with such a story (or why he would want to go anywhere with it). Holden is so full of despair and loneliness that he is literally nauseated most of the time. He realizes how different he is from other people, yet his own personality barely exists. He is filled with a penetrating nothingness, and for all the advice he gets, no one can tell him what he must do. There is no rational way he can discover a way out of his dilemma, yet he must take action of some sort, and suicide is not it.

From *J. D. Salinger* (New York: Ungar, 1979), pp. 37–53, 55–68.

In describing Holden's predicament, one cannot avoid using existential platitudes, for Holden is, undoubtedly, in the midst of an existential crisis. Yet for all his despair, Holden is not a character who adequately illustrates the bitter pessimism and seriousness of a character out of the writings of Sartre, nor does he convey the simple message of popular existentialism as suggested by Camus—choose a path, commit yourself, be yourself, realize your own dignity. Salinger conceives of character much the same way Sartre and Camus do, but his use of language, his humor, and his ultimate willingness to look elsewhere for his answers make him a far different writer, even though he begins at the same point: The world with all its obscenities.

The way Holden Caulfield sees the world is stated in the novel's most famous line: "If you had a million years to do it in, you couldn't rub out even *half* the 'Fuck you' signs in the world" (p. 262). It is ironic that this sentence is the one that is most responsible for the various bannings of the novel in the years following its appearance. The Detroit Police did not understand Salinger's point at all when they pulled the book out of the city's bookstores—that the controversial line, instead of being obscene itself, is directed, as almost all of Salinger's fiction is, *against* obscenity. Holden tries to explain to us not only what is offensive, disgusting, and repulsive to him in human behavior, but also what goes against prevailing notions of modesty and decency. "The things that Holden finds so deeply repulsive are things he calls 'phony,'" writes Dan Wakefield, "and the 'phoniness' in every instance is the absence of love, and, often, the substitution of pretense for love."[2] Holden is a rebel, but he is hardly a rebel without a cause: He begins in a screaming rage against a society of convention, immorality, and the patently false, but he ends by establishing love and acceptance as a saving grace.

When Holden first introduces himself to us, it is difficult to believe that he is going to establish anything. He comes across as the classic screw-up. He has been thrown out of a series of schools, the latest being Pencey Prep in Agerstown, Pennsylvania, and he is undergoing psychiatric treatment in California. A remark by Stradlater, his old roommate at Pencey, seems to pretty well define his character: "You don't do *one damn thing* the way you're supposed to" (p. 53). Holden fails all of his subjects but one (English) his last term at Pencey, he succeeds in alienating himself from the other students, and he even fails as manager of the fencing team (he loses the team equipment on the subway). Yet he is a character type who has his own fascination for the reader. As Arthur Heiserman and James E. Miller, Jr., emphasize, "American literature seems fascinated with the outcast, the person who defies traditions in order to arrive at some pristine knowledge, some personal integrity."[3]

Integrity—or at least frankness—is one of Holden's most engaging qualities as he starts his story with an extended flashback to the day he left Pencey, the kind of school that advertises itself in the back pages of certain magazines with a picture of a guy on a horse jumping over a fence (Holden says that he has never seen a horse anywhere near the place). It is the day of the year's last football game, but Holden goes instead to see "old Spencer," his history teacher, who asked him to stop by before leaving school. Spencer, in a question that echoes throughout the book, asks Holden, "What's the matter with you, boy?" (p. 14). As Spencer tries to lecture him, telling him that he flunked history because he simply did not know anything, Holden's mind wanders to a question of his own, one he returns to time after time in the novel. He wonders what happens to the ducks in the lagoon near Central Park South when winter comes. It is now winter for Holden, and what will happen to him?

Much has been made critically of Holden's obsession with the ducks, and in some ways the symbolism seems too obvious. But the ducks are another one of Salinger's signs, and they suggest a verse from the New Testament: "The foxes have holes and the birds have nests, but the Son of Man has no place to lay his head." Holden, in his perception of the phony, in his outrage against the obscene, and in his own ineptitude is estranged from both his society and nature. He is not, in this respect, a Christ-figure, but he is most certainly a fool for Christ. Once he leaves Pencey, he does not have a place to rest, and his odyssey becomes the story not of a seeker after truth so much as the story of one who seeks relief from his madness through some saving grace, through some healing stroke.

Holden has often been compared to earlier characters in literature. A substantial amount has been written showing his relationship to Huckleberry Finn—a connection that seems obvious enough given the first-person narration, the colloquial language, the emphasis on the problems of adolescence, and the motif of the journey.[4] Holden has also been compared to the hero of Goethe's *The Sorrows of Young Werther,* Byron's Childe Harold in *Childe Harold's Pilgrimage,* and, more significantly, to Fitzgerald's Gatsby in *The Great Gatsby.* The latter point has considerable validity, because both Gatsby and Holden are model characters of innocence and illusion in American literature, and as one critic has stressed, "The central common characteristic of both Gatsby and Holden is the adherence to a powerful, abiding illusion, while around them swirls a corrupt, hostile, essentially phony world."[5] Salinger even goes so far as to have Holden say, "I liked Ring Lardner and *The Great Gatsby* and all. I did, too. I was crazy about *The Great Gatsby.* Old Gatsby. Old sport" (p. 183). Surprising similarities to William Saroyan's *The Human Comedy* (1943) have been noted.[6] In both novels there is an objectionable boy named Ackley, and the name of Saroyan's hero, Homer Macauley, bears some metrical and orthographical similarity to Holden Caulfield. Each of the characters has a sister and two brothers (with one of the brothers either dead or dying), each gets into trouble in a history course, and each has an encounter with a prostitute. But the similarities, as great as they are, end there between Saroyan and Salinger: Holden is a much more memorable character than is Homer Macauley, and *The Catcher in the Rye* is, without argument, a much more important book than is *The Human Comedy;* its story is more subtle, its structure more complex, and its humor more outrageous.

Holden himself suggests another literary comparison that has not been given much emphasis in interpretations of the novel. About half-way through his monologue, Holden says, "If you want to know the truth, the guy I like best in the Bible, next to Jesus, was that lunatic and all, that lived in the tombs and kept cutting himself with stones. I like him ten times as much as the Disciples, that poor bastard" (p. 130). Holden *is* the lunatic in the tombs. He lives surrounded by death. One of his obsessions is his younger brother, Allie, who died from leukemia at the age of ten. Another one of his obsessions is James Castle, a boy at one of his former schools, Elkton Hills, who committed suicide by jumping from a window after being cruelly harassed by some of the other students. Holden is also like the lunatic in another way—he keeps hurting himself as he masochistically puts himself in one situation after another that can only lead to pain and revulsion. He goes places where he should not be, he calls up people who do not really want to see him or even begin to understand him, and he dwells on thoughts that can only cause him pain. Like the lunatic, he is possessed by not one demon, but many (the lunatic's name is "Legion" because of his multiple possession)—the demon of fate and death, the demon of emptiness and meaninglessness, the demon of guilt and condemnation, the demon of despair, and the demon of jealousy. The casting forth of these evil spirits is what his story ultimately comes down to.

The extent of his possession is indicated early in the book when he learns that his roommate Stradlater's date for the evening is Jane Gallagher, a girl Holden met the summer before last and with whom he is vaguely and uncertainly in love. After Stradlater leaves, Holden sits in his room and begins to think about what Stradlater might do to Jane. "God, how I hated him. . . ." Holden later explains. "Most guys at Pencey just *talked* about having sexual intercourse with girls all the time . . . but old Stradlater really did it. . . . That's the truth" (pp. 55, 63). He is driven by his jealousy to provoke a fight with Stradlater, who knocks him down and bloodies his face—the first of several injuries that Holden manages to inflict on himself in the course of the novel. But he is unable to stop thinking of Jane and Stradlater, and his own sexual insecurities along with his despair over the obscenity he sees all around him (Stradlater had a way of calmly sweet-talking girls into believing that he actually cared for them) send him off on a self-destructive spiral that, paradoxically, leads to his redemption at the end.

Holden's demonic possession is apparent when he catches the train to New York with the idea of staying in a cheap hotel until the day when his parents expect him home. A lady boards the train at Trenton, notices the Pencey sticker on Holden's luggage, and asks him if he knows her son at the school. Holden automatically adopts another personality. He tells her that his name is Rudolph Schmidt, casually lies to her about how popular and respected her obnoxious son is, and explains his own early departure by saying he is going to have an operation for a brain tumor. He evokes sympathy from her, and she is pleased with what he had said about her son, but it is all deception. In a phony world, phoniness works, but Holden's actions become increasingly those of a madman who seems less and less in control of them.

He goes into a phone booth at Penn Station, but he cannot think of anyone he could reasonably call at that late hour. He gets a cab, mistakenly gives the driver his home address, asks him to turn around, and then asks him if he knows what happened to the ducks in the winter. The driver thinks Holden is nothing more than a wise guy, and drops him off at the Edmont Hotel. Holden checks in, goes up to his room, and finds no comfort in his anonymity and isolation. He looks out his window and watches a transvestite dressing up and parading in front of a mirror in a room on the other side of the hotel. In another window he sees a man and woman squirting water at each other out their mouths. "Sex is something I really don't understand too hot" (p. 82), he says. He impulsively decides to call up a woman named Faith Cavendish, a part-time prostitute, whose number he obtained from a Princeton student a few months before, and asks her if she would like to have a drink with him. She offers to meet him the next day, but he loses his courage and backs off.

Shaken by his encounters with the inexplicable and the obscene, he goes down to the bar in the Lavender Room of the hotel and begins to think of his sister, Phoebe, one of Salinger's infuriatingly precocious children. "You should see her," Holden says. "You never saw a little kid so pretty and smart in your whole life" (p. 87). The same age as Allie was when he died (ten), Phoebe, like him, has had nothing but A's since she started school. She has learned the dialogue of her favorite movie, *The 39 Steps,* by heart. And she writes books about a girl detective named "Hazle" Weatherfield. Phoebe and Allie symbolize innocence to Holden, but they are more than that. A major theme in the New Testament is that to enter the Kingdom of Heaven one must have the purity of heart that can be achieved only by becoming like little children. Or, as Robert G. Jacobs has stated it, "For Salinger, childhood is the source of the good in human life; it is in that state that human beings are genuine and open in their love for one another. It is when people become conscious in their relationships to one another, become adults, that they become 'phony' and logical and come to love the reasons for love more than the loved person."[7]

That Holden himself sees childhood as the source of good in human life is indicated in the title of the novel. At one point in his wanderings through New York, he sees a father, a mother, and their six-year-old son who had all apparently just come out of church. The parents are talking to one another, paying no attention to the child who is walking in the street, next to the curb, with traffic zooming by dangerously close. Disturbed and fascinated by the scene, Holden gets close enough to hear the boy singing a song, "If a body catch a body coming through the rye." Late that night he sneaks into his parents' apartment to see Phoebe and tries to explain to her why he has left school by saying that he did not like anything that was happening at Pencey. She replies by suggesting that perhaps his problem is just that—that he does not like *anything,* that he does not want to become *anything* (a lawyer, for instance, like his father), and that he does not want to do *anything.* Holden pauses, and then he tells her what he would like to be. He asks her if she knows the song the boy in the street was singing. Wise child that she is, she of course knows that it is a poem by Robert Burns and, furthermore, that Holden has the words wrong. It actually goes, "If a body meet a body coming through the rye"—a significant difference, because it indicates Holden's subconscious desire to "rewrite," to change an order of things that he finds unacceptable. His reply to Phoebe is one of the most famous passages in the novel:

> "I thought it was 'If a body catch a body,'" I said. "Anyway, I keep picturing all these little kids playing some game in this big field of rye and all. Thousands of little kids, and nobody's around—nobody big, I mean—except me. And I'm standing on the edge of some crazy cliff. What I have to do, I have to catch everybody if they start to go over the cliff—I mean if they're running and they don't look where they're going I have to come out from somewhere and *catch* them. That's all I'd do all day. I'd just be the catcher in the rye and all. I know it's crazy, but that's the only thing I'd really like to be. I know it's crazy." (pp. 224–225)

The "fall" he is talking about is the fall from the innocence of childhood into the obscenity of adulthood. Holden, in his anger at the phoniness of Pencey Prep and other institutions imposed upon the young by the old, wants a world populated by sweet children whose skates need lacing and by nuns who can teach English literature and be untouched by the sexual overtones in it.

The problem with all of this for Holden is that he is sixteen; he cannot remain a child—he cannot stand at the edge of the cliff and be the catcher; he must fall off into adulthood. But there are ways to fall and ways not to fall, a lesson that is pointed out to Holden after he sneaks back out of the apartment and goes to visit Mr. Antolini, his old English teacher at Elkton Hills and now an instructor at N.Y.U. Mr. Antolini cannot approve of Holden's behavior, and tells him, in a thematic echo of the wish to be the catcher in the rye that Holden expresses to Phoebe, that Holden is riding for a fall. "This fall I think you're riding for—it's a special kind of fall, a horrible kind," Mr. Antolini explains. "The man falling isn't permitted to feel or hear himself hit bottom. He just keeps falling and falling. The whole arrangement's designed for men who, at some time or other in their lives, were looking for something their own environment couldn't supply them with. . . . So they gave up looking. They gave it up before they ever really even got started" (pp. 243–244). In other words, one may fall into disillusionment, giving up on the possibilities in life as the innocent dreams of childhood are by necessity abandoned. Or one may break the fall, may even land, by realizing that indeed there are things one's environment simply cannot supply, such as innocence, selfless love, freedom from obscenity.

Mr. Antolini expands his lecture to Holden by reading him a quotation from Wilhelm Stekel, a psychoanalyst who was the colleague of Freud and Jung and the author of numerous works expressing his theories on the relationship between infantilism and maturity.[8] "'The mark of the immature man is that he wants to die nobly for a cause,'" Mr. Antolini cites, "'while the mark of the mature man is that he wants to live humbly for one'" (p. 244). Holden's immaturity on this point is apparent: As the catcher in the rye, he sees himself risking his own life (in fact denying it through his refusal to grow up and through his wish to keep other children from doing so) on the edge of the "crazy cliff." His conception is an overdramatized vision of himself as a "savior," nobly sacrificing himself for the sake of preserving what he takes to be the innocent and the good. What he needs is to find something he can *live* for, instead of something he wants to die for.

At the center of Holden's difficulties is the dangerous symbolism of childhood and its innocence. His disgust with the adult world is so great that he is blinded to the realities of childhood. Infantile sexuality was once considered one of the most shocking aspects of Freudian thought. And one does not have to be a social worker to know that children often delight in writing the words on walls that Holden finds so offensive. Even Phoebe is depicted as being much more worldly than Holden perceives her as being. For example, she indicates that she knows quite clearly what is going on when a boy in her class, Curtis Weintraub, persists in following her around. What Holden must come to understand is that the scriptures do not say that one can become a child again—or even that it is ever possible, even when a child, to be what the word implies. Sin and corruption are too much with us from the day we are born. But we can become *like* a child in believing in the *possibility* of goodness despite the obscenity that surrounds us.

Coming to such a realization is by no means easy, for even in the midst of truth one must deal with corruption. Holden's experience with Mr. Antolini is a case in point. Mr. Antolini illuminates Holden's life, but Mr. Antolini's own life is representative of the kind of "maturity" that is shallow and phony in itself. He has married an older woman for her money, and it is apparent that he does not love her. He is an alcoholic, and he is drunk when he is talking to Holden. His practical suggestion concerning Holden's future is a lame and unthinking defense of "applying" oneself in school and pursuing a conventional academic career. And in the middle of the night, as Holden is asleep on the couch, Mr. Antolini makes a homosexual advance toward him. All of this provides Holden with an emblem of what the adult world he has fallen into is like—the true and the obscene all mixed together. "The more I thought about it, though, the more depressed and screwed up about it I got" (p. 253), he concludes when he wakes up the next morning in the waiting room of Grand Central Station.

Thought is not going to be any help to him. When he first starts talking to Mr. Antolini, he indicates that, subconsciously at least, he senses this. He is trying to explain to Mr. Antolini why he flunked his class in oral expression at Pencey. The teacher, Mr. Vinson, spent most of his time arguing the importance of sticking to the point and avoiding digression. The trouble with this idea, Holden maintains, is that he likes listening to a speech better when someone digresses. He says this of Mr. Vinson: "He could drive you crazy sometimes, him and the goddam class. I mean he'd keep telling you to *unify* and *simplify* all the time. Some things you just can't *do* that to" (p. 240). The same thing is true of Holden's own story—it is not unified and simplified; it is in itself an extended digression leading in fits and starts toward a movement of illumination that is not the result of logical, ordered thought.

This has made for problems in reading *The Catcher in the Rye*, because the logic of the conclusion is present only metaphorically. Like the lunatic in the tombs, Holden goes through an exorcism that works, but he is not quite certain how it has worked. He leaves the waiting room and is suddenly surrounded by the trappings of Christmas—Santa Clauses on every streetcorner and displays in the stores. As he walks, he sees some workmen unloading a Christmas tree off a truck, one of them saying to the other, "Hold the sonuvabitch *up!* Hold it *up,* for Chrissake!" (p. 255). Holden starts to laugh and then he is overcome by nausea—his dual reaction to the duality of the world. As the humor in his monologue shows, Holden perceives the comic nature of human life, yet this comedy is often the result of a depressing juxtaposition of the sacred and the profane, a juxtaposition that is central to Salinger's art. As Ihab Hassan has stressed, "Revulsion and holiness make up the rack on which Salinger's art still twitches."[9] How to maintain a sense of the holy in the midst of obscenity is what Holden's character development is all about.

As he walks up Fifth Avenue, he experiences an hallucination that brings together all of his anxieties at once. Every time he comes to the end of a block and steps off the curb, he has the feeling that he will never get to the other side of the street; he will fall off the curb and disappear. He begins to pray to his brother, Allie, not to let him disappear. In the midst of his anxieties over fate and death, emptiness and meaninglessness, guilt and condemnation, and despair, he appeals to Allie to save him, yet the memories of Allie and the seeming sacrilege of his death embody all of those anxieties in themselves. What he is actually praying for is a means of saving himself from himself through himself.

He rests for a time sweating on a park bench and thinks about escaping by hitchhiking out west and getting a job working at a filling station. He would pretend to be a deaf-mute so he would not have to talk to anyone, and he would live by himself out in the woods in a log cabin. This is both a theme and a means of escape that runs through American literature—and through the adolescent mind. Holden, in what turns out to be the last gasp of his rebellion, buys the idea. He decides that he will go away, that he would never go home again, and that he would never go to another school. But first he must say good-by to Phoebe. He goes to her school and leaves a note telling her that he is leaving town and that she should meet him at the Museum of Natural History at quarter past twelve if she can.

While he is waiting for her, he goes into his favorite room in the museum—the mummies' tomb. He likes the room because it is always the same, just as he would like his world to be (it is significant that the only thing that interested him in his history course at Pencey is the ancient Egyptians' secret of preservation). But then, in what leads to a moment of revelation, he notices an obscenity written with a child's red crayon on the wall. "That's the whole trouble," he finally realizes. "You can't ever find a place that's nice and peaceful, because there isn't any. You may *think* there is, but once you get there, when you're not looking, somebody'll sneak up and write 'Fuck you' right under your nose" (p. 264). He even concludes that when he dies, someone will write "Fuck you" on his tombstone. Right away he is sickened and goes to the toilet, where he passes out and falls to the floor. This fall, which results from his realization of the essential obscenity of life itself, is the one he has been dreading, the fall from adolescence into adulthood. But he survives, although he is not sure why. "I was lucky, though," he says. "I mean I could've killed myself when I hit the floor, but all I did was sort of land on my side. It was a funny thing, though. I felt better after I passed out. I really did" (p. 265).

This is a lucky fall, a "fortunate" fall. Only through coming to terms with the fallen nature of the world through his own fall can Holden achieve release. And in the next scene, when he goes to the zoo with Phoebe and sits on a bench in the park watching her ride the carrousel, we see that he has left his idea of being the catcher in the rye behind. "All the kids kept trying to grab for the gold ring, and so was old Phoebe," he says quietly, "and I was sort of afraid she'd fall off the goddam horse, but I didn't say anything or do anything. The thing with kids is, if they want to grab for the gold ring, you have to let them do it, and not say anything. If they fall off, they fall off, but it's bad if you say anything to them" (pp. 274–275). And suddenly Holden is surrounded by symbols that suggest rebirth, blessing, and hopefulness. It is raining, it is Christmas, and in the carrousel's circular movement he obtains a true and vital vision of eternity to replace his old lunatic's love for the mummies' tombs.

In the epilogue, we learn that Holden did finally go home, that he got sick, and that he wound up out in California in the psychiatric ward—an ending that at first seems to be another digression or, much worse, that contradicts the joyous scene at the zoo with Phoebe and the carrousel. But the final chapter works to show the progress Holden has made in moving toward authenticity and understanding the essential question that is behind every good novel: What is the nature of reality? The answer resides in the dynamic relationship between childhood and maturity, between the static and the changeable, between thought and action, and between the outer and inner worlds—a reality that is "an existentialist datum of physical and emotional experience."[10] This datum, which has its immediate basis in Christian thought, finds its ultimate rationale in Buddhism—a crucial point in understanding the end of the novel, an ending that points directly to *Nine Stories*.

One of the mistakes in reading *The Catcher in the Rye* is to assume, since Holden is under the treatment of a psychoanalyst, that the novel closes with some unsettled psychoanalytical questions concerning Holden's experiences and his future. This is not the case at all. Holden has been sick, but he has already been cured, and the resources of his personality are strong at the end, so strong that it is he, not the psychoanalyst, who possesses the insights. This can be seen in the three seemingly puzzling statements he makes in the final chapter. The first is when he responds to the doctor's question of whether or not he is going to apply himself when he goes back to school, by saying, "I mean how do you know what you're going to do till you *do* it?" (p. 276). The second is when his brother, D.B., asks him what he thinks about the story he has just finished telling, and Holden replies, "If you want to know the truth, I don't *know* what I think about it" (pp. 276–277). And the third is when he ends by saying that he misses everybody he told about, even the pimp who beat him up after a pathetic encounter with a prostitute at the Edmont Hotel, and adds, "Don't ever tell anybody anything. If you do, you start missing everybody" (p. 277). The meaning of these statements may be puzzling, but their purpose is not: They are intended as Zen riddles or *koan,* designed to present intellectual impasses that serve to indicate, sharpen, and define the elusiveness and indefinability of life. As Alan W. Watts explains it in *The Way of Zen,* "when the disciple comes to the final point where the *koan* absolutely refuses to be grasped, he comes also to the realization that life can never be grasped, never possessed or made to stay still. Whereupon he 'lets go,' and this letting go is the acceptance of life *as* life. . . ."[11] This is the insight, the illumination Holden has reached by the time his story is over and he has left his precept-laden anxieties behind.

Holden is thus not, as many of Salinger's critics have maintained, a tragic figure, a victim of modern society. He is not mentally defeated at the end, and he has surprisingly come to terms with the world in which he must live. Salinger's gospel is a positive one, showing "how exposure of the sensitive soul to the darkness of this present age can lead not only to sickness but also to healing."[12] ⟨. . .⟩

It is Salinger's use of language that is one of the most distinctive qualities of *The Catcher in the Rye,* and an analysis of that language is essential to an appreciation of just what Salinger accomplishes artistically in the novel. If we look at the language in isolation, it is crude, profane, and obscene—by the standards of most people even in 1979 as well as in 1951. But if we look at the language and its relationship to the overall effect of the novel, another conclusion emerges. "Given the point of view from which the novel is told," Edward P. J. Corbett argues in a sensible article on the whole matter of *The Catcher in the Rye* and censorship, "and given the kind of character that figures as the hero, no other language was possible. The integrity of the novel demanded such language."[13] It is not simply a matter of realizing that Holden's language·would not seem at all unusual or shocking to a real-life prep-school boy. His swearing is habitual and so unconsciously ritualistic that it contributes to, rather than diminishes, the theme of innocence that runs through the novel. In addition, Holden is characterized by a "desperate bravado"[14]—he wants to appear older than he is, and his rough language fits in with his concept of the corrupt adult world.

Holden's way of talking is, it must be realized, a device. Salinger is not directly interested in merely depicting the way a boy like Holden would actually speak—no more than Mark Twain was attempting to be "realistic" in the literal sense when he invented an idiom for Huckleberry Finn (an important thing to remember here is that Twain's novel, like Salinger's, was widely castigated for its language and even banned because of it). "Neither J. D. Salinger nor Mark Twain really 'copied' anything," Heiserman and Miller remind us. "Their books would be unreadable had they merely recorded intact the language of a real-life Huck and a real-life Holden. Their genius lies in their mastery of the technique of first-person narration which, through meticulous selection, creates vividly the illusion of life: gradually and subtly their narrators emerge and stand revealed, stripped to their innermost beings."[15] Or, as Mary McCarthy has observed, "The artless dialect is an artful ventriloquial trick of Salinger's, like the deliberate halting English of Hemingway's waiters, fishermen, and peasants—anyone who speaks it is a good guy, a friend of the author's, to be trusted."[16]

Salinger's genius does derive in large part from his ability as a literary ventriloquist. He is a writer concerned with messages, with stressing moral points, and suggesting ways to move from despair to illumination. Holden Caulfield thus comes to embody Salinger's thought, but the language Salinger chooses to give him is so artfully controlled that the voice seems to come from some other source than the author. The problem a ventriloquist must always get around is to make his audience forget that the figure on his knee is just a wooden dummy, not "real," and this is what Salinger succeeds in doing in *The Catcher in the Rye*—something that does not always happen in his later work, where it is often all too apparent that he is carrying on a pretended conversation with characters who are only lovable puppets.

But even though Holden's language is artful pretense, it never seems pretended. Donald P. Costello in his thorough and insightful study of Salinger's use of language in the novel has uncovered some of the reasons why this is so.[17] First of all, Salinger does know enough about authentic teenage speech to establish a basic level of believability that he never departs from in the novel. Holden never says anything that he conceivably could not have said. Salinger manages, however, to individualize Holden through having him make use of certain repetitions in an unusually significant way. Like other teenagers of his time and place, Holden repeats *and all* and *I really did,* as well as the famous, *if you want to know the truth.* But these repetitions have a purpose beyond simple realism. Holden repeats *I really did* to establish that he is not a phony. He repeats *and all* because of his eventual mystic ability to find the all in the one as he moves toward his final vision. And he repeats *if you want to know the truth* because that is what the book at last is about.

A second point about Salinger's language is that Holden's speech at first seems to be typical schoolboy vulgarity. But a closer look reveals that it is actually restrained to indicate Holden's sensitivity. After all, Holden is offended by certain uses of coarse language. The word *fuck* appears four times, but it is never a part of Holden's speech. Holden uses *goddam* often, but never the more offensive *Jesus Christ* or even *for Chrissake* except in repeating the speech of others. One soon notices that the crudity of language increases when Holden is reporting what others say and decreases significantly when he directly addresses the reader.

A third point concerns something Salinger has in common with Sinclair Lewis—

his love for slang words and expressions. But unlike Lewis's work, Salinger's does not seem strikingly dated in its reliance on jargon, because the slang words Salinger selects are narrow in choice and carefully repeated—words like *lousy, pretty, crumby, terrific, quite, old*, and *stupid*. The repetition of identical words and expressions in different situations is, however, humorous and also shows the American characteristic of adapting nouns into adjectives and nouns into adverbs. He turns nouns into adverbs simply by adding a *y*, and we have *vomity-looking, show-offy, pimpy*, and *perverty*. Perhaps more distinctive is his ability to use nouns as adverbs: "She sings it very Dixieland and whorehouse, and it doesn't sound at all mushy" (p. 149).

But Holden is no mere illiterate adolescent. He reveals his education in the way he discourses on two levels at once. He uses, for example, the colloquial *take a leak* at one time and then the more genteel *relieve himself* at another—a shift in word-choice that contributes to the humor in the novel. Like a typical kid his age might do, Holden does violate some rules of grammar. He consistently misuses *lie* and *lay*, is uncertain about relative pronouns, and is a devotee of the double negative. But he is extremely conscious of his own speech and is especially critical of the language of others. His character builds through this consciousness, and his eventual self-awareness is made more acceptable through his ability to recognize the phony, the untrue, in his objections to the overuse of such words as *grand, prince, traveling incognito*, and *little girls' room*. And it is often forgotten that Holden, in revealing his character, is *speaking*, not writing. If he were writing, his grammatical mistakes would be fewer and he would never write so many fragments.

A close look at the language in *The Catcher in the Rye* leads to a conclusion stated memorably by Costello: "The language of *The Catcher in the Rye* is an authentic rendering of a type of informal, colloquial, teenage American spoken speech. It is strongly typical and trite, yet often somewhat individual; it is crude and slangy and imprecise, imitative yet occasionally imaginative, and affected toward standardization by the strong efforts of schools. But authentic and interesting as this language may be, it must be remembered that it exists . . . as only one part of an artistic achievement."[18] But it is certainly a powerful part of Salinger's artistry and is a reminder of how careful a writer he is. His relatively small output is not due to a limited imagination; it is more likely due to his extreme care in choosing the words he is going to use.

Salinger's attitudes toward language further suggest a conceptual relationship between him and the philosopher of what was called the school of Linguistic Analysis, Ludwig Wittgenstein (1889–1951), an Austrian who did much of his work at Oxford University. Wittgenstein concluded that there is no discoverable reality outside of language, that we live in a world of words that is much more important to us than the illusory world of facts we think we live in. He reached the point where he even argued that the human desire to understand the world is an outdated folly because there is an impenetrable veil between the world of words and the world of fact. Wittgenstein's ideas are hardly easy and they cannot be easily applied to Salinger, but Holden Caulfield does live in a world of words, and the memory one has of *The Catcher in the Rye* is less of what Holden describes about the world of facts than of how his description is in itself a world of words.

An interesting sidenote about Wittgenstein is that his development and personality bear some resemblance to Salinger's. Wittgenstein was austere and ascetic, known for his integrity and, after he gave up professing at Oxford, achieved a reputation as something of an intellectual saint. He began as an engineering student, but he moved from science to philosophy through the study of religion. In the years after World War I, Wittgenstein was greatly influenced by Tolstoy's religious writings and became a simple village schoolmaster, even thinking about becoming a monk (one thinks of Holden's question to Ackley about what it takes to join a monastery).

But whatever the relationship between the two, both Salinger and Wittgenstein, in line with contemporary "structuralist" linguistics, stress the importance of language dimensions in understanding the nature of reality. We are, they both seem to agree, the prisoners of our language, an irrational structure from which we cannot escape. We think largely as language directs us to think, a process we can observe clearly as we read *The Catcher in the Rye*. Holden is so dominated by his language that he *is*, indeed, his language. He is deposited in a strange world of which he can make no sense and from which he seems cut off. But through his scrutiny of language, through his scrutiny of the structure that *thinks him*, he plays a series of word games that endow his condition with meaning. This is what the *koans* at the end of the book come down to. And a good part of Salinger's achievement in the novel is the way the book works to elucidate the language of everyday life.

The climate of ideas surrounding *The Catcher in the Rye* is, as even a brief consideration of the theories of language in the novel suggests, more dense, more diverse, than was realized when the book was published. While it is dangerous to argue that *The Catcher in the Rye* derives from any particular earlier work or school of thought, it does, in many ways, embody the general intellectual interests of the 1950s. There was, for instance, considerable interest in anthropology and psychology in the decade. Margaret Mead's *Coming of Age in Samoa* (1928) and Ruth Benedict's *Patterns of Culture* (1934) became popular and influential when they appeared as paperbacks after World War II. Depth psychology, with its emphasis on the unconscious and the impact of myth, ritual, and archetype on the theory of instincts and man's primordial nature, shows up in Joseph Campbell's *The Hero with a Thousand Faces* (1949), C. G. Jung's *Psychology and Alchemy* (1953), Lionel Trilling's *Freud and the Crisis of Our Culture* (1955), and Otto Rank's *The Myth and Birth of the Hero* (1959). Holden Caulfield's story is not only told against a background of myth and archetype (like Ulysses, he is on a quest, and at the end of the novel we see him going through a symbolic death and resurrection), it is also an anthropological study of the rites of passage from adolescence into adulthood for an American youth of Holden's type.

It has often been assumed that, because of the internalization of plot in *The Catcher in the Rye*, the novel is not much of a reflection of its times nor much of a commentary on the society from which it emerges. Maxwell Geismar makes such an objection when he writes, "Just as the hero's interest in the ancient Egyptians extends only to the fact that they created mummies, so Salinger's own view of his hero's environment omits any reference to its real nature and dynamics."[19] This is hardly the case. *The Catcher in the Rye* should be seen as one of many books published in the postwar era that serve as significant cultural criticism of conformity in a mass society. Alfred Kinsey in his two works, works that were even more controversial than *The Catcher in the Rye, Sexual Behavior of the American Male* (1948) and *Sexual Behavior of the American Female* (1953), raises, through statistical study, the whole question of sexual normality. Holden's concern over still being a virgin at age sixteen and his admission that his sexual experience has been retarded would have been seen against the background of the Kinsey report by Salinger's readers in the 1950s. The same thing is true of Salinger's indirect but nonetheless constant commentary on how money is made and how success is achieved in America. Holden's attitude toward D.B.'s sell-out to Hollywood, his reluctance to even consider becoming a lawyer like his father, and the ridicule he directs at the distinguished Pencey alumnus who made a fortune through establishing a chain of cut-rate funeral parlors, all point toward similar criticisms of American democracy in C. Wright Mill's *White Collar* (1951) and *The Power Elite* (1956), William H. Whyte's *The Organization Man* (1956), Vance Packard's *The Hidden Persuaders* (1957), and John Kenneth Galbraith's *The Affluent Society* (1958).

But of all the books of this sort, the one that is most closely tied to *The Catcher in the Rye* is David Riesman's *The Lonely Crowd* (1950). Like Salinger, Riesman deals with the peculiar and often contradictory pressures to conform exerted upon the individual by a mass society. Riesman invented two terms that were very much discussed during the 1950s—"inner direction" and "outer direction." The first term indicates the character taught to children in the nineteenth century when the most important social aim was production. At a time when most goods were produced by individuals or small manufacturers, self-reliance, self-assurance, and an inflexible set of principles were the necessary virtues for success. The puritan ethic is an example. As Riesman writes, "the source of direction for the individual is 'inner' in the sense that it is implanted early in life by the elders and directed toward generalized but nonetheless inescapably destined goals."[20] But since about 1920, the productive process has been taken over by machines owned by giant corporations. Success suddenly demanded a more flexible and compromising personality. The nineteenth-century man who took pride in being able "to go it on his own" and "to be as honest as the day is long" had little place in the executive structure of a manufacturing conglomerate. What was needed was someone who could "play the game," who could "get along with others," who could "fit in." This person was "other-directed" in that others, his contemporaries, his friends, neighbors, and business associates are his source of direction, and his goals shift as the signals he picks up from others shift. The social pressures that serve to create an "other-directed" personality are reinforced by economic pressures to be a good consumer of what the machines have produced. Being a good consumer means being sensitive to one's neighbors; keeping up with the Joneses means becoming aware of whatever new consumer product is going to bring status. And this, of course, makes the "other-directed" person especially vulnerable to the mass media, which is constantly redefining which product, which style, which look, and even which ideas are the most prestigious.

While Riesman does not argue that the "other-directed" personality is necessarily bad for the future of civilization and that a return to the rigidity of nineteenth-century values is desirable, he does develop a conception of modern corporate society into which the dilemma of Holden Caulfield fits. One of Riesman's main concerns in *The Lonely Crowd* is with the difficulties "other direction" brought on in child raising. "Inner direction" implied certainties in the spheres of work and social relations that made bringing up children easier. Children were once raised to move easily and without trauma from childhood into adulthood, from the world of play into the world of work, because their play was directed toward production, and where it stopped being play and suddenly became work was undefinable. The blacksmith's son begins, for example, by playing in the shop, and soon he is helping. An important point to consider here is that in the nineteenth century, the ideas of "teenager" and "adolescent" were not at all current. But in an "other-directed" society, the movement from childhood to adulthood is seldom a smooth one because there is a built-in dissonance.

Without an "inner direction" to implant in their children, parents are forced to encourage them to develop "outer direction" through extensive and "permissive" contact with other children from nursery school and even earlier. Just how early was emphasized in Dr. Benjamin Spock's best-selling *Baby and Child Care* (1946). Spock taught that there are no problem children, only problem parents, and he repudiated the rigid schedules that almost all previous child-care books had endorsed. Instead, he claimed that children should be fed according to their own rhythms. They should not be taught certain skills, such as reading and writing, until they are ready. And it is important that they be given the opportunity to learn from each other, not only from authority figures. The result was the "open" classroom where children supposedly developed their personalities in a relaxed and friendly atmosphere with the teachers serving as opinion leaders.

One difficulty eventually comes up, however. The new approach to childraising and education tried, as much as possible, to keep children free from rigid timetables. But the corporation cannot allow people to remain children for long; it can permit permissiveness only up to a point. Eventually it is no longer socially functional to encourage independence. Sooner or later, the child will be asked to join an economic system that is rigidly defined, that is run according to timeclocks, working days, and production quotas. But what if the children do not want to? What if they rebel? What if they refuse to become organization men? When that happens, a character like Holden Caulfield emerges.

Holden refuses to relate to others the way his society with its idea of "other direction" would have him do. He refuses to go to the football game and cheer his heart out for old Pencey the way most of his fellow students do. He refuses to participate in his classes the way he is expected to. He rejects the attitudes toward sex that he is supposed to learn from the more experienced Stradlater. And he buys and wears a red deer-hunting cap not because it is the fashion or because he has been encouraged by advertising to buy it; he wears it simply because *he* thinks he looks good in it. He is uncomfortable in his twentieth-century social setting and the demands it places on him, and it is his desire to return to the older, "inner-directed" world (his dream is to go out west and live in a log cabin the way people used to do in the nineteenth century). He cannot actually do this, but his enlightenment and apparent peace at the end is the result of an "inner" process that leads to a way of resisting the conformity that his parents, his schools, and his doctors have been trying to encourage him to accept.

Holden's suspicion of and final rejection of "other-directed" society can be seen no better than in his sarcasm concerning movies in the novel. Holden indicates that he likes to read, and lists a fairly impressive selection of favorite books ranging from Thomas Hardy's *The Return of the Native* to Isak Dinesen's *Out of Africa*. Reading is associated with the era of inner-direction; it is something Holden does all by himself. Movie-going is another matter. Even if one attends alone, the viewing is a communal matter. The experience itself depends on the reactions of other people in the audience; it is a matter of "other direction." Holden's dislike of the movies is not so much of the films themselves as it is of the way he sees other people reacting to them. He is relieved when he does not have to go to the movie with Brossard and Ackley the night he leaves Pencey. "I didn't care about not seeing the movie, anyway," he explains. "It was supposed to be a comedy, with Cary Grant in it, and all that crap. Besides, I'd been to the movies with Brossard and Ackley before. They both laughed like hyenas at stuff that wasn't even funny. I didn't even enjoy sitting next to them in the movies" (p. 48). His reaction is much the same when, to kill some time the next day in New York, he goes to the movies at Radio City. The movie, he says, is "putrid" but what really bothers him is that the woman sitting next to him cries all the way through it. "The phonier it got, the more she cried," he complains. "You'd have thought she did it because she was kindhearted as hell, but I was sitting right next to her, and she wasn't. She had this little kid with her that was bored as hell and had to go to the bathroom, but she wouldn't take him. She kept telling him to sit still and behave himself. She was about as kindhearted as a goddam wolf. You take somebody that cries their goddam eyes out over phony stuff in the movies, and nine times out of ten they're mean bastards at heart. I'm not kidding" (p. 181).

In his suspicions of the movies and other forms of other-directed mass media, Holden is a rebel against what he takes to be a life-threatening phoniness in his society. His suspicion can be seen as part of the generalized paranoia that accompanied the McCarthy era, the Korean War, and the fear of atomic attack that produced the so-called "silent generation" of gray-flannel conformists. But Holden is not silent. His monologue is a noisy one that proclaims an alternative, a way of defying and even escaping from other-directed mass society by learning to perceive reality from the inside, by learning how to find meaning from within.

The influence of Holden's example on an entire generation of readers is impossible to measure, but it is difficult to ignore in considering the development of the "counterculture" of white American youth in the 1960s. The conventional virtues they rejected—competitive masculinity, military supremacy, and the emphasis on self-discipline in order to channel energy into economic achievement—are all virtues rejected by Holden. And the belief that non-Western thought could provide humanizing answers that centuries of Christianity and European philosophy had not is as much a part of Salinger and *The Catcher in the Rye* as it is of the Beat movement. Like Gary Snyder, Salinger suggests the use of Zen Buddhism as a means of discipline necessary to cleanse the mind of certain untruths promoted by mass culture in America. Holden Caulfield's long digression is a pilgrimage to find meaning, one he has doubtless encouraged others to follow on the path back to a revitalized sense of inner direction.

But however extensive the influence of Salinger's most notorious character, he is a major reason for Salinger's fame and popularity. In the real and relevant idiom of Holden, Salinger caught and dissected modern society through a symbolic structure of language, motif, and episode that is as masterful as anything in contemporary literature. *The Catcher in the Rye* is a novel that fights obscenity with an amazing and divine mixture of vulgarity and existential anguish, and it does this through a style that moves the narrative effortlessly along on a colloquial surface that suddenly parts to reveal the terror and beauty of the spiritual drama that Holden enacts. It may be Salinger's only novel, but it is still one of the best we have.

NOTES

[1] J. D. Salinger, *The Catcher in the Rye* (Boston: Little, Brown, 1951). All subsequent page references are to this edition.
[2] Dan Wakefield, "The Search for Love," in *Salinger: A Critical and Personal Portrait,* ed. Henry Anatole Grunwald (New York: Harper & Row, 1962), p. 180.
[3] Arthur Heiserman and James E. Miller, Jr., "Some Crazy Cliff," in *Salinger: A Critical and Personal Portrait,* p. 197.
[4] See *If You Really Want to Know: A Catcher Casebook,* ed. Malcolm M. Marsden (Chicago: Scott, Foresman, 1963) for a collection of articles on the Holden-Huck relationship.
[5] Mario D'Avanzo, "Gatsby and Holden Caulfield," *Fitzgerald Newsletter,* Summer 1967, pp. 4–6.
[6] Frederick L. Gwynn and Joseph L. Blotner, *The Fiction of J. D. Salinger* (Pittsburgh: University of Pittsburgh Press, 1958), p. 47.
[7] Robert G. Jacobs, "J. D. Salinger's *The Catcher in the Rye:* Holden Caulfield's 'Goddam Autobiography,'" *Iowa English Yearbook,* Fall 1959, p. 13.

[8] Stekel's best known work in an English translation is probably *Peculiarities of Behavior: Wandering Mania, Dipsomania, Pyromania and Allied Impulsive Acts* (New York, 2 vols., 1924 and 1943).

[9] Ihab Hassan, *Radical Innocence: Studies in the Contemporary American Novel* (Princeton: Princeton University Press, 1961), p. 288.

[10] Carl F. Strauch, "Kings in the Back Row," in *If You Really Want to Know: A* Catcher *Casebook*, p. 115.

[11] Alan W. Watts, *The Way of Zen* (New York: Pantheon, 1957), p. 75.

[12] Kenneth Hamilton, *J. D. Salinger: A Critical Essay* (Grand Rapids, Mich.: Eerdmans, 1967), p. 39.

[13] Edward P. J. Corbett, "Raise High the Barriers, Censors," in *J. D. Salinger and the Critics*, ed. William F. Belcher and James W. Lee (Belmont, Cal.: Wadsworth, 1962), p. 55.

[14] Corbett, p. 56.

[15] Arthur Heiserman and James E. Miller, Jr., "Some Crazy Cliff," in *Salinger: A Critical and Personal Portrait*, p. 203.

[16] Mary McCarthy, "J. D. Salinger's Closed Circuit," *Harper's*, October 1962, p. 46.

[17] Donald P. Costello, "The Language of *The Catcher in the Rye*," in *Salinger: A Critical and Personal Portrait*, pp. 266–276. I am indebted to Costello for much of the discussion of Salinger's language that follows.

[18] Costello, p. 276.

[19] Maxwell Geismar, "The Wise Child and the *New Yorker* School of Fiction," in *If You Really Want to Know: A* Catcher *Casebook*, p. 44.

[20] David Riesman, *The Lonely Crowd: A Study of the Changing American Character* (New Haven: Yale University Press, 1950), p. 15.

Edwin Haviland Miller

IN MEMORIAM:
ALLIE CAULFIELD

Although J. D. Salinger's *Catcher in the Rye* deserves the affection and accolades it has received since its publication in 1951, whether it has been praised for the right reasons is debatable. Most critics have tended to accept Holden's evaluation of the world as phony, when in fact his attitudes are symptomatic of a serious psychological problem. Thus instead of treating the novel as a commentary by an innocent young man rebelling against an insensitive world or as a study of a youth's moral growth,[1] I propose to read *Catcher in the Rye* as the chronicle of a four-year period in the life of an adolescent whose rebelliousness is his only means of dealing with his inability to come to terms with the death of his brother. Holden Caulfield has to wrestle not only with the usual difficult adjustments of the adolescent years, in sexual, familial and peer relationships; he has also to bury Allie before he can make the transition into adulthood.[2]

Life stopped for Holden on July 18, 1946, the day his brother died of leukemia. Holden was then thirteen, and four years later—the time of the narrative—he is emotionally still at the same age, although he has matured into a gangly six-foot adolescent. "I was sixteen then," he observes concerning his expulsion from Pencey Prep at Christmas time in 1949, "and I'm seventeen now, and some times I act like I'm about thirteen."[3]

On several occasions Holden comments that his mother has never gotten over Allie's death, which may or may not be an accurate appraisal of Mrs. Caulfield, since the first-person narrative makes it difficult to judge. What we can deduce, though, is that it is an accurate appraisal of Holden's inability to accept loss, and that in his eyes his mother is so preoccupied with Allie that she continues to neglect Holden, as presumably she did when Allie was dying.

The night after Allie's death Holden slept in the garage and broke "all the goddam windows with my fist, just for the hell of it. I even tried to break all the windows on the station wagon we had that summer, but my hand was already

From *Mosaic* 15, No. 1 (Winter 1982): 129–40.

broken and everything by that time, and I couldn't do it. It was a very stupid thing to do, I'll admit, but I hardly didn't even know I was doing it, and you didn't know Allie" (p. 39). The act may have been "stupid"—which is one of his pet words to denigrate himself as well as others—but it also reflects his uncontrollable anger, at himself for wishing Allie dead and at his brother for leaving him alone and burdened with feelings of guilt. Similarly, the attack on the station wagon may be seen as his way of getting even with a father who was powerless either to save Allie or to understand Holden. Because he was hospitalized, he was unable to attend the funeral, to witness the completion of the life process, but by injuring himself he received the attention and sympathy which were denied him during Allie's illness. His actions here as elsewhere are inconsistent and ambivalent, but always comprehensible in terms of his reaction to the loss of Allie.

So too is Holden's vocabulary an index to his disturbed emotional state—for all that it might seem to reflect the influence of the movies or his attempts to imitate the diction of his older brother, D.B. At least fifty times, something or somebody *depresses* him—an emotion which he frequently equates with a sense of isolation: "It makes you feel so lonesome and depressed" (p. 81). Although the reiteration of the word reveals the true nature of his state, no one in the novel recognizes the signal, perceiving the boy as a kind of adolescent clown rather than as a seriously troubled youth. As his depression deepens to the point of nervous breakdown, furthermore, Holden—who at some level of awareness realizes that he is falling apart—seeks to obscure the recognition by referring to everything as "crazy" and by facetiously likening himself to a "madman."

"Crap," another word he uses repeatedly, is similarly self-reflexive. Although it is his ultimate term of reductionism for describing the world, like "crazy" it serves to identify another of his projections. He feels dirty and worthless, and so makes the world a reflection of his self-image. Similarly, if he continually asserts, almost screams, that the phony world makes him want to "puke," it is because Holden's world itself has turned to vomit. In his troubled, almost suicidal state he can incorporate nothing, and, worse, he believes there is nothing for him to incorporate. In turn, the significance of his repeated use of variations on the phrase "that killed me" becomes almost self-evident: reflecting his obsession with death, it tells the unsuspecting world that he wishes himself dead, punished and then reunited with Allie.

Although his consistently negative and hostile language thus reflects Holden's despair and is his way of informing the world of his plight, if no one listens it is primarily his own fault. For with the usual fumbling of the hurt he has chosen a means which serves his purposes poorly. While his language may serve to satisfy his need to act out his anger, at the same time it serves to isolate and to punish him further. If in his hostile phrases he is calling for help, he makes certain that he does not receive it. Ashamed of his need—a sixteen-year-old crying for emotional support—and unable to accept kindness since in his guilt he feels he does not deserve it, Holden is locked into his grief and locked out of family and society.

In this respect, the first paragraph of *Catcher in the Rye* is one of the most deceptively revealing possible. Although Holden, the would-be sophisticate, relegates his familial background to "David Copperfield kind of crap," he talks about little else except his "lousy childhood." Arguing that he will not divulge family secrets so as not to cause pain, and pretending to respect the feelings of his parents, he verbally mutilates them, and in an ugly way; but if he is to suffer, so must they. He retaliates in kind, not in kindness. Yet the aggressive, assertive tone masks a pitiful, agonized call for emotional support and love.

Equally revealing of Holden's problem is his observation, as he stands alone on a hill that cold December, his last day at Pencey Prep, looking down at the football field where his classmates are participating collectively in one of the rites of adolescence: "it was cold as a witch's teat, especially on top of that stupid hill" (p. 4). What he wants is the good mother's breast. And why he needs this maternal comfort so much is implicitly suggested when he descends the hill to say good-by to his history teacher, who cannot understand why in answering a question about Egyptian history on an examination Holden should have begun and ended with a description of the preservation of mummies. The teacher cannot know that Holden has no interest in the Egyptians, only in what happened to Allie, and that he cannot focus on ancient history until he has come to terms with his own past. Nor can he know that Holden has misinterpreted as rejection his father's concern for his future, that the boy wants to be at home, and that to accomplish his goal he has failed in four different schools.

But lest one think that this insensitivity is a fault of the older generation, Salinger next portrays the response of one of Holden's peers to the first of a number of roles he will play in his desperate attempt to disguise his obsession with Allie's death, on the one hand, and his need for parental comfort, on the other. Thus when Holden pulls his red hunting cap over his eyes and says histrionically, "I think I'm going blind. . . . Mother darling, everything's getting so *dark* in here. . . . Mother darling, give me your *hand*," the response of his classmate is: "You're nuts. . . . For Chrissake, grow up" (pp. 21–22). Ackley cannot know that Holden assumes Allie's red hair when he puts on the red cap, that the simulated blindness is descriptive of Holden's state, or that he uses the script as a (futile) means of asking for the maternal hand that he believes has been denied to him.

If Ackley does not appreciate the extent to which the death of Holden's red-haired brother informs his posturing, even less is his room-mate Stradlater aware of the chain of associations that he sets off when he asks Holden to write a composition for him. Unable to write about a "room or a house" Holden writes about Allie's baseball mitt—an object which is a complex version of a child's security blanket, a sacred relic of the living dead, at the same time that it reminds Holden of betrayal. And thus as he writes about the mitt, we learn directly for the first time of Allie's death and of Holden's self-punishing rage.

By coincidence, Stradlater has a date that evening with Jane Gallagher, the girl to whom Holden had shown the glove in a combined attempt to sympathize with her for her unhappy childhood and to solicit her sympathy for himself. Worried that Stradlater will make "time" with an attractive girl with whom Holden plays checkers—the only kind of play of which the self-styled sex maniac is capable—Holden presses to know what has happened on the date. And when Stradlater implies that he got what he wanted, Holden lashes out with the hand he injured on the day of Allie's death. Subsequently pinned to the floor until he promises to stop his ridiculing insults, as soon as he is released, Holden shouts, "You're a dirty stupid sonuvabitch of a moron," and then he receives the blow that subconsciously he wants. "You asked for it, God damn it," Stradlater says, and he is right for reasons he does not understand (pp. 44–45).

And so on his last day at Pencey Prep Holden makes a clean sweep of it: he writes off the school, his chums, and even Jane. There is no Tom Sawyer to rescue him when he eventually quotes Huck Finn: "I felt so lonesome, all of a sudden. I almost wished I was dead" (p. 48). Suddenly Holden decides to leave late that evening even though his family is not expecting him until the following Wednesday. His Mark Cross luggage packed, he is "sort of crying. I don't know why. I put my red hunting hat on, and turned the peak around to the back, the way I liked it, and then I yelled at the top of my goddam voice, 'Sleep tight, ya morons!'" Thus, in his usual hostile fashion, Holden makes sure that he will be rejected. Protected only by the red hat, which he now wears like a baseball catcher as he evokes Allie's favorite sport, he stumbles down the stairs and "damn near broke my crazy neck" (p. 52).

On the train to New York he strikes up a conversation with a Mrs. Morrow, who turns out to be the mother of one of his former classmates. He lies through his teeth praising her son who is "about as sensitive as a goddam toilet seat" (p. 55). But "Mothers are all slightly insane. The thing is, though, I liked old Morrow's mother," who happens to be proud of her moronic son. When she wonders whether Holden is leaving school before the beginning of vacation "because of illness in the family," he casually informs her, "I have this tiny little tumor on the brain" (p. 58). The fib achieves the expected result, Mrs. Morrow's genuine sympathy for an ill "son."

Though Holden plans to spend the next few days in a hotel, he is "so damn absent-minded" that he gives the cab driver his home address. After he realizes his "mistake," they drive through Central Park, and Holden asks the driver whether he knows what happens to the ducks in the pond during the winter. The "madman" replies angrily, "What're ya tryna do, bud? . . . Kid me?" (p. 60). Worried that he has antagonized the man, Holden invites him for a drink. When the driver refuses, Holden, "depressed," retaliates against "father": "He was one of those bald guys that comb all their hair over from the side to cover up the baldness" (p. 61).

In the hotel he is bored but "feeling pretty horny" (p. 63), as a sixteen-year-old is supposed to feel, and he calls up a whore but lets her put him off ("I *really* fouled that up"). Then he thinks of telephoning his sister Phoebe, who "has this sort of red hair, a little bit like Allie's was" (p. 67), but he is afraid his mother will answer. He goes to the bar in the hotel and dances with some older women from Seattle who are in New York to see the celebrities, not to provide Holden with entertainment or solace. He punishes them for neglecting him when he fibs that Gary Cooper has just left the room. On the way to a bar frequented by his older brother D.B., who is now, according to Holden, prostituting himself in Hollywood, he asks a cabby named Horwitz about the ducks in the lagoon in Central Park. Horwitz gets "sore" and counters in a typical New York taxi discussion that "The *fish* don't go no place" (p. 82). Desperate for companionship, Holden invites Horwitz for a drink. The driver refuses and has the last word: "If you was a fish, Mother Nature'd take care of *you,* wouldn't she? Right? You don't think them fish just *die* when it gets to be winter, do ya?" (p. 83). Holden does not comment, but Horwitz unwittingly summarizes the boy's dilemma.

Later, in D.B.'s nightclub Holden glosses over his loneliness by observing the behavior of the phonies in the club, and then rejects the invitation of one of D.B.'s girl friends as others have rejected him. When Holden returns to his hotel, an elevator operator named Maurice sets him up with a call girl, but when "Sunny" arrives, he is "more depressed than sexy" (p. 95), and asks her to stay and talk. He pays her $5.00 and then "depressed" begins "talking, sort of out loud, to Allie" (p. 98).

Maurice returns with Sunny and demands another $5.00 for services not rendered. Holden tries to defend his rights but begins to cry. Sunny wants to leave quietly after she takes money from Holden's wallet, but Maurice "snapped his finger very hard on my pajamas. I won't tell you *where* he snapped it, but it hurt like hell." (The sudden self-protective chastity is an amusing and effective detail.) When Holden calls Maurice "a stupid chiseling moron," for the second time that evening he is smacked, with a "terrific punch" in his stomach (p. 103). Hardly able to breathe, fearing he is drowning, he stumbles toward the bathroom. "Crazy," he acts out a scenario: with a bullet in his gut, he goes down the stairs and puts six shots into Maurice's "fat hairy belly," and then throws the gun down the elevator shaft. He calls up Jane, who comes over and bandages his wound: "I pictured her holding a cigarette for me to smoke while I was bleeding and all." Finally he goes to sleep: "What I really felt like, though, was committing suicide. I felt like jumping out the window. I probably would've done it too"—except for the "stupid rubbernecks" (p. 104).

Holden's protestations to the contrary, the associations in this scene are only superficially from the "goddam movies." Maurice threatens Holden with castration, even though he has not had sex with Sunny, and then pummels him in the stomach. In retaliation Holden commits parricide. In his fantasy he summons Jane, who is associated with Allie through her knowledge of the baseball mitt, and has her play the role of mother.

When Holden thinks of jumping out the window, he is recalling an event which the reader does not learn about until later. A few years earlier Jimmy Castle, a classmate, was so tortured and brutalized, presumably genitally, by a bunch of students that he leaped from a window, wearing Holden's turtleneck sweater. As though Holden is not sufficiently burdened with his unresolved grief for Allie, he has had to cope with this tie to an unfortunate classmate. Sunny, the prostitute, anticipates the appearance of Phoebe, who is both the kid sister and by mythic association the sun goddess. Sunny offers Holden sex, Phoebe will offer him love. Unable to handle sex, Holden wants Sunny to be a confidante, a role which she is unable to handle. Yet she tries unsuccessfully to protect him from Maurice's aggression, which may be Holden's construction of his mother's ineffectual role in the Caulfield household.

At breakfast on the following morning he meets two nun school teachers, and begins a conversation which shortly turns to *Romeo and Juliet*. If the scene with Sunny reveals that Holden is not ready for sexual relationships—he is a "sex maniac" only in his head—his comments on the tragedy solely in terms of Romeo's culpability in Mercutio's death confirm the arrestment. He is attracted to the nuns, or mothers, who remind him of "old Ernest Morrow's mother" (p. 112), but they also remind him that his father was a Catholic until he "married my mother." This leads him to recall some unpleasant associations with Catholics, and when he says good-by to the nuns, "by mistake I blew some smoke in their face. I didn't mean to, but I did it" (p. 113). In atonement for his unkindness Holden makes a symbolic apology to the nuns when he imagines them standing in front of a department store raising money for charity. He tries "to picture my mother or somebody, or my aunt, or Sally Hayes's crazy mother, standing outside some department store and collecting dough for poor people in a beat-up old straw basket. It was hard to picture." Since his "picture" of his mother is too harsh, and anxiety-producing, he guiltily corrects it: "Not so much my mother, but those other two" (p. 114).

Walking along the street, he sees a family coming from church—"a father, a mother, and a little kid about six years old." Holden "sees" the family, but only in terms of his own situation. Without evidence he initially assumes that the parents are neglecting the boy who walks along the curb singing to himself, "If a body catch a body coming through the rye"—or so Holden imagines. For it is doubtful that the six-year-old, if he knows the poem in the first place, duplicates Holden's misreading of the famous lines. What Holden "hears" anticipates the grandiose fantasy he will later relate to Phoebe in which he catches and saves children. For a moment he is charmed with his fantasy of a self-contained kid whose parents are at hand to protect him: "It made me feel not so depressed any more" (p. 115).

In the afternoon Holden escorts Sally Hayes to a Broadway show and goes ice skating at Rockefeller Center. Then they sit down for a chat—about Holden. He pours out his anger at the phony world, and when Sally tries to be sensible, he almost screams at her, "I don't get hardly anything out of anything. I'm in bad shape. I'm in *lousy* shape" (p. 131). Sally can hardly be expected to understand how empty he feels, or know how to respond to his cry for sympathy. Then he proposes what he knows she cannot agree to, that they run off together to New England. When she objects to the scheme, he verbally assaults her but not without self-pity: "she was depressing the hell out of me" (p. 133).

After this rejection, which in his usual fashion he makes inevitable, he tries to lift the depression by evoking earlier, happier days when the Caulfield family was intact. He goes to Radio City Music Hall, where, with the parents in another part of the theater, Allie and he had sat by themselves watching a favorite drummer. But pleasant memories of Allie cannot rescue him, and he goes to a bar to meet a former classmate named Luce. Although Holden wants Luce's companionship and assistance, he subjects him to an offensive, crude interrogation about his sex life. Twice Luce asks, repeating the question put earlier by Ackley, "When are you going to grow up?" (p. 144). After Holden confesses that his sex life "stinks," Luce reminds him that once before he had advised him to see an analyst. At once Holden asks for more information and comes as close as his pride permits to begging for the kind of aid which Luce of course cannot provide. When Luce gets ready to leave for his date, Holden implores, "Have just one more drink. Please. I'm lonesome as hell" (p. 149).

Now "*really* drunk" and wounded, because Luce like the others betrays him, he replays the scenario of "that stupid business with the bullet in my guts again. I was the only guy at the bar with a bullet in their guts. I kept putting my hand under my jacket, on my stomach and all, to keep the blood from dripping all over the place. I didn't want anybody to know I was even wounded. I was conce*a*/ing the fact that I was a wounded sonuvabitch" (p. 150). Even in fantasy his self-pity turns into self-disparagement: he hates himself as he screams for attention.

He decides to call up Jane Gallagher, but by "mistake"—it is almost a comedy of errors—he dials Sally Hayes and makes up for his insults. Then he goes to the men's room, dunks his head in a washbowl, and sits on a radiator to dry himself. When the pianist, a "flitty-looking guy," enters, Holden asks him to arrange a date with the singer at the club. The pianist tells him to go home.

> "You oughta go on the radio," I said. "Handsome chap like you. All those goddam golden locks. Ya need a manager?"
> "Go home, Mac, like a good guy. Go home and hit the sack."
> "No home to go to. No kidding—you need a manager?" (p. 152)

Holden, who needs "a manager," is crying as he goes for his coat. When the middle-aged attendant gives him his coat even though he has lost his check, he returns the kindness by asking her for a date. She laughs, but not derisively, and, intuiting the role he wants her to play, makes him put on his red hunting hat. His teeth chattering, Holden goes to Central Park to "see what the hell the ducks were doing" (p. 153). On the way, one "accident" following another, he drops the phonograph record he has bought for Phoebe. If, as he believes, nothing has been given to him, he cannot give even to his favorite sister and must punish her as he has been punished. When he finds the pond he nearly falls in. "Still shivering like a bastard," he imagines that he has pneumonia and dies.

In this fantasy he acts out his anger against his parents and inflicts upon them the ultimate punishment, his death. His funeral is mobbed and everybody cries: "They all came when Allie died, the whole goddam stupid bunch of them." He feels "sorry as hell for my mother and father. Especially my mother, because she still isn't over my brother Allie yet" (p. 155). In this reenactment of Allie's funeral he displaces his brother and enjoys exclusively the love of his mother. But not for long, since his "picture" cannot lift his guilt, dissolve his rage, or make over reality. People will not mourn him long, no longer than they mourned Allie, and life in the phony world will go on without him. Like Allie he will lie in the cemetery exposed to the elements.

To take his "mind off getting pneumonia and all," he skips "the quarters and the nickel" across the lagoon. "I don't know why I did it, but I did it." Perhaps he imitates a game Allie and he played together, but when he throws away his money, there is only one place he can go—home. Which he does, although he disguises the desire by preserving his fantasy: he goes there to see Phoebe "in case I died and all" (p. 156). In the foyer of the Caulfield apartment he recognizes "a funny smell that doesn't smell like any place else" (p. 158), and he finds Phoebe asleep in D.B.'s bed: "I felt swell for a change" (p. 159). Safe and protected, he begins to relax and no longer worries "whether they'd catch me home or not" (p. 163). What he does not say is that he would like to be caught. At first Phoebe is "very affectionate" until she guesses that he has been kicked out of Pencey Prep. Then, hurt and angry, a reaction which he cannot understand, she beats him with her fists and says over and over, "Daddy'll *kill* you!" At last Holden tellingly replies, "No, he won't. The worst he'll do, he'll give me hell again, and then he'll send me to that goddam military school. That's all he'll do to me" (p. 166).

In this climactic scene Phoebe plays a double role. About Allie's age when he died, she is the sister disappointed in the failures of her idealized brother, but she is also an underaged, undersized mother figure. Firmly but affectionately Phoebe presses Holden to explain why he has been expelled. He pours forth all his phony rationalizations, most of which begin and end with something or somebody "depressing" him. When Phoebe suggests that the fault may be his—"You don't like *any*thing that's happening"—he is "even more depressed" (p. 169). She insists, now perhaps not unlike the lawyer father, that he name some things he likes. Unable to "concentrate" on her disturbing questions, Holden thinks of the two nuns and of Jimmy Castle's suicide—kind mothers and a dead son. Relentlessly but not without a concession, Phoebe asks him to tell her "one thing" he likes.

> "I like Allie," I said. "And I like doing what I'm doing right now. Sitting here with you, and talking, and thinking about stuff, and—"
>
> "Allie's *dead*— You always say that! If somebody's dead and everything, and in *Heaven,* then it isn't really—"
>
> "I know he's dead! Don't you think I know that? I can still like him, though, can't I? Just because somebody's dead, you don't just stop liking them, for God's sake—especially if they were about a thousand times nicer than the people you know that're *alive* and all." (p. 171)

Phoebe is silent. Holden believes that "she can't think of anything to say." More perceptive than her older brother, she gives him time to recognize the significance of what he has said: that Allie is dead. Then, like the parents and the teachers, but with an affection that dilutes his anger, she tries to direct Holden to a consideration of a future which—as she tactfully does not say—must be lived without Allie. When she suggests that he may want to be a lawyer, Holden is unable to reply precisely, not merely because he is trapped in his negations, but also because, in spite of his anger, he can only attack the father by indirection. "Lawyers are all right, I guess," he replies, with wayward antecedents, "but it doesn't appeal to me." He draws a picture of lawyers "saving innocent guys' lives"—which is another rescue fantasy and a disguised self-reference. When he discusses, from his hurt viewpoint, the role of the corporation lawyer, he deflects the indictment of his father through use of the second-person pronoun: "All you do is make a lot of dough and play golf and play bridge and buy cars and drink Martinis and look like a hot-shot" (p. 172). Ironically, Holden emulates his father's behavior, from his Mark Cross luggage to his drinking and "hot-shot" attacks on phonies.

Soon Holden confides his most heroic fantasy, undeterred when Phoebe corrects the misquotation of Burns's poem on which it is based.

> "I thought it was 'If a body catch a body,' " I said. "Anyway, I keep picturing all these little kids playing some game in this big field of rye and all. Thousands of little kids, and nobody's around—nobody big, I mean—except me. And I'm standing on the edge of some crazy cliff. What I have to do, I have to catch everybody if they start to go over the cliff—I mean if they're running and they don't look where they're going I have to come out from somewhere and *catch* them. That's all I'd do all day. I'd just be the catcher in the rye and all. I know it's crazy, but that's the only thing I'd really like to be. I know it's crazy." (p. 173)

This is the most complex of all the rescue fantasies. Holden has the "crazy" idea that he should have saved Allie, and that in the future he will save children abused by adults. If he is savior, he is also victim. For he himself is at "the edge of some crazy cliff" and feels himself, as he puts it later, going "down, down, down" (p. 197). He acts out the role he wants the adult world, particularly his father, to play: that of rescuer.

When a moment later Phoebe and Holden horse around and dance about the bedroom, the youth's delight illuminates his desire for a childhood where there are no fears, only joy and protection. The idyll ends abruptly when the parents come home, and Holden, fearing rejection, hides in a closet. Before he leaves, he borrows Phoebe's Christmas money. For the fourth time he begins to cry: "I couldn't help it. I did it so nobody could hear me, but I did it." For the first time he achieves what he has cried for from the beginning: Phoebe, now the mother, not the little sister, "put her old arm around my neck, and I put my arm around her, too, but I still couldn't stop for a long time" (p. 179). Before he goes, he almost tells the truth about himself as well as about the catcher-in-the-rye fantasy. "I didn't give much of a damn any more if they caught me. I really didn't. I figured if they caught me, they caught me. I almost wished they did, in a way" (p. 180).

Holden leaves to spend the night with a former teacher at a preparatory school, now an English professor at New York University. Antolini has been a role model, a good father, for Holden: he carried the body of Jimmy Castle to the infirmary after his suicide, and he banters in the witty style of D.B. Holden is disappointed when Antolini informs him that he has had lunch with Mr. Caulfield and shares the father's concern that "you're riding for some kind of a terrible, terrible fall" (p. 186). The professor tries intellectually to check the boy's self-destructive tendencies, as Phoebe does in her quite different way. Antolini puts the boy to bed on a couch in the living room, and says "Good night, handsome." Later Holden wakens to find "something on my head, some guy's hand" (p. 191). "Shaking like a madman," he concocts an excuse to leave and spends the rest of the night sleeping on a bench in Grand Central Station. "I think," he writes, "I was more depressed than I ever was in my whole life" (p. 194).

Although initially Holden interprets Antolini's caress as a sexual advance, in the morning he has doubts, "I mean I wondered if just maybe I was wrong about thinking he was making a flitty pass at me" (pp. 194–95). Whatever his intentions, sexual or paternal, Antolini sets off the not unusual homosexual panic of adolescents. But Holden's problem is not primarily sexual. He cannot connect with anyone in any way until the burden of Allie's death is lifted.

Alone, depressed, he walks up Fifth Avenue in the morning looking for the two nuns—looking for mother—when something "very spooky" happens. "Every time I came to the end of a block and stepped off the goddam curb, I had this feeling that I'd never get to the other side of the street. I thought I'd just go down, down, down, and nobody'd ever see me again." Once more he is at the cliff, and there is no one to catch him, to keep him from going "down, down, down"— except Allie. He cries out, "Allie, don't let me disappear" (pp. 197–98).

Holden has at last touched bottom, although he is not to be spared further indignities, some of his own making. Never again will he summon Allie, which means that he begins to turn from the past and death and to move into the present and toward the living. The inevitable fantasy that he creates in moments of crisis subtly changes. He plans to go "out West where it was very pretty and sunny and where nobody'd know me" (p. 198). When Holden proposes to Sally that they run off to Vermont or Massachusetts, the flight is in the direction of Maine, where Allie died. In going west he moves toward the living, for D.B. is in Hollywood. Still damaged and still hungering for security, he pictures himself as a deaf mute working at a filling station and—most important—married to another deaf mute. "If we had any children," he declares, with obvious reference to his own lot, "we'd hide them somewhere. We could buy them a lot of books and teach them how to read and write by ourselves" (p. 199). At last Holden's locked world is opening up.

He goes to Phoebe's school to say good-by and to return her Christmas money. He is upset to find "Fuck you" scrawled on a wall, no doubt more upset than the kids who share neither his naive ideas of purity, despite his verbal profanities, nor his fears of sexuality. While he waits for Phoebe at the museum, two boys ask the way to the mummies. As Holden leads them to the Egyptian room, he begins to repeat the information given in his history examination at Pencey Prep about the process of preservation, and frightens the lads who do not share his obsession with death. Instead of a savior or a catcher, Holden turns out to be a bogey man—as unfeeling as the unfeeling adults who have never understood him. Alone in the tomb, he is mocked again by the ugly epithet of sexual assault which he finds on the walls. Typically he overreacts and at the same time punishes himself as he pictures his tombstone: Holden Caulfield—"Fuck you" (p. 204).

If this debasement is not enough, he suddenly has diarrhea, and passes out on the floor of a toilet. It is as though he must experience an elemental purging—get all the "crap" out of his distorted picture of life and of himself. Compulsively he creates still another fantasy of flight. This time he is a thirty-five-year-old man living by himself: "I even started picturing how it would be when I came back. I knew my mother'd get nervous as hell and start to cry and beg me to stay home and not go back to my cabin, but I'd go anyway" (p. 205). If he is still punishing his mother—and himself—at least he pictures himself alive and at the middle of the journey.

When Phoebe comes to the museum with her luggage because she plans to go west too, once again she reaches out to her brother. The act of love is almost too much for Holden. "I got sort of dizzy and I thought I was going to pass out or something again" (p. 206). But he does not fall or pass out. Instead like the loved-hated parents or like a protective older brother—in short like all the other adults—he automatically advances all the sensible reasons why Phoebe's plans are "crazy." When he begins genuinely to think of some one else's lot, he assumes responsibility. He is no longer the kid who needs and demands everybody's attention.

When Phoebe proves stubborn, he returns her gift of love with another gift. He escorts her to Central Park, not to the duck pond—with its associations with death—but to the carrousel: "When she was a tiny little kid, and Allie and D.B. and I used to go to the park with her, she was mad about the carrousel" (p. 210). In the bedroom Holden and Phoebe had danced together like two kids, but at the carrousel Holden refuses to ride with her and watches her reach for the gold ring. In turn, when he promises to go home with Phoebe, he delights her and at the same time achieves the goal hinted at on the first page of his narrative: "I felt so damn happy all of a sudden, the way old Phoebe kept going around and around. I was damn near bawling, I felt so damn happy" (p. 213)...

In the epilogue, Chapter 26, Holden writes of himself at age seventeen in an institution near Hollywood, not far from D.B. After a period of rest and therapy there has been no fabulous transformation, although there has been change. His language is no longer negative, nor is his attitude. He is not sure that he is going to apply himself when he returns to school in September: "I *think* I am, but how do I know? I swear it's a stupid question" (p. 213). Although he has to put up token resistance—after all, he is Holden Caulfield—he is ready to go "around and around" in the game of life and no longer needs Allie's mitt or hat to protect him. Nor must he picture himself as the victim of insensitive adults; the psychoanalyst's advice is not "bull."

When D.B. asks him about "all this stuff I just finished telling you about," he replies truthfully, without a defensive wisecrack. "About all I know is, I sort of *miss* everybody I told about." At last he cuts through his "crap," his evasions and hostile defenses. He wants, as he has always wanted, to establish connections, and he is well on his way to doing just that, for in his narrative he has at least established connections with readers.

"Don't ever tell anybody anything," he writes at the conclusion; "if you do, you start missing everybody" (p. 214). But telling is precisely what he has been doing and in the process Holden has finished mourning. Allie now rests in peace.

NOTES

[1] Holden Caulfield has been called "a lout," a saint, a "sad little screwed-up" neurotic, and a "beatnik Peter Pan," but he deserves none of these epithets, positive or negative. The novel has been read as a critique of "the academic and social conformity of its period" (Maxwell Geismar), as a modern version of the Orestes-Iphigeneia story (Leslie Fiedler), as a commentary on the modern world in which ideals "are denied access to our lives" (Ihab Hassan), or as a celebration of life (Martin Green). These essays appear in *Salinger—A Critical and Personal Portrait,* ed. Henry Anatole Grunwald (New York, 1962).
[2] James Bryan recognizes that "the trauma" behind Holden's problems is the death of his brother Allie, but he proceeds to examine the work in terms of Holden's psychosexual growth when clearly the youth's development is emotionally arrested. See "The Psychological Structure of *The Catcher in the Rye,*" *PMLA,* 89 (1974), 1065–74.
[3] J. D. Salinger, *The Catcher in the Rye* (New York, 1964), p. 9.

R. J. Huber

ADLERIAN THEORY AND
THE CATCHER IN THE RYE

$\mathbf{A}$lfred Adler felt that observations of the great writers were invaluable assets to the contemporary psychologist, and, in particular, he found the Bible, Goethe, and Shakespeare extremely helpful in his understanding of human nature.[1] He also engaged in literary interpretation through his comments on the works of Alfred Berger, Dostoevsky, and the diary of the Russian ballet great, Nijinsky.[2] Contemporary Adlerians have shown a sustained interest in literary analysis in articles over the past several years that have appeared in their principle English language journal, *The Journal of Individual Psychology.*[3] In a recent book Leon Edel has stressed the cogency of Adlerian psychology to understanding literature.[4] The compatibility between literature and Adlerian psychology exists because the writer and the Adlerian psychologist are about the same task, as Phyllis Bottome, a novelist and one of Adler's biographers, states: "Not what happens to people, but how people take what happens to them has always been the chief part of the novelist's task to reveal."[5] The Adlerian psychologist, similarly, is most interested in how one interprets his or her environment. The world view of the individual is a proper beginning for a discussion of Adlerian literary analysis; however, before this topic can be pursued it is necessary to paint a miniature sketch of Adlerian theory.

While it is true that Adler was a member of the original Vienna Psychoanalytic Society, one should not regard him as a disciple of Freud. There is a great deal of evidence indicating that Adler's ideas differed significantly from those of Freud before the two men were acquainted. In his first publication Adler emphasized social factors in the occupational diseases of tailors; this emphasis dominated his thought before, during, and after his association with Freud.[6] It is this difference and others that nurtured the split of Adler from Freud in 1911 because Freud insisted on orthodoxy of thought. In 1911 Adler and his co-workers founded the school of Individual Psychology, which adhered to principles that are the cornerstones of

From *Psychological Perspectives on Literature: Freudian Dissidents and Non-Freudians, a Casebook,* edited by Joseph Natoli (Hamden, CT: Archon, 1984), pp. 43–52.

many contemporary theories of personality. Carl Rogers and Abraham Maslow accepted the concept of the creative self and the individual frame of reference as fundamental postulates for their theories.[7] These writers as well as others accepted the idea that the human is a continually evolving, striving being. Indeed, Adler's approach to motivation suggests that the prime human motive is not biological in the traditional sense; certainly he felt that the desire to grow, to be more, and to be significant transcended physiological desires such as hunger, thirst, and sex. From this perspective, the death-inviting exploits of someone like Evel Knievel become readily understandable.

To the lay person, Adler is most famous for his complementary concepts of the inferiority and superiority complexes. When Adler spoke of the human striving for superiority, he was, however, actually speaking of something that can be more properly labeled a growth urge. That anyone can always be more than they are is clearly summarized in Adler's statement, "I would like to stress that the life of the human soul is not a 'being' but a 'becoming'."[8] Striving for completion, therefore, is a lifelong process that is never accomplished. The growth urge is differentiated from a pathological striving. Many literary characters are examples, par excellence, of the type of striving that involves an attempt on the part of the individual to achieve an almost godlike state to compensate for felt feelings of inferiority. George Orwell's depiction of a wretched albino who attempts to rule the world by becoming invisible and Albert Camus's description of a Parisian lawyer who tries to be superhuman are good examples of this inferiority complex.[9] It is unfortunate that fewer literary works have depicted the self-actualized individual.[10] Not all compensatory striving rests on deep-seated feelings of inferiority. Some strivings are more normal types of adjustment that are the result of a temporarily induced feeling of inferiority. An example here would be Thomas Aldrich's depiction of the moody behavior of a young boy who finds that his ardent love is not reciprocated by a mature young woman.[11]

Adler's psychology is known as Individual Psychology, yet there is nothing in his description of striving for superiority to account for the uniqueness of the individual. To account for individual differences, we must describe what Adler called one's scheme of apperception, or one's world view. One's world view gives direction to striving. There are myriads of ways in which one can assert oneself in the world. As William James noted, the individual selects the sphere in which he or she tries to exert influence.[12] The stamp collector may care little if he or she is a miserable chess player, and similarly the chess player may care little for stamps. There are even people who achieve feelings of self-worth by arranging words on pages and then covering them with cloth or paper covers. Others, perhaps rightfully so, cannot fathom how this could be a satisfying pursuit. Thus, the world view gives direction to the striving. The world view also influences how one interprets so-called objective events. Adlerian psychologists, therefore eschew causal explanations of human behavior. Having a snake placed on one's lap, for example, is open to a variety of interpretations. To most this would be a revolting event, and the perpetrator of this deed would be viewed as unfriendly. The same act, neverthe-less, may be viewed by a budding herpetologist as a token of interest and friend-ship. From this perspective no behavior is psychologically nonsensical, and thus behavior is in accord with the individual's world view. What, then, separates psy-chological functioning that is commonly viewed as nonsensical from that usually viewed as normal? To answer this question, which has been considered the most significant aspect of Adlerian theory, we must consider social interest.[13]

Social interest is the common English translation of the German term *gemein-schaftsgefuhl*, a term that is one of the cornerstones of Maslow's description of the self-actualized individual. I have described social interest as an empathic cooperative style of living where empathy is the cognitive aspect and cooperation is the be-havioral aspect of social interest.[14] Adler felt that the socially interested individual saw with the eyes of another, heard with the ears of another, and felt with the heart of another. Social interest is the criterion for assessing one's world view and consequent behavior. On the one hand, if one's behavior springs from a world view imbued with empathy and a cooperative spirit, it is easily understood. While on the other hand, if one's behavior springs from a world view that is private and ego-centric, it appears illogical. John Hinckley, for example, tried to assassinate the President in order to show his love for the movie star Jodie Foster and to achieve fame. This act from his perspective was most logical. It does not, however, evoke a responsive note in the world view of others; he can thus be viewed as insane, and indeed a jury ruled him innocent by reason of insanity.

Adler did indeed feel that humans were inextricably social creatures.[15] He often stated that he ". . . refused to recognize the isolated human being." This contention has its roots in a biological theory that holds that most species live better in aggregate than in isolation.[16] The implications of this view for Adler were that the person must be considered as part of a social situation involving what he regarded as the three life problems: love, occupation, and community.[17] Thus, Adler was interested in the psychological development of the individual insofar as that devel-opment either fostered or hindered the development of social interest. And he considered five factors that he believed affected the development of social interest in the individual: pampering, neglect, organ inferiorities, birth order, and creativity.[18] The first four of these factors may adversely affect the development of social interest. The pampered individual like Nellie Olson in Laura Ingalls Wilder's *Little House* books for children is ill prepared for the reciprocity necessary for social living, while the neglected child such as Smike in Dickens's *Nicholas Nickleby* is never introduced to the world of love and social interest.

Physical deformities can predispose one to feel inferior and thus cause one to strive for superiority in a socially useless manner. Shakespeare vividly describes this in Richard III, who is portrayed as the ugly yet successful seducer of women he seeks for conquest rather than love. Adler also believed that birth order can affect one's view of the world. The firstborn is more likely to feel dethroned and ne-glected, while the youngest is most likely to be pampered. McLaughlin describes these dynamics in relation to the tragedy of *King Lear*.[19] And, finally, it is an individual's possession of creative power that relegates the first four factors to a nondeterministic level. Objective events provide probabilities only of what *may* be, since all events are answered by the styled creative power of the individual as expressed in his or her world view.

Adler believed that each person was, to a large extent, the author and actor of his or her own play of life. The individual, therefore, can never be explained. He or she can only be understood by accurately assessing his or her world view. Literature, similarly, is not to be explained; it is to be understood from the psychological viewpoint of its characters. An Adlerian approach to literature is mutually beneficial. In Adler's words,

> We have no desire to tamper with the marvellous outpourings of our poets and thinkers and shall therefore attempt merely to determine, through their creations, to what extent we are on the right path and how much of their work can be understood by reference to the working methods of Individual Psychology.[20]

An Adlerian View of Holden Caulfield

The word "analysis" is not appropriate from an Adlerian frame of reference, since the goal of literary interpretation from this point of view is a holistic understanding of a character's world view and consequent style of living in relation to his or her social situation. "Creative synthesis" would be a more appropriate description of the Adlerian approach to literature. In essence, an Adlerian psychologist, whether dealing with a client or a literary character, attempts through keen observation of behavioral minutiae to understand the individual's frame of reference. If the psychologist understands the frame of reference, a consistent psychological depiction of a character can be formed. If a character's prime goal is social victory at all costs, he or she may be a veritable Uriah Heep in one instance and a Simon Legree in another; the contradictory behaviors may serve the same ends.

To aid them in their understanding, many Adlerian literary interpreters have evaluated issues that are embodied in the following query: Is the individual striving for growth and fulfillment in a beneficent way with his fellow humans? Or is the individual striving for useless superiority because of feelings of inferiority in a manner that is inconsiderate of others and ultimately destructive of self? In short, the Adlerian is always interested in knowing whether one feels competent or inferior, and whether one strives with or without social interests in mind.

A wide range of literature has proved itself amenable to Adlerian interpretation—Shakespeare (including Philip Mairet's essay on Hamlet), German medieval and romantic literature, existential literature, science fiction, autobiography, and contemporary American literature.[21] This wide spectrum underscores the validity of the Adlerian approach in its applicability to many cultural contexts over a great expanse of time. Readers of the post–World War II era, the Eisenhower era, the Vietnam era, and the present have all been able to identify with the pangs of Holden Caulfield as he attempts to come of age in America. As many critics have indicated, Holden Caulfield has served as more than a character many adolescent readers can identify with. He has become an adolescent folk hero.[22] In one sense, he can be seen as a valiant knight struggling against an evil society. In another sense, Holden's cynical world view can be seen as much more than the typical view of a typical rebellious adolescent. In fact, from an Adlerian perspective, Holden is more prototypical of maladjustment in general than of normal adolescence. Even a cursory inspection of Salinger's classic character reveals deep-seated inferiority feelings and a compensatory striving for grandiosity.

If Holden Caulfield is a prototype of a maladjusted person, why has he so often been considered an adolescent hero? The Adlerian response is that one's schema of apperception, one's world view, is never *completely* mistaken. The neurotic is right up to a point. In some instances, Holden aptly describes flaws in our society. For example, he indicates the callousness of a headmaster who dotes on wealthy parents and ignores parents of less affluent students. Similarly, many would agree with Holden that the Radio City Christmas pageant is only quasi-religious in nature. One must, however, take a look at Holden's total life context. The question to be asked is: Are the above instances parts of an empathic and cooperative life-style, or are they parts of a life-style filled with inferiority feelings and self-seeking grandiosity? As one describes Holden's style of living in detail, it is obvious that the latter is true. It seems that Holden selectively attends to and retains the negative aspects of his world, and then depreciates others and his surroundings in order to compensate for deep-seated feelings of inferiority. One would expect to find egocentricity and not social interest in such an individual. A closer look at Holden's world view, his schema of apperception, will reveal Holden's maladjustment rather than his folk-hero proportions.

Since one's world view pervades all one's life, Holden's every action and attitude should be closely integrated parts of his total personality. Adler connects actions and meaning:

> If we close our ears to his words and observe his actions, we shall find that he has his own individual 'meaning' of life and that all his postures, attitudes, movements, expressions, mannerisms, ambitions, habits, and character traits accord with this meaning.[23]

Holden's world view is permeated with feelings of inferiority, and his self-perception mirrors these feelings. At various points in the novel, Holden depicts himself as a "moron," "yellow," "quite illiterate," "not too tough," "a liar," "the only dumb one," and "weak." He perceives himself as a "loser in life." When one of his former professors, Mr. Spencer, states that life is a game, Holden retorts with the following:

Game, my ass. Some game. If you get on the side where all the hot-shots are, then it's a game, all right—I'll admit that. But if you get on the *other* side, where there aren't any hot-shots, then what's a game about it? Nothing. No game.[24]

Clearly, as Adler would put it, Holden sees himself in a minus situation. He definitely is not a hotshot. Holden describes himself as extremely slender, abnormally tall, prematurely gray, very weak. He has respiratory problems and a disfigured hand. But there is an even more dramatic congruence between Holden's world view and his physical life, physical expressions of his psychic state. His intense feelings of inferiority are manifested in a somesthetic awareness. Toward the end of the novel, Holden has a psychotic episode when he steps off a curb and feels he will descend "down, down, down," and be lost forever. The downward direction is indicative of his intense feeling of failure and inferiority.

Given Holden's negative interpretation of his life position, it is logical to find a negative behavioral counterpart. Holden adopts a hesitating attitude, one in which he attempts to avoid life's problems and yet preserve his frail self-esteem. The hesitating attitude "offers an alibi to the neurotic."[25] The neurotic lives according to the formula "yes-but." The goal to be attained is the "yes," and the "but" is the fictive excuse that arrests the individual's goal-oriented strivings. Holden exemplifies this hesitating "yes-but" attitude when dealing with members of the opposite sex. When Jane Gallagher, a friend from the previous summer, is in the lobby of his dorm, Holden avoids meeting her by saying he is not "in the mood," even though it is more than obvious that he would like to see her. Similarly, having hired a prostitute, Holden once again uses the fictive excuse of not being in the mood to avoid a sexual encounter. However, Holden does not merely avoid members of the opposite sex. He avoids most social contact. He excludes others from his social sphere by adopting an "all or nothing" attitude. This "all or nothing" attitude is characteristic of the individual who feels he is living in "enemy territory" and shows the oversensitivity of one threatened by defeats. Holden's oversensitivity is seen when he is driven "damn near crazy" when he sees "fuck you" written on the wall of his sister's school. This to him is proof positive that the entire world is an evil place and that the plight of man is hopeless. Holden uses his oversensitivity to exclude himself from society, and therefore he is able to cleverly protect his self-esteem. Adler terms this the exclusion tendency:

> ... anything that does not fit in with his early adopted attitudes is more or less excluded; or it is wholly or in part stripped of its intellectual content and objective meaning and is interpreted, always in accordance with the individual's view of the world.[26]

Inferiority and superiority feelings work in a dialectical fashion, that is, the greater the feelings of inferiority the more grandiose the goal. "... an increased insecurity feeling in childhood causes a higher and more unalterable goal setting, a striving which goes beyond human measure..."[27] This active upward striving to overcome inferiorities always includes maintenance of the self-esteem. Given Holden's avoidance of the problems of life, he employs, as one would expect, other safeguarding mechanisms in addition to hesitating and all-or-nothing attitudes as means of achieving a sense of grandiosity and godlikeness. Holden uses his unrealistic imagination to place himself over others and thus succeeds in enhancing his self-esteem. Fantasy helps to give a neurotic ". . . an illusory view of enhancement of his self-esteem, usually spurring him on . . ."[28] When Holden's grandiose self-image is threatened, he imagines himself as a dying hero, similar to those seen in Saturday matinees, to achieve a sense of grandiosity. He often sees himself wounded and ". . . holding onto my guts, blood leaking all over the place." Thus, Holden's fantasies give him an illusory view of increased personal worth, and compel him to view himself as a hero in the manner of John Wayne, a manner Adler describes as masculine protest.

Means of safeguarding the self-esteem through "masculine protest" follows the schematic formula "I want to be a real man." Instead of a dashing hero, however, Holden is a caricature of a "real man." Consider, for example, his frequent offer to buy cocktails for those he meets. In an attempt to be suave, he asks numerous people to join him for a drink, but they are people who have no time for a drink—cabdrivers, waitresses, etc. The inappropriateness of his offers reveals their overdriven quality. Similarly, Holden's repetitive use of profanity is indicative of his masculine protest, an empty protest serving a useless goal. Adler emphasizes that to understand an individual, one must understand his or her goals, an important part of one's world view, one's line of direction. Holden's goal is one of useless grandiosity—to be a catcher in the rye—to be the person who catches small children running through a field of rye before they go over a cliff. Holden sees himself as a savior of the children of the world. This unique sort of striving for godlikeness is characteristic of the compulsive neurotic, who ". . . tries to represent himself . . . as a demigod, who exalts himself above humankind."[29] Appropriately, Holden states that there would be "nobody big . . . except me . . . ," indicating his wish to be superior in every way.

In addition to his godlike image, Holden strives for superiority in a most ungodlike manner, namely through depreciation. Like the neurotic ". . . who exalts himself above mankind and depreciates everyone else and puts them in the shade . . . ," Holden repeatedly belittles his environment.[30] A key word in his vocabulary is "phony," a word that reflects his general view of society. His school ". . . was a terrible school no matter how you looked at it." The hotel he stayed in had "vomity-looking chairs," and was "full of perverts." This depreciatory attitude blends well with Holden's hesitating attitude. He feels it is not worthwhile to get involved with the world he sees. Considering this negative view, it is comprehensible that his social interest is low.

It is, in Adler's view, always a lack of social interest that causes insufficient preparation for all of the problems of life—love, society, and occupation. Life's problems are of a social nature and therefore demand social interest for their

successful solution. Holden inadequately copes with the problems of life by hesitating and avoiding love and communal relationships and striving for a useless goal.
His low social interest is further indicated by his desire to isolate himself from the
rest of mankind. He attempts to do so through language, ". . . a common creation
of mankind. . . ."[3] Holden wishes, in fact, to be a deaf-mute, to be cut off from
mankind's common base, language. He prefers to seek the company of a dead
brother, and through this positive orientation with someone dead, reveals his
tendency to isolate himself. He can have an idealized but not ideal (socially interested) relationship. He is in enemy territory, mute and sure only that his safest
social relationship is with a dead brother. This kind of estrangement is poignantly
revealed at the beginning of his narration. He depicts himself as alone, on a hill
above others, watching the homecoming football game of his school. He literally
feels that others are his enemies, a feeling that is evident when he describes his red
hunting hat, bought on a recent trip to New York City, as a "people shooting hat."
This aggressive attitude is one Adler would expect from someone with a low
degree of social interest and a high degree of activity, that is, a choleric type.

And truly Holden's adventures are indicative of someone with a great deal of
energy. In the span of two days, he goes to a movie, leaves school, checks in and
out of a hotel, goes to several bars, attends a Broadway show, goes ice skating, visits
home, visits a former teacher, and takes several long walks. Even when he is in one
place, he is constantly moving—dancing, shouting, drumming on the table, striking
matches. And he even wants to jump out the window. In an Adlerian view, suicide
is a real possibility when someone has a low social interest and a high degree of
activity. Holden's ultimate end is what Mr. Antolini, a former teacher, tries to warn
Holden about. He quotes Wilhelm Stekel: "The mark of the immature man is that
he wants to die nobly for a cause while the mark of a mature man is that he wants
to live humbly for one." Mr. Antolini seemed to realize, as did Adler, that those
who have contributed little to the general good and have not given life meaning
cannot endure into the future. It is interesting to note that Adler felt that any work
of art was a reflection of the life-style of its creator. In one famous passage in *The
Catcher in the Rye,* Salinger has Caulfield state at length how he would like to live
in a cabin in Vermont where he would rarely have to speak to anyone. This has
been the fate of J. D. Salinger himself.

NOTES

[1] R. Rom and H. L. Ansbacher, "An Adlerian Case or a Character by Sartre?" *Journal of Individual
Psychology* 21 (1965): 32–41.
[2] Alfred Adler, "Individual Psychological Remarks on Alfred Berger's *Hofrat Eysenhardt,*" in *The Practice
and Theory of Individual Psychology* (Totowa, N.J.: Littlefield, 1959); Alfred Adler, "Preface to the Diary
of Vaslav Nijinsky," *Archives of General Psychology* 38, no. 7 (1981), 834–35.
[3] In 1982 this journal merged to form a new quarterly, *Individual Psychology.*
[4] Leon Edel, *Stuff of Sleep and Dreams: Experiments in Literary Psychology* (New York: Harper & Row,
1982).
[5] Phyllis Bottome, *Alfred Adler* (New York: Vanguard, 1957), 195.

[6] See H. Ellenberger's *The Discovery of the Unconscious* (New York: Basic Books, 1970) for a discussion of the association of Freud and Adler.

[7] Carl Rogers, *A Way of Being* (Boston: Houghton Mifflin, 1980); *On Becoming a Person* (Boston: Houghton Mifflin, 1961); Abraham Maslow, *Motivation and Personality* (New York: Harper & Row, 1970).

[8] Alfred Adler, *The Problem Child* (New York: Capricorn Books, 1963).

[9] M. E. Skorburg, "An Adlerian Interpretation of H. G. Wells," *Journal of Individual Psychology* 31 (1975): 85–96; E. Sachs, *"The Fall* by Albert Camus: A Study in Adlerian Psychology," *Journal of Individual Psychology* 28 (1972): 76–80.

[10] See J. J. McLaughlin and R. R. Ansbacher, "Sane Ben Franklin: An Adlerian View of His Autobiography," *Journal of Individual Psychology* 27 (1971): 189–207.

[11] Thomas Aldrich, *The Story of a Bad Boy* (Philadelphia: Winston, 1927), 224.

[12] William James, *Principles of Psychology* (New York: Holt, 1890).

[13] H. L. Ansbacher, "The Concept of Social Interest," *Journal of Individual Psychology* 31 (1968): 131–49.

[14] R. J. Huber, "Social Interest Revisited," *Character Potential* 7 (1975): 64–77.

[15] Alfred Adler, *The Individual Psychology of Alfred Adler* (New York: Basic Books, 1956); *Superiority and Social Interest* (Evanston, Ill.: Northwestern University Press, 1964); *Cooperation between the Sexes* (New York: Doubleday, Anchor, 1978).

[16] W. C. Alee, *Cooperation among Animals* (New York: Schuman, 1951); R. J. Huber et al., "Evolution: Struggle or Synergy?" *Journal of Individual Psychology* 34 (1978): 210–20; E. O. Wilson, *Sociobiology: The New Synthesis* (Cambridge, Mass.: Harvard University Press, 1975).

[17] Alfred Adler, *What Life Should Mean to You* (New York: Capricorn Books, 1958).

[18] Ibid.

[19] J. J. McLaughlin, "The Dynamics of Power in *King Lear:* An Adlerian Interpretation," *Shakespeare Quarterly* 29 (1978): 37–43.

[20] Adler, "Individual Psychological Remarks," 267.

[21] Philip Mairet, "Hamlet as a Study of Individual Psychology," *Journal of Individual Psychology* 25 (1969): 71–88; McLaughlin, "Dynamics of Power"; R. C. J. Endres, "Understanding the Life Style of a Medieval Literary Character," *Journal of Individual Psychology* 30 (1974): 251–64; Adler, "Individual Psychological Remarks"; S. Osherson, "An Adlerian Approach to Goethe's *Faust,"* *Journal of Individual Psychology* 21 (1965): 194–98; Rom and Ansbacher, "An Adlerian Case"; Sachs, *"The Fall:* A Study"; Skorburg, "An Adlerian Interpretation"; McLaughlin and Ansbacher, "Sane Ben Franklin"; J. Irving, *"The Catcher in the Rye:* An Adlerian Interpretation," *Journal of Individual Psychology* 32 (1976): 81–92; R. J. Huber and G. Ledbetter, "Holden Caulfield, Self-Appointed Catcher in the Rye: Some Additional Thoughts," *Journal of Individual Psychology* 33 (1977): 250–56.

[22] See as an example, L. Unger, ed., *American Writers: A Collection of Literary Biographies,* vol. 3 (New York: Scribner, 1961).

[23] Adler, *What Life Should Mean to You,* 14.

[24] J. D. Salinger, *The Catcher in the Rye* (New York: Modern Library, 1951).

[25] Adler, *Superiority and Social Interest.*

[26] Ibid., 103.

[27] Adler, *The Individual Psychology.*

[28] Ibid., 21.

[29] Adler, *Superiority and Social Interest,* 117.

[30] Ibid., 117.

[31] Adler, *The Individual Psychology,* 253.

Alan Nadel

HOLDEN AND
THE COLD WAR

If, as has been widely noted, *The Catcher in the Rye* owes much to *Adventures of Huckleberry Finn*,[1] it rewrites that classic American text in a world where the ubiquity of rule-governed society leaves no river on which to flee, no western territory for which to light out. The territory is mental, not physical, and Salinger's Huck spends his whole flight searching for raft and river, that is, for the margins of his sanity. A relative term, however, "sanity" merely indicates conformity to a set of norms, and since rhetorical relationships formulate the normative world in which a speaker functions, a fictional text—whether or not it asserts an external reality—unavoidably creates and contains a reality in its rhetorical hierarchies, which are necessarily full of assumptions and negations.[2] This aspect of fiction could not be more emphasized than it is by Holden Caulfield's speech, a speech which, moreover, reflects the pressures and contradictions prevalent in the Cold War society from which it was forged.

I. Caulfield's Speech

An obsessively proscriptive speaker, Caulfield's essay-like rhetorical style—which integrates generalization, specific examples, and consequent rules—prevails throughout the book, subordinating to it most of the description, narration, and dialogue by making them examples in articulating the principles of a rule-governed society. In one paragraph, for example, Caulfield tells us that someone had stolen his coat (example), that Pencey was full of crooks (generalization), and that "the more expensive a school is, the more crooks it has" (rule) (4). In a longer excerpt, from Chapter 9, we can see how the details Caulfield sees from his hotel window— "a man and a woman squirting water out of their mouths at one another"—become examples in a series of generalizations, rules, and consequent evaluations:

From *Centennial Review* 32, No. 4 (Fall 1988): 351–71.

> The trouble was, [principle] that kind of junk is sort of fascinating to watch, even if you don't want it to be. For instance, [example] that girl that was getting water squirted all over her face, she was pretty good-looking. I mean that's my big trouble. [generalization] In my *mind*, I'm probably the biggest sex maniac you ever saw. Sometimes [generalization] I can think of *very* crumby stuff I wouldn't mind doing if the opportunity came up. I can even see how it might be quite a lot of fun, [qualification] in a crumby way, and if you were both sort of drunk and all, [more specific example] to get a girl and squirt water or something all over each other's face. The thing is, though, [evaluation] I don't *like* the idea. It [generalization] stinks, if you analyze it. I think [principle arrived at deductively through a series of enthymemes] if you don't really like a girl, you shouldn't horse around with her at all, and if you *do* like her, then you're supposed to like her face, and if you like her face, you ought to be careful about doing crumby stuff to it, [specific application] like squirting water all over it. (62)

Caulfield not only explains his world but also justifies his explanations by locating them in the context of governing rules, rendering his speech not only compulsively explanatory but also authoritarian in that it must demonstrate an authority for *all* his statements, even if he creates that authority merely through rhetorical convention.

With ample space we could list all the rules and principles Caulfield articulates. Here are a few: it's really hard to be roommates with people if your suitcases are better than theirs; "grand" is a phony word; real ugly girls have it tough; people never believe you; seeing old guys in their pajamas and bathrobes is depressing; don't ever tell anybody anything, if you do you start missing everybody. We could easily find scores more, to prove the book a virtual anatomy of social behavior. The book, however, also anatomizes Caulfield's personal behavior: he lies; he has a great capacity for alcohol; he hates to go to bed when he's not even tired; he's very fond of dancing, sometimes; he's a pacifist; he always gets those vomity kind of cabs if he goes anywhere late at night, etc.

As the author of the two anatomies, Caulfield thus manifests two drives: to control his environment by being the one who names and thus creates its rules, and to subordinate the self by being the one whose every action is governed by rules. To put it another way, he is trying to constitute himself both as subject and as object; he is trying to read a social text and to write one. When these two drives come in conflict, there are no options left.

Although reified in the body of Holden Caulfield—a body, like the collective corpus of Huck and Jim, that longs for honesty and freedom as it moves more deeply into a world of deceit and slavery—this lack of options reveals an organization of power which deeply reflects the tensions of post–WWII America from which the novel emerged. The novel appeared in 1951, the product of ten years' work. Especially during the five years between the time Salinger withdrew from publication a 90-page version of the novel and revised it to more than double its length, the "cold war" blossomed.[3]

Richard and Carol Ohmann have related *Catcher's* immense success to the political climate of the Cold War by trying to show that Caulfield provides a critique of the phoniness "rooted in the economic and social arrangements of capitalism and their concealment" (29). Although they tend, unfortunately, to oversimplify both the text and the relationship between literature and history,[4] *Catcher* may indeed reveal what Fredric Jameson has termed the political unconscious, a narrative in which "real social contradictions, unsurmountable in their own terms, find purely formal resolution in the aesthetic realm" (79). As we shall see, Caulfield not only speaks the speech of the rule contradictions embedded in the voice of his age but also displaces it by internalizing it. He thus converts his rhetoric into mental break-down and becomes both the articulation of "unspeakable" hypocrisy and its critic. Finally, he becomes, as well, for his audience a sacrificial escape from the implications of such an articulation.[5]

II. The Search for Phonies

Victor Navasky describes the cold war as a period having

three simultaneous conflicts: a global confrontation between rival imperialisms and ideologies, between capitalism and Communism . . . a domestic clash in the United States between hunters and hunted, investigators and investigated . . . and, finally a civil war amongst the hunted, a fight within the liberal community itself, a running battle between anti-Communist liberals and those who called themselves progressives. . . . (3)

These conflicts took not only the form of the Korean War but also of lengthy, well-publicized trials of spies and subversives, in ubiquitous loyalty oaths, in Senate (McCarthy) and House (HUAC) hearings, in Hollywood and academic purges, and in extensive "anti-Communist" legislation. Even three years before Senator Joseph McCarthy's infamous speech alleging 57 Communists in the State Department, President Truman had created a Presidential Commission on Employee Loyalty and the Hollywood Ten had been ruined by HUAC.[6] Constantly, legislation, hearings, speechs, and editorials warned Americans to be suspicious of phonies, wary of associates, circumspect about their past, and cautious about their speech. A new mode of behavior was necessary, the President's Commission noted, because America was now confronted with organizations which valorized duplicity: "[these organizations] while seeking to destroy all the traditional safe-guards erected for the protection of individual rights are determined to take unfair advantage of those selfsame safe-guards."

Since uncovering duplicity was the quest of the day, in thinking constantly about who or what was phony, Caulfield was doing no more than following the instructions of J. Edgar Hoover, the California Board of Regents, *The Nation,* the Smith Act, and the Hollywood Ten, to name a very few. The President's Loyalty Commission, for example, announced as its purpose both to protect the government from infiltration by "disloyal persons" and to protect loyal employees "from unfounded accusations." The Commission's dual role, of course, implied dual roles for all citizens: to be protected *and* exonerated. Potentially each citizen was both the threat and the threatened. Because the enemy was "subversive," furthermore, one could never know whether he or she had been misled by an enemy pretending to be a friend; without a sure test of loyalty, one could not sort the loyal from the disloyal and therefore could not know with whom to align. The problem—elevated to the level of national security and dramatized most vividly by the Hiss case—was to penetrate the duplicity of phonies.

This problem manifests itself in Caulfield's rhetoric not only in his diatribe against "phonies" but also through a chronic pattern of signifiers which indicate the truthfulness of Caulfield's testimony. He regularly marks the narration with such phrases as "it (he, she, I, they) really does (do, did, didn't, was, wasn't, is, isn't, can, had, am)," "if you want to know the truth," "I (I'll, I have to) admit (it)," "if you really want to know," "no (I'm not) kidding," "I swear (to God)," "I mean it." The word "really" additionally appears at least two dozen more times in the narration, often italicized. These signifiers, along with those which emphasize the intensity of an experience (e.g. "boy!") or the speaker's desire for clarity (e.g. "I mean. . . .") make Caulfield's speech one which asserts its own veracity more than once for every page of narration.[7]

Because it is so important to Caulfield that the reader not think he is a phony, he also constantly provides ample examples and illustrations to prove each assertion, even his claim that he is "the most terrific liar you ever saw in your life" (16). Examples of such rhetorical performances abounded in the media during the novel's five-year revision period. Like many of the ex-Communist informers of the period, Caulfield's veracity rests on the evidence of his deceitfulness. This paradox is especially foregrounded by a discussion Caulfield has on the train with Mrs. Morrow, the mother of another boy at Pencey. In that discussion, he convinces the reader of his truthfulness with the same signifier he uses to make Mrs. Morrow believe his lies. Although Caulfield feels her son, Ernie, is "doubtless the biggest bastard that ever went to Pencey," he tells her, " 'He adapts himself very well to things. He really does. I mean he really knows how to adapt himself.' " Later he adds: " 'It really took everybody quite a long time to get to know him.' " Having used "really" as a false signifier, Caulfield in confessing to the reader italicizes part of the word: "Then I *really* started chucking the old crap around." The evidence which follows should thus convince the reader that the italicized "real" can be trusted, so that the more he demonstrates he has duped his fellow traveler, the more the reader can credit the veracity of the italicized "real". The *real* crap is that Ernie was unanimous choice for class president but wouldn't let the students nominate him because he was too modest. Thus Caulfield proves his credibility to the reader: he *is* a good liar, but when he italicizes the "real" he can be trusted. In trying to convince Mrs. Morrow, however, he adds: " 'Boy, he's *really* shy' " and thus destroys the difference between italicized and unitalicized signifier (54–57).

III. The Meaning of Loyalty

Although presented as a trait of Caulfield's character formalized in his speech, these inconsistencies reflect as well the contradictions inherent in a society plagued by loyalty oaths. Swearing that something is true doesn't make it true, except at the expense of anything not-sworn-to. There exists, in other words, some privileged set of "true" events marked by swearing. The swearing, of course, marks them not as true but as important to the speaker—the things that he or she wants the audience to believe, cares about enough to mark with an oath. In this way, Caulfield creates a rhetorical contract—the appeal to ethos—which legitimizes the discourse. It does so, however, at the cost of all those items not stipulated: they reside in the margins by virtue of being so obvious that they can be taken for granted or so unimportant that they need not be substantiated. Thus grouped together as the "unsworn," the taken-for-granted and the not-*necessarily*-so become indistinguishable parts of the same unmarked set. This is exactly what, as Americans were discovering, loyalty oaths did to the concept of loyalty. For all constitutions bind those loyal to them, and the failure to take that for granted becomes the failure to grant a group constituted by a common social contract. It leaves the "we" of "We the People" without a known referent and makes it impossible to distinguish the real American from the phony—the one so disloyal that he or she will swear false allegiance, will italicize *real* commitment in order to dupe others.

Since social contracts rely upon rhetorical contracts, the problem then is one of language. But Communism according to its accusers acknowledged neither the same social nor rhetorical contracts. According to a major McCarthy witness, ex-Communist Louis Budenz, Communists often used "Aesopean" language so that, "no matter how innocent the language might seem on its face, the initiate understood the sinister underlying message" (Navasky 32). Because no court recognizes a contract binding on only one party, in dealing with those outside the social and rhetorical contracts, the traditional constitutional rules no longer applied. In his 1950 ruling upholding the Smith Act, under which eleven leaders of the American Communist Party were sentenced to prison, Judge Learned Hand indicated that when challenged by an alternative system, "Our democracy . . . must meet that faith and that creed on its merits, or it will perish. *Nevertheless,* we may insist that the rules of the game be observed, and the rules confine the conflict to the weapons drawn from the universe of discourse" [emphasis added]. Because the Communists do not function in the same universe of discourse, the same rules do not apply to them. But, as the need for loyalty tests proved, it was impossible to distinguish those for whom the rules did not apply from those for whom they did.

To do so requires a position outside the system, from which to perceive an external and objective "truth." In other words, one needs a religion, which as Wayne Booth implies is the only source of a truly reliable narrator.[8] All other narration must establish its credibility rhetorically by employing conventions. One of Caulfield's conventions is to acknowledge his unreliability by marking specific sections of the narration as extra-reliable. As we have seen, however, marked thus by their own confessions of unreliability, Caulfield's oaths become one more series of questionable signs, indicating not reliability but its myth. Roland Barthes has astutely demonstrated that a myth is an empty sign, one which no longer has a referent but continues to function as though it did, thus preserving the status quo. The loyalty oath is such a myth in that it preserves the idea of a "loyalty" called into question by its own presence, and in that it is executed at the expense of the field in which it plays—the constituted state to which the mythical loyalty is owed.

Like Caulfield's oaths, loyalty oaths in the public realm also proved insufficient. In a truly Orwellian inversion, the "true" test of loyalty became betrayal. Unless someone were willing to betray friends, no oath was credible. With the tacit and often active assistance of the entire entertainment industry, HUAC very effectively imprinted this message on the public conscience through half a decade of Hollywood purges. As has been clearly shown, investigating the entertainment industry was neither in the interest of legislation nor—as it could be argued that an investigation of the State Department was—in the interest of national security. It was to publicize the ethic of betrayal, the need to name names.[9]

IV. The Importance of Names

If the *willingness* to name names became the informer's credential, furthermore, the *ability* to do so became his or her capital. Thus the informer turned proper nouns into public credit that was used to purchase credibility. Caulfield too capitalizes names. The pervasive capitalization of proper nouns marks his speech; he compulsively names names. In the first three chapters alone, the narration (including the dialogue attributed to Caulfield) contains 218 proper nouns—an average of nine per page. They include people, places, days, months, countries, novels, cars, and cold remedies. Many of the names, moreover, are striking by virtue of their unimportance. Does it matter if "old Spencer" used "Vicks Nose Drops" or read *Atlantic Monthly?* Is it important that these items are named twice? Caulfield's speech merely mirrors the convention of the Hollywood witness by demonstrating the significance of his speech lay in alacrity, not content:

> A certain minimum number of names was necessary; those who ... could convince HUAC counsel that they did not know the names of enough former comrades to give a persuasive performance ... were provided with names. The key to a successful appearance ... was the *prompt* recital of the names of a few dozen Hollywood Reds [emphasis added]. (Ceplair and Englund 18)

Nor was the suspicion of Hollywood one-sided. Suspected by the right of being potentially subversive, it was suspected by liberals of being inordinately self-censored. Carey McWilliams, writing in *The Nation,* in 1949, bemoans the effects of the "graylist." Intimidated out of dealing realistically with social issues, the movies, McWilliams fears, were becoming more and more phony.

Not surprisingly, Caulfield too equates Hollywood with betrayal and prostitution. The prostitute who comes to his room, furthermore, tells him she is from Hollywood, and when she sits on his lap, she tries to get him to name a Hollywood name: " 'You look like a guy in the movies. You know. Whosis. *You* know who I mean. What the heck's his name?' " When Caulfield refuses to name the name, she tries to encourage him by associating it with that of another actor: "Sure you know. He was in that pitcher with Mel-vine Douglas. The one that was Mel-vine Douglas's kid brother. *You* know who I mean" (97). In 1951, naming that name cannot be innocent, because of its associations. Douglas, a prominent Hollywood liberal (who in 1947 supported the Hollywood Ten and in 1951 distanced himself from them), was, more importantly, the husband of Helen Gahagan Douglas, the Democratic Congresswoman whom Richard Nixon defeated in the contest for the California Senate seat. Nixon's race, grounded in red-baiting, innuendos, and guilt by association, attracted national attention and showed, according to McCarthy biographer David Oshinsky, that " 'McCarthyism' was not the exclusive property of Joe McCarthy" (177).

If Caulfield is guilty by virtue of his association with Melvyn Douglas, then guilty of what? Consorting with prostitutes? Naming names? Or is it of his own hypocrisy, of his recognition, also inscribed in his rhetoric, that he hasn't told the truth in that he actually loves the movies, emulates them, uses them as a constant frame of reference. The first paragraph of the book begins "if you want to know the truth" and ends with the sentences: "If there's one thing I hate, its the movies. Don't even mention them to me." Despite this injunction, Caulfield's speech is full of them. He acts out movie roles alone and in front of others, uses them as a pool of allusion to help articulate his own behavior, and goes to see them, even when he believes they will be unsatisfactory.[10]

This marked ambivalence returns us again to the way historical circumstances make Caulfield's speech, like all public testimony, incapable of articulating "truth" because the contradictions in the conditions of public and private utterance have become visible in such a way as to mark all truth claims "phony." In their stead come rituals of loyalty, rituals which do not manifest truth but replace it. In presenting advertised, televised, confessionals, which were prepared, written, and rehearsed, and then were performed by real-life actors, the HUAC Hollywood investigations not only replicated the movies, but they also denied the movies distance and benignity, in short their claim to artificiality. The silver (and cathode-ray) screen is everywhere and nowhere, presenting an act of truth-telling hard to distinguish from its former fabrications, stories for the screen which may or may not have been encoded, subversive messages. So too in "real life"—the viewers of these confessions may have been duped, made inadvertently to play a subversive role, followed an encoded script produced by a secret conspiracy of the sort they're used to seeing in the movies. And of course the movies *can* be believed, for if they cannot what is all the worry about? Why bother investigating the harmless? This was the mixed message of the HUAC hearings: movies were dangerous because they *could* be believed, and movies were dangerous because they *could not*. One cannot escape such a message by discovering the "truth," but only by performing the ritual that fills the space created by the impossibility of such a discovery. In this light, perhaps, Phoebe Caulfield's role in her school play should be read. When Caulfield asks her the play's name she says:

> " 'A Christmas Pageant for Americans.' It stinks, but I'm Benedict Arnold. I have practically the biggest part . . . It starts out when I'm dying. This ghost comes in on Christmas Eve and asks me if I'm ashamed and everything. You know. For betraying my country and everything. . . ." (162)

The passage accurately summarizes the ideal HUAC witness. The former traitor now starring in a morality play that honors the state through a form of Christian ritual, the goal of which is not the discovery of truth, but the public, "educational" demonstration of loyal behavior, in which the fiction's paragon of innocence and the nation's historical symbol of perfidy validate one another by exchanging roles.

V. Simple Truth and the Meaning of Testimony

Phoebe's play unites the two central loci for phonies in Caulfield's speech, the worlds of entertainment and of education. In questioning the phoniness of all the schools and teachers he has seen, Caulfield again articulates doubts prevalent in the public consciousness, especially as he is most critical of the Eastern Intellectual Establishment. That establishment, with Harvard as its epitome, came to represent for the readers of *Time,* for example, a form of affluence and elitism that could not be trusted. In their education section, the week of June 5, 1950, for example, *Time* quoted I. A. Richards at length on college teaching:

> "You are never quite sure if you are uttering words of inspired . . . aptness, or whether you are being completely inept. Often you will find yourself incompetent enough to be fired at once if anybody was intelligent enough to see you as you are. . . .
> " 'Am I, or am I not, a fraud?' That is a question that is going to mean more and more to you year by year. At first it seems agonizing; after that it becomes familiar and habitual." (65–66)

Again we have the same confessional paradigm. Richards gains credibility by confessing he was a fraud. He also suggests an encoded language meant to deceive the average person—anybody *not* "intelligent enough to see you as you are"; by implication, those who *were* intelligent enough participate in the conspiracy to keep the fraudulence hidden.

This issue becomes particularly germane in a period when teachers and professors were being forced to sign loyalty oaths and/or were being dismissed because of present or past political beliefs. The central issue, many faculty argued, was that academic personnel were being judged by non-academic standards.[11] Yet

Richards' statement could suggest that "true" academic standards were really a myth created by those intelligent enough to know better. Intelligence thus signified the capacity for fraud: only someone intelligent enough to see them as they are had something to hide. Because they knew more, intellectuals were more likely to know something they should confess, and not confessing hence signified probable disloyalty rather than innocence.

Time (1/23/50) made the same inferences about the psychiatrists who testified in Alger Hiss's defense, pointing out that Dr. Murray (like Dr. Binger and Hiss) was a Harvard graduate: "He backed up his colleague, Binger. Chambers ... was a psychopathic personality.... He had never seen Chambers but this did not faze him. He had psychoanalyzed Adolph Hitler *in absentia,* correctly predicting his suicide" (14).

If, filtered through *Time's* simplifying voice, these doctors seemed foolish accomplices, Hiss himself came to stand for everything that needed exposure and rejection. About his conviction, *Time* (1/30/50) wrote: "[Hiss] was marked as a man who, having dedicated himself to Communism under a warped sense of idealism, had not served it openly but covertly; a man who, having once served an alien master, lacked the courage to recant his past, but went on making his whole life an intricate, calculated lie" (12). Thus the past existed to be recanted, not recounted. The recounted past—the truth of one's past—became living a lie, while recanting revealed Truth, discovered not in past actions but in ideological enlightenment, enlightenment which reveals that one's life was a lie. Analysis is intellectual lying, *Time* had suggested in its treatment of Hiss's "authorities," part of the Intellectual conspiracy that did not revere the Truth but rather suggested that facts could be contravened by an unseen, subversive presence, knowable only to a trained elite whom the general population had to trust without evidence. For *Time,* truth was less ambiguous, existing in a transparent connection between physical phenomena and accepted beliefs, and with its authority lying outside the speaking subject. Hiss had transgressed by seeking to intervene, to analyze, to apply principles not grounded in Truth but in the trained intellect of a fallen mortal, fallen because he believed in the power of human intervention, the ability of the intellect to discern and interpret.

This too is Caulfield's failing, and he must recognize the error of locating himself as the discoverer, interpreter and arbiter of truth and phoniness. In other words, if his speech constitutes him both as subject and as object, it also constitutes him as testifier and judge, accuser and accused. It has the quality of testimony—the taking of oaths and the giving of evidence to support an agenda of charges. And like much of the most publicized testimony of its day, it has no legal status. As Navasky pointed out about the Hollywood hearings:

> [T]he procedural safeguards ... were absent: there was no cross examination, no impartial judge and jury, none of the exclusionary rules about hearsay or other evidence. And, of course, the targets from the entertainment business had committed no crime.... (xiv)

In such a context, it was hard to regard testimony as a form of rhetoric in a forensic argument. Although sometimes masked as such, it rarely functioned in the way Aristotle defined the concept. Rather it more often resembled testimony in the religious sense of confessing publicly one's sins. Caulfield's speech thus simultaneously seeped in conventions of both forensic testimony and spiritual, reveals the incompatability of the two, in terms of their intended audience, their intended effect, and their relationship to the speaker. Most important, forensic testimony presumes truth as something arrived at through the interaction of social and rhetorical contract, whereas spiritual testimony presumes an external authority for truth; its rhetoric *reveals* the Truth, doing so in such a way as to exempt the speech from judgment and present the speaker not as peer but as paragon.

These distinctions apply particularly to the concept of incrimination. A witness giving forensic testimony always risks self-incrimination; recognizing this, our laws allow the witness to abstain from answering questions. The paragon, who gives spiritual testimony, however, is above such self-incrimination; the paragon knows the Truth and has nothing to fear. Exercising the legal protection against self-incrimination (as many HUAC witnesses chose to do) meant the speaker was offering forensic testimony not spiritual, had thus not found the Truth, and therefore could not be trusted. Designed to protect the individual from self-incrimination, the Fifth Amendment then became the instrument of that self-incrimination. In a society that determined guilt not by evidence but by association and/or the failure to confess, people often found that the only way not to incriminate others was to claim they would be incriminating themselves. Since that claim became self-incriminating, they purchased silence by suggesting guilt. They thus internalized the dramatic conflict between social contract and personal loyalty, with the goal not of catharsis but silence. Autobiography, always potentially incriminating, had become recontextualized as testimony, but testimony itself had been freed of its evidenciary contexts and become an unbound truth-of-otherness. It potentially revealed the other—the subversive—everywhere but in the place he or she was known to be, even in the audience of investigators and/or in the speaker. The speaker, by virtue of testimony's two voices and self-incrimination's merger with its own safeguard, was as much alienated in the face of his or her own speech as in the face of his or her silence.

VI. The Case for Silence

The battle waged internally by so many during the Cold War, between spiritual and forensic testimony, public and personal loyalty, recounting and recanting, speech and silence, created a test of character. No matter how complex and self-contradictory the social text, the individual was supposed to read it and choose correctly. This is exactly the dilemma Caulfield's speech confronts from its first words:

> If you really want to hear about it, the first thing you'll probably want to know is where I was born, and what my lousy childhood was like, and how my parents were occupied and all before they had me, and all that David Copperfield kind of crap, but I don't feel like going into it, if you want to know the truth. In the first place, that stuff bores me, and in the second place, my parents would have about two hemorrhages apiece if I told anything pretty personal about them. (I)

Caulfield will try to tell the truth to this "hearing" without incriminating himself or his parents. But at every turn he fails, constantly reflecting rather than negotiating the contradictions of his world. Against that failure weighs the possible alternative, silence, in the extreme as suicide. The memory of James Castle's suicide haunts the book. Castle, the boy at Elkton Hills, refused to recant something he had said about a very conceited student, and instead committed suicide by jumping out a window. Caulfield too contemplated suicide in the same manner after the pimp, Maurice, had taken his money and hit him (104). This image of jumping out the window not only connects Caulfield with Castle but also epitomizes the fall from which Caulfield, as the "catcher in the rye," wants to save the innocent.

The image of jumping out the window also typified, as it had during the stock market crash of 1929, admission of personal failure in the face of unnegotiable social demands. In 1948, for example, Lawrence Duggan fell or threw himself from the window of his New York office. Immediately Congressman Karl Mundt announced the cause was Duggan's implication in a Communist spy ring; along with five other men, his name had been named at a HUAC meeting. The committee would disclose the other names, Mundt said, "as they jump out of windows."

On April 1, 1950, F. O. Matthiessen, "at the time," in the words of William O'Neill, "the most intellectually distinguished fellow traveler in America" (173), jumped to his death from a Boston hotel window. In his suicide note, he wrote: ". . . as a Christian and a socialist believing in international peace, I find myself terribly oppressed by the present tensions" (Stern 31). Although Matthiessen did not commit suicide solely for political reasons, for the general public his death symbolized the culpability and weakness of the Eastern Intellectual Establishment. His powerful intellect, his political leanings and, especially, his longstanding affiliation with Harvard identified him clearly as the kind of analytic mind that typified the intellectual conspiracy *Time*, Joseph McCarthy, et al. most feared and despised. Like Hiss, he was led astray by his idealism which, in true allegorical fashion, led to deceit and ultimately the coward's way out. *Or:* like many dedicated progressives, he was hounded by witch hunters forcing him to choose between the roles of betrayer and betrayed, and leading him ultimately to leap from melodrama into tragedy. Hero or coward, Christ or Judas—in either case, in the morality drama of his day, he graphically signified the sort of fall from innocence against which Caulfield struggles.[12]

But, in the end, Caulfield renounces this struggle, allowing that one cannot catch kids: ". . . if they want to grab for the gold ring, you have to let them do it, *and not say anything.* If they fall off, they fall off, *but it's bad if you say anything to them"* [emphasis added] (211). Thus the solution to Caulfield's dilemma becomes renouncing speech itself. Returning to the condition of utterance, stipulated in his opening sentence, which frames his testimony, he says in the last chapter—"If you want to know the truth . . ." (213), this time followed not with discourse but with the recognition that he lacks adequate knowledge for discourse: ". . . I don't *know* what I think about it" (213–14). From this follows regret in the presence of the named names:

> I'm sorry I told so many people about it. About all I know is, I sort of *miss* everybody I told about. Even old Stradlater and Ackley, for instance. I think I even miss goddam Maurice. It's funny. Don't ever tell anybody anything. If you do, you start missing everybody. (214)

These last sentences of the book thus replace truth with silence. The intermediary, moreover, between Caulfield's speech—deemed unreasonable—and his silence is the asylum, and we could say that the whole novel is speech framed by that asylum. It intervenes in the first chapter, immediately after Caulfield asks "if you want to know the truth" and in the last, immediately before he says he does not know what to think. In this way, the asylum functions in the manner Foucault has noted—not to remove Caulfield's guilt but to organize it "for the madman as a consciousness of himself, and as a non reciprocal relation to the keeper; it organized it for the man of reason as an awareness of the Other, a therapeutic intervention in the madman's existence" (247).

> Incessantly cast in this empty role of unknown visitor, and challenged in everything that can be known about him, drawn to the surface of himself by a social personality silently imposed by observation, by form and mask, the madman is obliged to objectify himself in the eyes of reason as the perfect stranger, that is, as the man whose strangeness does not reveal itself. The city of reason welcomes him only with this qualification and at the price of this surrender to anonymity. (249–50)

In this light, we can see that the asylum not only frames Caulfield's speech but also intervenes throughout as an increasing awareness of his otherness, marked by such phrases as "I swear to God, I'm a madman." Given the novel's frame, it is not astonishing that Caulfield's speech manifests traits of the asylum. In that his speech also manifests the contradictions of McCarthyism and the Cold War, the novel more interestingly suggests that the era in many ways institutionalized traits of the asylum. To prove the validity of his "madman" oaths, Caulfield again must assume the dual roles of subject and object, for as Foucault demonstrates, the intervention of the asylum (and, by extension we can say the Cold War) functioned by three principal means: perpetual judgment, recognition by the mirror, and silence.[13]

NOTES

[1] Heiserman and Miller make this connection. Others examining the book's relationship to *Adventures of Huckleberry Finn* include: Aldridge (129–31), Branch, Fiedler, Kaplan, and Wells.

[2] The relationship between reality and rhetoric has been most fully developed, of course, by Auerbach and, in some ways, modified and extended by Iser's concept of the "implied reader" who is led by an author's strategies of omission to complete the text's implied reality. It is important to note, therefore, that I am not using the word "negation" here in the sense that Iser does, but rather to suggest the "blanks" of Lacanian discourse—something akin to the "blindness" of a text which, for de Man, its rhetoric signifies. For Lacan, de Certeau notes, " 'literary' is that language which makes something else heard than that which it says; conversely psychoanalysis is a literary practice of language.... At issue here is rhetoric, and no longer poetics" (53).

[3] Grunwald (20) and French (26) mention this shorter 1946 version.

[4] Miller's response demonstrates that their reading tends to be reductive and ignores much significant textual evidence.

[5] For discussion of Caulfield as Christ figure, surrogate, saint, or savior, see: Barr, Baumbach 55–67, French 115–17, and Rupp 114–18.

[6] See Oshinsky's discussion of "The Red Bogey in America, 1917–1950" (85–102). The literature on American history and politics in the five-year period following WWII is, of course, extensive. Caute provides an excellent bibliography (621–50) for additional references beyond my necessarily selective citations.

[7] Approximately one third of the novel is dialogue rather than narration.

[8] As a result, the voice-of-God narrator, as typified in the Book of Job, serves as the paradigm of authority against which Booth analyzes other forms of narrative.

[9] See Navasky, Ceplair, and Englund 254–98, 361–97; Caute 487–538.

[10] Oldsey discusses the movies in the novel.

[11] See Caute 403–45.

[12] Stern: "Those were years in which a person searching for a community of shared socialist and Christian concerns needed the greatest personal support and fortitude to keep from the bottle, from an ignominious abandonment of all previous social concerns, or from the window ledge. Matthiessen chose to end his life, but others of his contemporaries I have known who shared his ideas at some point gave up lifelong commitments to socialism for goals far less honorable during the period" (30).

[13] See Foucault 241–78.

REFERENCES

Aldridge, John W. *In Search of Heresy: American Literature in an Age of Conformity.* New York: McGraw-Hill, 1956.

" 'Am I a Fraud?' " *Time* 5 January 1950: 65–66.

Auerbach, Eric. *Mimesis: The Representation of Reality in Western Literature.* Trans. Willard R. Trask. Princeton: Princeton UP, 1953.

Barthes, Roland. *Mythologies.* Trans. Annette Lavers. New York: Hill & Wang, 1978.

Baumbach, Jonathan. *The Landscape of Nightmare: Studies in the Contemporary American Novel.* New York: New York UP, 1965.

Booth, Wayne. *The Rhetoric of Fiction.* Chicago: U of Chicago P, 1961.

Branch, Edgar. "Mark Twain and J. D. Salinger: A Study in Literary Continuity." *American Quarterly* 9 (1957): 144–58.

Caute, David. *The Great Fear: The Anti-Communist Purge under Truman and Eisenhower.* New York: Simon & Schuster, 1978.

Ceplair, Larry, and Steven Englund. *The Inquisition in Hollywood: Politics in the Film Community 1930–1960.* Garden City, NY: Doubleday-Anchor, 1980.

Certeau, Michel de. *Heterologies: Discourse on the Other.* Trans. Brian Massumi. Theory and History of Literature, vol. 17. Minneapolis: U of Minnesota P, 1986.

de Man, Paul. *Blindness and Insight: Essays in the Rhetoric of Contemporary Criticism.* New York: Oxford UP, 1971.

Fiedler, Leslie. "The Eye of Innocence." *Salinger.* Ed. Henry Anatole Grunwald. New York: Harper, 1962.

Foucault, Michel. *Madness and Civilization: A History of Insanity in the Age of Reason.* Trans. Richard Howard. New York: Random-Vintage, 1973.

French, Warren. *J. D. Salinger.* New York: Twayne, 1963.

Galloway, David D. *The Absurd Hero in American Fiction.* Revised edition. Austin: U of Texas P, 1970.

Grunwald, Henry Anatole. "The Invisible Man: A Biographical Collage." *Salinger.* Ed. Grunwald. New York: Harper, 1962.

Hassan, Ihab. *Radical Innocence: Studies in the Contemporary American Novel.* Princeton: Princeton UP, 1961.

Heiserman, Arthur, and James E. Miller. "J. D. Salinger: Some Crazy Cliff." *Western Humanities Review* 10 (1956): 129–37.

Iser, Wolfgang. *The Implied Reader: Patterns of Communication in Prose Fictions from Bunyan to Beckett.* Baltimore: Johns Hopkins UP, 1974.

Jameson, Fredric. *The Political Unconscious: Narrative as a Socially Symbolic Act.* Ithaca: Cornell UP, 1981.

Kaplan, Charles. "Holden and Huck: The Odysseys of Youth." *College English* 18 (1956–57): 76–80.

Lacan, Jacques. *Speech and Language in Psychoanalysis.* Trans. Anthony Wilden. Baltimore: Johns Hopkins UP, 1968.

Lundquist, James. *J. D. Salinger.* New York: Ungar, 1979.

McWilliams, Carey. "Graylist." *The Nation* 19 Oct. 1949: 491.

Navasky, Victor. *Naming Names.* New York: Viking, 1980.

Ohmann, Carol, and Richard Ohmann. "Reviewers, Critics, and *The Catcher in the Rye.*" *Critical Inquiry* 3 (1976): 64–75.

Oldsey, Bernard S. "The Movies in the Rye." *College English* 23 (1961): 209–15.

O'Neill, William L. *A Better World: Stalinism and the American Intellectuals.* New York: Simon & Schuster, 1982.

Oshinsky, David M. *A Conspiracy So Immense: The World of Joe McCarthy.* New York: Macmillan–Free Press, 1983.

Rupp, Richard H. *Celebration in Postwar American Fiction 1945–1967.* Coral Gables, FL: U of Miami P, 1970.

Salinger, J. D. *The Catcher in the Rye.* 1951. New York: Bantam, 1964.

Stern, Frederick C. *F. O. Matthiessen: Christian Socialist as Critic.* Chapel Hill: U of North Carolina P, 1981.

"Trials—Some People Can Taste It." *Time* 23 Jan. 1950: 14.

"Trials—The Reckoning." *Time* 30 Jan. 1950: 11–12.

Wells, Arvin R. "Huck Finn and Holden Caulfield: The Situation of the Hero." *Ohio University Review* 2 (1960): 31–42.

CONTRIBUTORS

HAROLD BLOOM is Sterling Professor of the Humanities at Yale University and Henry W. and Albert A. Berg Professor of English at the New York University Graduate School. He is a 1985 MacArthur Foundation Award recipient, served as the Charles Eliot Norton Professor of Poetry at Harvard University (1987–88), and is the author of eighteen books, the most recent being *Ruin the Sacred Truths: Poetry and Belief from the Bible to the Present* (1989). Currently he is editing the Chelsea House series Modern Critical Views and The Critical Cosmos, and other Chelsea House series in literary criticism.

DONALD P. COSTELLO is Professor of American Studies at the University of Notre Dame. He is the author of *The Serpent's Eye: Shaw and the Cinema* (1965) and *Fellini's Road* (1983).

ARVIN R. WELLS is Professor of English at Ohio University. He is the author of *Jesting Moses: A Study in Cabellian Comedy* (1962).

VERA PANOVA, who lived in Leningrad, is considered one of the most prominent women prose writers of the postwar era. The author of many stories, novels, and plays, she won various Soviet literary awards. Her works published in English include *The Train* (1949), *Looking Ahead* (c. 1951), and *On Faraway Street* (1968).

JONATHAN BAUMBACH is Professor of English at Brooklyn College. He has written several works of fiction, of which his most recent are *Chez Charlotte and Emily* (1979), *The Return of Service* (1979), *My Father, More or Less* (1982), and *The Life and Times of Major Fiction* (1986).

CLINTON W. TROWBRIDGE is former Professor of English at Adelphi Suffolk College. He has published essays on Flannery O'Connor, Saul Bellow, and Arthur Miller.

DAVID J. BURROWS is former Professor of English at Douglass College of Rutgers University. He is the editor of several collections of modern writing, among them *Alienation: A Casebook* (1969) and *Myths and Motifs in Literature* (1973; with Frederick R. Lapides and John T. Shawcross).

WILLIAM GLASSER is President/Chancellor at Southern Vermont College. He has published essays on Herman Melville, Harriet Beecher Stowe, Stephen Crane, and Henry James.

DUANE EDWARDS is Professor of English at Fairleigh Dickinson University. He has published essays on English and American literature in *Southern Humanities Review* and *Ball State University Forum.*

JAMES LUNDQUIST is Professor of English at St. Cloud State University. He is the author of *Theodore Dreiser* (1974), *Chester Himes* (1976), *Kurt Vonnegut* (1977), and *Jack London: Adventures, Ideas, and Fiction* (1987).

EDWIN HAVILAND MILLER is former Professor of English at New York University. He is the author of *Walt Whitman's Poetry: A Psychological Journey* (1968), *Melville* (1975), and *Walt Whitman's "Song of Myself": A Mosaic of Interpretations* (1989).

R. J. HUBER is Professor of Psychology at Meredith College. He has contributed numerous articles based on Adlerian theories to psychology journals.

ALAN NADEL is Associate Professor of English at Rensselaer Polytechnic Institute. He is the author of *Invisible Criticism: Ralph Ellison and the American Canon* (1988).

BIBLIOGRAPHY

Bank, Stanley. "A Literary Hero for Adolescents: The Adolescent." *English Journal* 58 (1969): 1013–20.

Behrman, S. N. "The Vision of the Innocent." *New Yorker,* August 11, 1951, pp. 64–68.

Belcher, William F., and James W. Lee, ed. *J. D. Salinger and the Critics.* Belmont, CA: Wadsworth Publishing Co., 1962.

Bloom, Harold, ed. *J. D. Salinger.* New York: Chelsea House, 1987.

Bowden, Edwin T. *The Dungeon of the Heart.* New York: Macmillan, 1961, pp. 54–65.

Brown, Rosellen. "On Willa Cather and 'Paul's Case.'" In *The American Short Story,* Volume 2, ed. Calvin Skaggs. New York: Dell, 1980, 188–94.

Bryan, James. "The Psychological Structure of *The Catcher in the Rye.*" *PMLA* 89 (1974): 1065–74.

Bryant, Jerry H. *The Open Decision: The Contemporary American Novel and Its Intellectual Background.* New York: Free Press, 1970, pp. 236–40.

Burack, Boris. "Holden the Courageous." *CEA Critic* 27 (1965): 1.

Cohen, Hubert I. "'A Woeful Agony Which Forced Me to Begin My Tale': *The Catcher in the Rye.*" *Modern Fiction Studies* 12 (1966–67): 355–66.

Conrad, Robert C. "Two Novels about Outsiders: The Kinship of J. D. Salinger's *The Catcher in the Rye* with Heinrich Böll's *Ansichten eines Clowns.*" *University of Dayton Review* 5 (1968–69): 23–27.

Daughtry, Vivian F. "A Novel Worth Teaching: Salinger's *The Catcher in the Rye.*" *Virginia English Bulletin* 36 (1986): 88–94.

Deer, Irving, and John H. Randall, III. "J. D. Salinger and the Reality Beyond Words." *Lock Haven Review* No. 6 (1964): 14–29.

DeLuca, Geraldine. "Unself-Conscious Voices: Larger Contexts for Adolescents." *The Lion and the Unicorn* 2 (1978): 89–108.

Dodge, Stewart. "The Theme of Quest: In Search of 'The Fat Lady.'" *English Record* 8 (1957): 10–13.

Ely, Mary. "A Cup of Consecrated Chicken Soup." *Catholic World* 202 (1965–66): 298–301.

Fleissner, Robert F. "Salinger's Caulfield: A Refraction of Copperfield and His Caul." *Notes on Contemporary Literature* 3 (May 1973): 5–7.

Foran, Donald J. "A Doubletake on Holden Caulfield." *English Journal* 57 (1968): 977–79.

Fowler, Albert. "Alien in the Rye." *Modern Age* 1 (1957): 193–97.

French, Warren. "Holden's Fall." *Modern Fiction Studies* 10 (1964–65): 389.

———. *J. D. Salinger.* New York: Twayne, 1963.

———. *J. D. Salinger, Revisited.* Boston: G. K. Hall, 1988.

Furst, Lilian R. "Dostoyevsky's *Notes from the Underground* and Salinger's *The Catcher in the Rye.*" *Canadian Review of Comparative Literature* 5 (1978): 72–85.

Gale, Robert L. "Redburn and Holden—Half-Brothers One Century Removed." *Forum* [Houston] 3, No. 12 (Winter 1963): 32–36.

Giles, Barbara. "The Lonely War of J. D. Salinger." *Mainstream* 12 (February 1959): 2–13.

Goldhurst, William. "The Hyphenated Ham Sandwich of Ernest Hemingway and J. D. Salinger: A Study in Literary Continuity." *Fitzgerald/Hemingway Annual 1970,* pp. 136–50.

Hainsworth, J. D. "Maturity in J. D. Salinger's *The Catcher in the Rye.*" *English Studies* 48 (1967): 426–31.

Hamilton, Ian. *A Search for J. D. Salinger.* New York: Random House, 1988.

Hamilton, Kenneth. *J. D. Salinger: A Critical Essay.* Grand Rapids, MI: Eerdmans, 1967.

Handa, Takuya. "On Interpretations of J. D. Salinger's *The Catcher in the Rye.*" *Kyushu American Literature* 21 (1980): 42–53.

Hassan, Ihab H. "The Victim: Images of Evil in Recent American Fiction." *College English* 21 (1959–60): 140–46.

Heiserman, Arthur, and James E. Miller, Jr. "J. D. Salinger: Some Crazy Cliff." *Western Humanities Review* 10 (1956): 129–37.

Hendin, Josephine. *Vulnerable People: A View of American Fiction since 1945.* New York: Oxford University Press, 1978, pp. 113–15.

Jacobs, Robert G. "J. D. Salinger's *The Catcher in the Rye:* Holden Caulfield's 'Goddam Autobiography.'" *Iowa English Yearbook* No. 4 (Fall 1959): 9–14.

Kaplan, Charles. "Holden and Huck: The Odysseys of Youth." *College English* 18 (1956–57): 76–80.

Laser, Marvin, and Norman Fruman, ed. *Studies of J. D. Salinger: Reviews, Essays, and Critiques of* The Catcher in the Rye *and Other Fiction.* New York: Odyssey Press, 1963.

Lettis, Richard. "Holden Caulfield: Salinger's 'Ironic Amalgam.'" *American Notes & Queries* 15 (1976): 43–45.

Livingston, James T. "J. D. Salinger: The Artist's Struggle to Stand on Holy Ground." In *Adversity and Grace: Studies in Recent American Literature,* ed. Nathan A. Scott, Jr. Chicago: University of Chicago Press, 1968, pp. 113–32.

Luedtke, Luther S. "J. D. Salinger and Robert Burns: *The Catcher in the Rye.*" *Modern Fiction Studies* 16 (1970–71): 198–201.

MacLean, Hugh. "Conservatism in Modern American Fiction." *College English* 15 (1953–54): 315–25.

McNamara, Eugene. "Holden as Novelist." *English Journal* 54 (1965): 166–70.

Marks, Barry A., Donald H. Reiman, and Dexter Martin. "Rebuttal: Holden in the Rye." *College English* 23 (1961–62): 507–8.

Marsden, Malcolm M., ed. *If You Really Want to Know: A* Catcher *Casebook.* Chicago: Scott, Foresman, 1963.

Noon, William T. "Three Young Men In Rebellion." *Thought* 38 (1963): 559–77.

O'Hara, J. D. "No Catcher in the Rye." *Modern Fiction Studies* 9 (1963–64): 370–76.

Ohmann, Carol, and Richard Ohmann. "Reviewers, Critics and *The Catcher in the Rye.*" *Critical Inquiry* 3 (Autumn 1976): 15–37.

Olan, Levi A. "The Voice of the Lonesome: Alienation from Huck Finn to Holden Caulfield." *Southwest Review* 48 (1963): 143–50.

Oldsey, Bernard S. "The Movies in the Rye." *College English* 23 (1961–62): 209–15.

Peavy, Charles D. "'Did You Ever Have a Sister?' Holden, Quentin, and Sexual Innocence." *Florida Quarterly* 1 (1968): 82–95.

———. "Holden Courage Again." *CEA Critic* 28 (1965): 1, 6, 9.

Peterson, Virgilia. "Three Days in the Bewildering World of an Adolescent." *New York Herald Tribune Book Review,* July 15, 1951, p. 3.

Pilkington, John. "About This Madman Stuff." *University of Mississippi Studies in English* 7 (1966): 65–75.

———. "Mummie and Ducks." *University of Mississippi Studies in English* 6 (1965): 15–22.

Pinsker, Sanford. *"The Catcher in the Rye* and All: Is the Age of Formative Books Over?" *Georgia Review* 40 (1986): 953–67.

Roper, Pamela E. "Holden's Hat." *Notes on Contemporary Literature* 7 (May 1977): 8–9.

Rosen, Gerald. "A Retrospective Look at *The Catcher in the Rye." American Quarterly* 29 (1977): 547–62.

———. *Zen in the Art of J. D. Salinger.* Berkeley: Creative Arts Book Co., 1977.

Salzberg, Joel. *Critical Essays on Salinger's* The Catcher in the Rye. Boston: G. K. Hall, 1990.

Seng, Peter J. "The Fallen Idol: The Immature World of Holden Caulfield." *College English* 23 (1961–62): 203–9.

Severin-Lounsberry, Barbara. "Holden and Alex: A Clockwork from the Rye?" *Four Quarters* 22 (Summer 1973): 27–38.

Simonson, Harold P., and Philip E. Hager, ed. *Salinger's* Catcher in the Rye: *Clamor vs. Criticism.* Lexington, MA: D. C. Heath, 1963.

Smith, Harrison. "Manhattan Ulysses, Junior." *Saturday Review,* July 14, 1951, pp. 12–13.

Starosciak, Kenneth. *J. D. Salinger: A Thirty-Year Bibliography 1938–1968.* St. Paul, MN: The Croixide Press, 1971.

Stashower, Daniel M. "On First Looking into Chapman's Holden: Speculations on a Murder." *American Scholar* 52 (1982–83): 373–77.

Stern, James. "Aw, the World's a Crumby Place." *New York Times Book Review,* July 15, 1951, p. 5.

Strauch, Carl F. "Kings in the Back Row: Meaning through Structure—A Reading of Salinger's *The Catcher in the Rye." Wisconsin Studies in Contemporary Literature* 2 (1961): 5–30.

Sublette, Jack R. *J. D. Salinger: An Annotated Bibliography 1938–1981.* New York: Garland, 1984.

Theroux, Joseph. "Holden Caulfield Comes to Samoa." *English Journal* 70 (1981): 42–46.

Vail, Dennis. "Holden and Psychoanalysis." *PMLA* 91 (1976): 120–21.

Wakefield, Dan. "Salinger and the Search for Love." *New World Writing, No. 14.* New York: New American Library, 1958, pp. 68–85.

Warner, Deane M. "Huck and Holden." *CEA Critic* 27 (1965): 4a–4b.

Wiegand, William. "J. D. Salinger's Seventy-eight Bananas." *Chicago Review* 11 (1958): 3–19.

Wiener, Gary A. "From Huck to Holden to Bromden: The Nonconformist in *One Flew Over the Cuckoo's Nest." Studies in the Humanities* 7 (1979): 21–26.

Zapf, Hubert. "Logical Action in *The Catcher in the Rye." College Literature* 12 (1985): 266–71.

ACKNOWLEDGMENTS

"New Novels in the News" by T. Morris Longstreth from *Christian Science Monitor,* July 19, 1951, © 1951 by the Christian Science Publishing Society. Reprinted by permission of *The Christian Science Monitor.*

"Case History of All of Us" by Ernest Jones from *Nation,* September 1, 1951, © 1951 by The Nation Company, Inc. Reprinted by permission of *The Nation.*

"The Society of Three Novels" by John W. Aldridge from *In Search of Heresy: American Literature in an Age of Conformity* by John W. Aldridge, © 1956 by John W. Aldridge. Reprinted by permission.

"Incommunicability in Salinger's *The Catcher in the Rye*" by Charles H. Kegel from *Western Humanities Review* 11, No. 1 (Winter 1957), © 1957 by the University of Utah. Reprinted by permission of *Western Humanities Review.*

"The Adolescent in American Fiction" by Frederic I. Carpenter from *English Journal* 46, No. 6 (September 1957), © 1957 by The National Council of Teachers of English. Reprinted by permission.

"*The Catcher in the Rye* (1951)" by Frederick L. Gwynn and Joseph L. Blotner from *The Fiction of J. D. Salinger* by Frederick L. Gwynn and Joseph L. Blotner, © 1958 by the University of Pittsburgh Press. Reprinted by permission.

" 'Why the Hell *Not* Smash All the Windows?' " by Christopher Parker from *Salinger: A Critical and Personal Portrait,* edited by Henry Anatole Grunwald, © 1962 by Henry Anatole Grunwald, © 1990 renewed. Reprinted by permission of Harper & Row, Publishers, Inc.

"Salinger and 'Honest Iago' " by Patrick Costello from *Renascence* 16, No. 4 (Summer 1964), © 1964 by the Catholic Renascence Society, Inc. Reprinted by permission of *Renascence.*

"The Love Ethic" by David D. Galloway from *The Absurd Hero in American Fiction: Updike, Styron, Bellow, Salinger* by David D. Galloway, © 1966 by David D. Galloway. Reprinted by permission of the author and the University of Texas Press.

"Gatsby and Holden Caulfield" by Mario L. D'Avanzo from *Fitzgerald Newsletter* No. 38 (Summer 1967), © 1967 by Matthew J. Bruccoli. Reprinted by permission of Matthew J. Bruccoli.

"Hamlet and Holden" by Clinton W. Trowbridge from *English Journal* 57, No. 1 (January 1968), © 1968 by The National Council of Teachers of English. Reprinted by permission.

"Holden Caulfield: Adolescents' Enduring Model" by Bernard C. Kinnick from *High School Journal* 53, No. 8 (May 1970), © 1970 by the University of North Carolina Press. Reprinted by permission.

"Holden Caulfield: Super-Adolescent" by Nancy C. Ralston from *Adolescence* No. 24 (Winter 1971), © 1971 by Libra Publishers, Inc. Reprinted by permission.

"Holden, 50, Still Catches" by Fred Bratman from *New York Times,* December 21, 1979, © 1979 by The New York Times Company. Reprinted by permission.

"Copperfield and Caulfield: Dickens in the Rye" by John S. Martin from *Notes on Modern American Literature* 4, No. 4 (Fall 1980), © 1980 by Edward Guereschi and Lee J. Richmond. Reprinted by permission.

"The Language of *The Catcher in the Rye*" by Donald P. Costello from *American Speech* 34, No. 3 (October 1959), © 1959 by Columbia University Press. Reprinted by permission of the author.

"Huck Finn and Holden Caulfield: The Situation of the Hero" by Arvin R. Wells from *Ohio University Review* 2 (1960), © 1960 by Ohio University. Reprinted by permission of *The Ohio Review.*

"On J. D. Salinger's Novel" by Vera Panova from *Soviet Criticism of American Literature in the Sixties: An Anthology,* edited by Carl R. Proffer, © 1972 by Ardis Publishers. Reprinted by permission.

"The Saint as a Young Man" (originally titled "The Saint as a Young Man: A Reappraisal of *The Catcher in the Rye*") by Jonathan Baumbach from *Modern Language Quarterly* 25, No. 4 (December 1964), © 1964 by *Modern Language Quarterly.* Reprinted by permission of the editor and author.

"Character and Detail in *The Catcher in the Rye*" (originally titled "Salinger's Symbolic Use of Character and Detail in *The Catcher in the Rye*") by Clinton W. Trowbridge from *Cimarron Review* No. 4 (June 1968), © 1968 by the Board of Regents for Oklahoma State University. Reprinted by permission.

"Allie and Phoebe" (originally titled "Allie and Phoebe: Death and Love in J. D. Salinger's *The Catcher in the Rye*") by David J. Burrows from *Private Dealings: Modern American Writers in Search of Integrity,* edited by David J. Burrows, Lewis M. Dabney, Milne Holton, and Grosvenor E. Powell, © 1969 by Almqvist & Wiksell. Reprinted by permission.

"The Catcher in the Rye" by William Glasser from *Michigan Quarterly Review* 15, No. 4 (Fall 1976), © 1976 by The University of Michigan. Reprinted by permission of *Michigan Quarterly Review.*

" 'Don't Ever Tell Anybody Anything' " (originally titled "Holden Caulfield: 'Don't Ever Tell Anybody Anything' ") by Duane Edwards from *ELH* 44, No. 3 (Fall 1977), © 1977 by The Johns Hopkins University Press. Reprinted by permission.

"Against Obscenity" (originally titled "Against Obscenity: *The Catcher in the Rye*") by James Lundquist from *J. D. Salinger* by James Lundquist, © 1979 by Frederick Ungar Publishing Co., Inc. Reprinted by permission.

"In Memoriam: Allie Caulfield" (originally titled "In Memoriam: Allie Caulfield in *The Catcher in the Rye*") by Edwin Haviland Miller from *Mosaic* 15, No. 1 (Winter 1982), © 1982 by *Mosaic*. Reprinted by permission.

"Adlerian Theory and *The Catcher in the Rye*" (originally titled "Adlerian Theory and Its Application to *The Catcher in the Rye*—Holden Caulfield") by R. J. Huber from *Psychological Perspectives on Literature: Freudian Dissidents and Non-Freudians, a Casebook*, edited by Joseph Natoli, © 1984 by The Shoe String Press, Inc. Reprinted by permission.

"Holden and the Cold War" (originally titled "Rhetoric, Sanity, and the Cold War: The Significance of Holden Caulfield's Testimony") by Alan Nadel from *Centennial Review* 32, No. 4 (Fall 1988), © 1988 by The Centennial Review. Reprinted by permission of *The Centennial Review* and the author.

INDEX